Hard Road to Democracy

Hard Road to Democracy

Four Developing Nations

Michael G. Roskin
Lycoming College

UPPER SADDLE RIVER, NEW JERSEY 07458

Library of Congress Cataloging-in-Publication Data

Roskin, Michael
Hard road to democracy: four developing nations/Michael G. Roskin.
p. cm.
Includes bibliographical references and index.
ISBN 0-13-033418-9
1. Developing countries—Politics and government—Case studies.
2. Democratization—Developing countries—Case studies. 3. Political culture—Developing countries—Case studies. I. Title

JF60.R67 2001
320.3'09172'4—dc21 00-065278

VP, Editorial director: Laura Pearson
Assistant editor: Brian Prybella
Editorial assistant: Jessica Drew
Director of marketing: Beth Gillett Mejia
Editorial/production supervision: Kari Callaghan Mazzola
Prepress and manufacturing buyer: Ben Smith
Electronic page makeup: Kari Callaghan Mazzola and John P. Mazzola
Interior design: John P. Mazzola
Cover director: Jayne Conte
Cover photo: Brian Prybella, "Great Wall of China," 1996

This book was set in 10/11.5 Goudy by Big Sky Composition
and was printed and bound by Hamilton Printing Company.
The cover was printed by Phoenix Color Corp.

Printed in the United States of America
10 9 8 7 6 5 4 3 2 1

ISBN 0-13-033418-9

PRENTICE-HALL INTERNATIONAL (UK) LIMITED, *London*
PRENTICE-HALL OF AUSTRALIA PTY. LIMITED, *Sydney*
PRENTICE-HALL CANADA INC., *Toronto*
PRENTICE-HALL HISPANOAMERICANA, S.A., *Mexico*
PRENTICE-HALL OF INDIA PRIVATE LIMITED, *New Delhi*
PRENTICE-HALL OF JAPAN, INC., *Tokyo*
PEARSON EDUCATION ASIA PTE. LTD., *Singapore*
EDITORA PRENTICE-HALL DO BRASIL, LTDA., *Rio de Janeiro*

To my children—Alex, Pam, and Stancey—in the hope that they will live in a more democratic world

Contents

Feature Boxes

Chapter 1

Chapter 2

Chapter 3

Chapter 4

Chapter 5

Preface

Students know little about the Third World or Global South, and often graduate with no introduction to the five-sixths of humankind who live there. To fill this gap, Beth Gillett Mejia of Prentice Hall and I agreed to publish in separate format the chapters from my larger textbook—*Countries and Concepts: Politics, Geography, Culture, Seventh Edition*—that cover Third World countries. This enables instructors in a wide variety of courses—history, political science, geography, cultural diversity—to briefly acquaint their students with developing countries.

The following instructional features help emphasize key concepts and definitions:

- Key Terms: Chapters have running marginal glossaries, labeled "Key Terms," to make sure students are building their vocabularies as they read. The definitions listed are those of a political scientist; in other contexts one might find different definitions. For further review, a list of key terms appears at the end of each chapter. The page number that follows each listed key term indicates the page upon which the corresponding marginal definition box appears.
- Feature Boxes: Most of the feature boxes have category heads—Geography, Democracy, Political Culture, Comparison, or Key Concepts—to give them greater focus and continuity.

The four countries—China, Brazil, South Africa, and Iran—are not necessarily representative of, respectively, Asia, Latin America, Africa, and the Middle East. What countries are? Rather, these four serve as springboards for discussion on how they compare and contrast with other nations in their region. Beginners have to know some history, geography, culture, and politics of several lands before they can grasp more abstract patterns, and for this the country-by-country approach generally works well with students.

I am not an area expert and welcome the input of those who are. Please flag errors of fact or interpretation to me directly at roskin@lycoming.edu or snail-mail to me at Lycoming College, Williamsport, PA 17701.

Michael G. Roskin

Hard Road to Democracy

CHAPTER 1

What to Look For

Questions to Consider

1. What is the trouble with the term "Third World"?
2. What was the impact of colonialism on the Third World?
3. Why is becoming modern such a wrenching experience?
4. What is meant by "quarrels"?
5. What is GDP, "per cap," and PPP?
6. How does economic development relate to democracy?
7. What is a political institution?
8. What is political culture?
9. What is ideology? Does it run stronger in the Third World?
10. How are generalizations and theories related?

It is the thesis of this book that developing countries are as capable of democracy as advanced countries; they just need economic development. What West Europe and North America did first—and it wasn't quick or easy—most of the Third World will accomplish in the twenty-first century. Already some growth demons on the Pacific Rim have turned themselves into prosperous democracies (Taiwan and South Korea). Brazil is doing the same, only more slowly. The Third World is not locked in permanent backwardness; it is rapidly modernizing, and this is leading to **democracy**. Rates of economic growth in many developing countries are much faster than what the West or Japan enjoyed at similar stages.

In this book, we look at four Third World countries, considering each in five sections, each focusing on a subject area. We start with some of the underlying elements of the current situations of the four countries:

The Impact of the Past
The Key Institutions
The Political Culture

We study the past, including the country's geography, in order to understand the present. We are not looking for the details of history but for the major patterns that have set up present institutions and culture. We study institutions to see how power is structured because institutions *are* structures of power. We study culture to see how people look at their social and political system, how strongly they support it, and how political views differ among groups.

Key Term

democracy Political system of mass participation, competitive elections, and human and civil rights.

The Third World

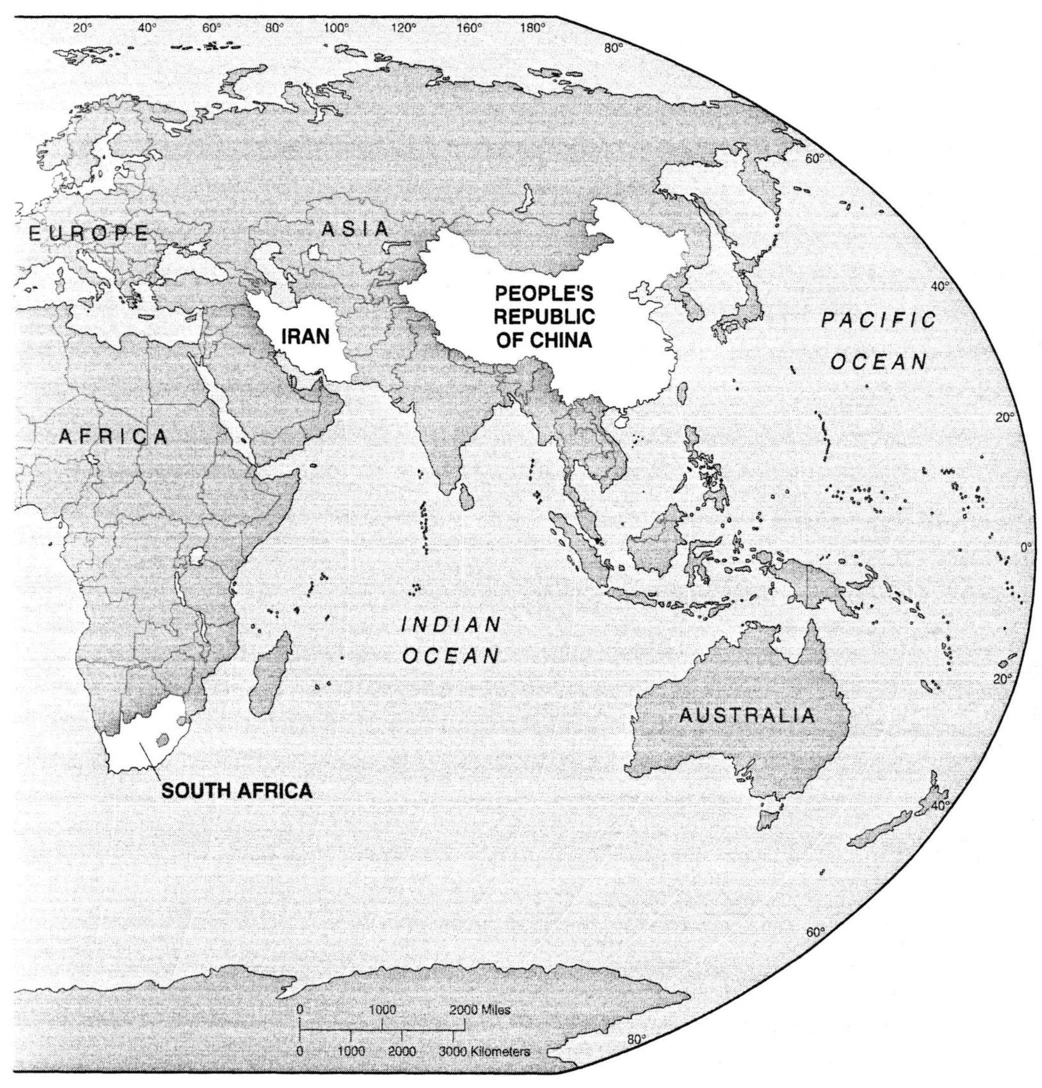
20°
40°
60°
80°
100°
120°
160°
180°
80°
60°
40°
20°
0°
20°
40°
60°
80°
EUROPE
ASIA
AFRICA
IRAN
PEOPLE'S REPUBLIC OF CHINA
PACIFIC OCEAN
INDIAN OCEAN
AUSTRALIA
SOUTH AFRICA
0 1000 2000 Miles
0 1000 2000 3000 Kilometers

GEOGRAPHY

WHAT IS THE THIRD WORLD?

Coined by French writers in the 1950s, *le Tiers Monde* (Third World) referred to the majority of humankind that was in neither the Western capitalist First World nor the Communist Second World. It is an awfully broad term that permits few firm generalizations. Now, with the collapse of communism in East Europe and the ex-Soviet Union, the Third World is simply everything that is not "the West," meaning Europe, the United States, Canada, Australia, and now Japan. Some say the only meaningful dividing line is now "the West and the rest."

The Third World is mostly poor, but some oil-producing countries are rich, and some of its lands have industrialized so fast that they are already affluent. It is mostly nonwhite. Almost all of it, at one time or another, was a colony of a European imperial power. Most of it is hot and closer to the equator than the rich countries, so some writers suggest we call it the Global South. The U.S. State Department and some international banks call it the LDCs (less-developed countries). The ones making fast economic progress are called NICs (newly industrializing countries). Business calls these countries the "emerging markets."

Call it what you will, one generalization stands up fairly well: It is politically unstable. The political institutions of almost all of its 120-plus countries are weak, and this is their chief difference from the West. Most Third World lands are wracked by political, social, and economic tensions that explode in revolution, coups, and upheavals and often end in dictatorship. Few have yet made it into the ranks of stable democracies, now the characteristic of all of the West. India is an amazing exception—although it went through a bout of authoritarian rule under Indira Gandhi. Pakistan is a more typical example: unstable elected governments alternating with military rule.

We should really come up with some better names than Third World to describe the complexity of the lands that are home to most of the human race, but until such a term has established itself, we use Third World.

Moving from the underlying factors to current politics brings us to the next two areas:

Patterns of Interaction
What People Quarrel About

Here, we get more specific and more current. The previous sections, we might say, are about the traditions, rules, and spirit of the game; the patterns of interaction are how the game is actually played. We look here for recurring behavior. The last section, the specific quarrels, represents the stuff of politics, the kind of things you see in a country's newspapers.

The Impact of the Past

We look first at a country's geography. *Physical geography* concerns the natural features of the earth, whereas **political geography** studies what is largely human-made. There is, of course, a connection between the two, as physical limits set by nature influence the formation, consolidation, and governing mentality of political systems.

Next, moving on to history, we ask, "Who first established this country, and how?" An ancient king? Or European colonialists? What language, religion, culture, and governing style did they lay down? Usages often persist for centuries, even after revolutions are supposed to have changed everything.

Long ago, some Third World countries were far in advance of Europe. China and Iran had magnificent civilizations when Europe wallowed in the Dark Ages. Europe moved ahead, starting more than half a millennium ago, while China and Iran stagnated. The causes are extremely complex. In Europe, monarchs became **absolutist** and competed among themselves with religion, war, technological innovation, economic growth, and overseas expansion. Much of Asia and the Middle East fell into the "sleep of the nations," partly due to **Mongol** conquest in the thirteenth century, to the bypassing of trade routes after European navigators rounded Africa, and to cultures uninterested in innovation and growth.

The regimes set up after independence from the Europeans and/or Americans are seldom democracies. Brazil was a monarchy until late in the nineteenth century, then a rigged democracy with repeated military takeovers until late in the twentieth century. China went from **authoritarian** rule under Chiang to **totalitarian** rule under Mao. Iran went from the Shah's modernizing tyranny to Khomeini's religious tyranny. Only South Africa moved directly into democracy, but a democracy under such pressure that some doubt it will endure.

Becoming "modern" is a wrenching experience. Industrialization, urbanization, and the growth of education and communications uproot people from their traditional villages and lifestyles and send them to work in factories, usually in cities. In the process, previously passive people become aware of their condition and willing to do something to change it. They become ready to participate in politics, demanding economic improvements, and often mobilized by new parties. It's a delicate time in the life of nations. If the traditional **elites** do not devise some way to take account of newly awakened **mass** demands, the system may be heading toward revolution. Elites are especially important in the transition to democracy and usually lead the way.

No country has industrialized in a nice way; it is always a process marked by low wages, bad working conditions, and usually by political repression. The longer in the past this stage has happened, the more peaceful and stable a country is likely to be. We must look for the stage of development a country is in. A country just undergoing industrialization can expect domestic tensions of the sort that existed earlier in Europe.

Religion is a crucial historical question. Does the country have its church-state relationship settled? If not, it's a lingering political problem, one that Iran is now struggling with.

Key Terms

political geography The ways territory and politics influence each other.

absolutism Royal dictatorship in which king amasses all power.

Mongols Thirteenth-century conquerors of Eurasia.

authoritarian Non-democratic or dictatorial politics.

totalitarian System in which state attempts total control.

elites The top or most influential people.

mass Most of the citizenry; everyone who is not an *elite*.

Key Concepts

The Impact of Colonialism

Almost all of the Third World was part of a European colonial empire. Starting half a millennium ago, West European monarchs began expanding overseas. **Colonialism** was terribly unfair to the "natives," but the dynamic, greedy Europeans encountered weaker civilizations and quickly subdued them by firearms, and, in the Americas, by disease. South Africa and Brazil were founded by colonists; China and Iran were reduced to semicolonial status by European soldiers and traders. European imperialism covered the globe; only Japan and to a lesser extent the Ottoman Turkish Empire held the West at bay. Japan engaged in a brilliant "defensive modernization" that eventually tried to beat the Europeans at their own game.

The Europeans brought technological progress to their colonies but exploited them economically and stunted their political progress for generations. In Latin America, Spaniards and Portuguese created new, artificial countries and saddled them with a feudal social structure: Iberians at the top, mestizos (persons of mixed Indian-Spanish descent) in the middle, and Indians and Africans at the bottom. The result: weak states that had a hard time keeping law and order. In Africa, the Europeans created a fragmented patchwork of artificial states in disregard of natural areas of tribes. The Europeans' "**divide and rule**" tactics created **tribalism** that rends Africa to this day.

How the colonies got out from under European rule forms dramatic chapters in each country's history. Brazil's independence was early and painless, but Brazil, like the rest of Latin America, maintained the feudal society implanted by the Iberian colonists. South Africa nominally became independent with its 1910 constitution but remained part of the British Commonwealth until 1961. *Apartheid* can be seen as a type of colonialism. The election of Nelson Mandela in 1994 finally marked the end of European rule.

China and Iran went through a series of convulsions in the twentieth century that ended the European presence and supervision. The first steps were the nationalistic takeovers by, respectively, Chiang Kai-shek and Reza Shah in the 1920s, but both still depended a great deal on outside, especially American, aid. The 1949 Chinese Communist revolution and 1979 Islamic revolution finally ousted all European and U.S. influence.

Key Terms

colonialism Gaining and ruling overseas territories.

divide and rule Roman and British ruling method of setting subjects against each other.

tribalism Identifying with tribe rather than country.

Finally, history establishes political symbols, which have the ability to awaken powerful emotions. Political symbols such as flags, religion, national holidays, and national anthems often serve as the cement that holds a country together, making the country's citizens feel that they are part of a common enterprise. To fully know a country, one must know its symbols, their historical origins, and their current connotations.

The Key Institutions

A political **institution** is a web of relationships lasting over time, an established structure of power. An institution may or may not be housed in an impressive building. With institutions we look for durable sets of human relationships, not architecture. One way to begin our search is to ask, "Who's got the power?" A nation's **constitution**—itself an institution—may give us some clues, but it does not necessarily pinpoint real power centers. Weak institutions are a hallmark of the Third World, where few institutions work as they are supposed to and many are hopelessly corrupt.

How powerful is the **parliament**? In most cases it is less powerful than the executive, especially in the Third World. Parliaments still pass laws, but most of them originate with the civil servants and cabinet and are passed according to party wishes.

How many parties are there? Are parties legal and well-organized or repressed and flimsy, as in Iran? Are we looking at a one-party system, such as China, or multiparty systems, such as Brazil and South Africa? One of the hallmarks of the Third World is its weak party systems.

Key Terms

institution Established rules and relationships of power.

constitution The written organization of a country's institutions.

parliament A national assembly that considers and passes laws.

GDP Gross Domestic Product; sum total of goods and services produced in a country in one year.

per capita GDP divided by population, giving an approximate level of well-being.

PPP Purchasing power parity; per capita GDP adjusted for cost of living.

DEMOCRACY

DEVELOPMENT AND DEMOCRACY

Scholars find a clear connection between economics and democracy. Countries with **per capita GDPs** above $6,000 (middle-income countries and higher) are almost all stable democracies and do not revert to authoritarianism. Countries with per capita GDPs below $5,000 have trouble establishing and sustaining democracy and often revert to authoritarianism. A quick look at the 1999 "per caps" (in **PPP**) of our four countries demonstrates this connection:

S. Africa	$6,900	(new democracy)
Brazil	6,150	(pretty firm democracy)
Iran	5,300	(working on democracy)
China	3,800	(stirrings of democracy)

Democracy requires a good-sized middle class to work right. As an economy grows, more and more people become middle class. They are educated and urban and no longer under the thumb of rural political bosses. They consume mass media and have a growing sense of their interests. The regime can no longer treat them like small children.

Americans may think elections are cures for all political ills, but elections in poor countries are seldom free and fair. Many are rigged by the ruling party, which uses threats and rewards, especially in rural areas, so that they always win. When the country attains middle-income status, things change. Mexico (with a per cap of $8,500) showed with its 2000 election of President Vicente Fox of PAN that it had modernized out of one-party rule. Mexico's PRI had won the previous fourteen elections.

Democracy

Waves of Democracy

Harvard political scientist Samuel P. Huntington saw democracy as spreading in three waves. The first wave, a long one, lasted from the American and French Revolutions through World War I. It gradually and unevenly spread democracy through most of West Europe. But between the two world wars, a "reverse wave" of communist and fascist authoritarian regimes pushed back democracy in Russia, Italy, Germany, Spain, Portugal, and Japan.

The second wave, a short one, lasted from World War II until the mid-1960s. It brought democracy to most of West Europe plus the many Asian and African colonies that got their independence. Most of Asia, Africa, and Latin America, however, quickly turned authoritarian.

Huntington's third wave began in the mid-1970s with the return of democracy to Portugal, Spain, and Greece, and thence to Latin America and East Asia. In 1989, as Communist regimes collapsed, it took over much of East Europe and even, with the Soviet collapse of 1991, Russia. At least on paper, roughly half of the world's 193 countries are democratic. But, warns Huntington, get ready for another reverse wave as some shaky democratic regimes revert to authoritarianism.

How powerful is the country's permanent civil service—its bureaucracy? In the Third World, especially Latin America, there are usually far too many bureaucrats, and they often strangle economic growth in taxes, regulations, and corruption. Trimming bureaucracies is an urgent task in much of the Third World.

Political Culture

By the late 1950s a new **political culture** approach to comparative politics became prominent; it sought to explain systems in terms of peoples' attitudes and psychology. Some thinkers believe this is the make-or-break for development in the Third World. With the right attitudes—trust in others, work hard, save a lot, educate your children—countries have enjoyed spectacular growth. Some political cultures are heavy on **cynicism**, fatalism, and passivity, and this harms their economic growth. This can be rapidly turned around, though; give people a sniff of a better life and they respond by quickly adopting new attitudes.

Legitimacy is a basic political attitude, originally meaning that the rightful king was on the throne, not a usurper. Now it means a mass attitude that people think the government's rule is valid and that it should generally be obeyed. Governments are not automatically legitimate; they have to earn the respect of their citizens. Legitimacy can be created over a long time as a government endures and governs well. Legitimacy can also erode as unstable and corrupt regimes come and go, never winning the

Key Terms

political culture The values and attitudes of citizens in regard to politics and society.

cynicism Mistrust; belief that a political system is wrong and corrupt.

legitimacy Mass perception that a regime's rule is rightful.

people's respect. One quick test of legitimacy is how many police officers a country has. With high legitimacy, it doesn't need many police because people obey the law voluntarily. With low legitimacy, a country needs many police. Many Third World regimes have weak legitimacy.

Regimes frequently espouse an **ideology**, a grand plan to save or improve the country (see box on page 10). Typically, leaders at the top of a system take their ideology with a grain of salt. But for mass consumption, the Chinese and Iranian leaders crank out reams of ideological propaganda (which, in fact, many people ignore).

Key Terms

ideology Belief system that society can be improved.

pragmatic Without ideological considerations, based on practicality.

autarchy Economic self-reliance with minimal imports.

Chinese Communists still espouse "socialism with Chinese characteristics"; Iran's mullahs proclaim "Islamic Revolution." Does every system have some sort of ideology? The opposite of ideological is **pragmatic**—if it works, use it. Typically, as Third World lands modernize, parties tone down their ideologies and become more pragmatic. Some have turned from **autarchy** and socialism to capitalist globalization.

Another contributor to political culture is a country's educational system. Almost universally, education is the main path to elite status. Who gets educated and in what way helps structure who gets political power and what they do with it. No country has totally equal educational opportunity. Even where schooling is legally open to all, social, economic, and even political screening devices work against some sectors of the population. Most countries have elite universities that produce a big share of their political leadership, at times a near monopoly. Elite views are a major determinant of a country's politics.

Political Culture

The Civic Culture Study

In a 1959 study, political scientists Gabriel Almond and Sidney Verba led teams that asked approximately one thousand people in each of five countries—the United States, Britain, West Germany, Italy, and Mexico—identical questions on their political attitudes. The Civic Culture study, which was a benchmark in cross-national research, discerned three types of political culture:

1. *Participant*, in which people know a lot about politics and feel they should participate in politics.
2. *Subject*, in which people are aware of politics but cautious about participating; they are more conditioned to obeying.
3. *Parochial*, narrow or focused only on their immediate concerns; one in which people are not even much aware of politics and do not participate.

Almond and Verba emphasized that each country is a mixture of these types, with perhaps one type dominating: participant in America, subject in West Germany and Italy, parochial in Mexico. Much of the Third World is now shifting out of parochial and, in the growth countries, even gaining a participant culture, the hallmark of young, urban, educated people.

Key Concepts

What Is "Ideology"?

Political ideologies can be an important part of political culture. They are belief systems—usually ending in *-ism*—that claim to aim at improving society. Believers in an ideology say: "If we move in this direction, things will be much better. People will be happier, catastrophe will be avoided, society will become perfected." An ideology usually contains four elements:

1. The *perception* that things are going wrong, that society is headed down the wrong path. Fanatic ideologies insist that catastrophe is just around the corner.
2. An *evaluation* or analysis of why things are going wrong. This means a criticism of all or part of the existing system.
3. A *prescription* or cure for the problem. Moderate ideologies advocate reforms; extremist ideologies urge revolution.
4. An effort to form a *movement* to carry out the cure. Without a party or movement, the above points are just talk without serious intent.

Marxism-Leninism is a perfect example of ideology. First, we have Marx's perception that capitalism is unjust and doomed. Second, we have his analysis that capitalism contains its own internal contradictions, which bring economic depressions. Third, we have a Marxist prescription: Abolish capitalism in favor of collective ownership of the means of production—socialism. And fourth, especially with Lenin, we have the determined movement to form a strong Communist party—the "organizational weapon"—to put the cure into effect by overthrowing the capitalist system.

An important point about ideologies is that they are always defective; that is, they never deliver what they promise: perfect societies and happy humans. China's warped version of Marxism-Leninism killed millions and kept China poor. Even Islamic fundamentalism did not make Iranians happy. After a while, ideological regimes tend to turn pragmatic.

Patterns of Interaction

Here we come to what is conventionally called "politics." We look for who does what to whom. We look for the interactions of parties, interest groups, individuals, and bureaucracies. Elites play a major role in these interactions. Even democratic politics is usually the work of a few. Most people, most of the time, do not participate in politics. But there are various kinds of elites, some more democratic and dedicated to the common good than others. How much of these interactions are an elite game with little or no mass participation?

Key Terms

generalization The finding of repeated examples and patterns.

theory Firm generalizations supported by evidence.

Do groups come together to compete or strike deals? How do political parties persuade the public to support them? We look not for one-time events but for things that occur with some regularity. Finding such patterns is the beginning of making **generalizations**, and generalizing is the beginning of **theory**. Once we have found a pattern, we ask why. The answer will be found partly from what we have learned about each country in preceding pages and partly from the nature of political life where struggle and competition are normal and universal.

Some interactions are open and public; others, especially elite interactions, are closed and secretive. A lot of politics happens behind closed doors and is known only by "**anecdotal evidence.**" The interactions of parties and citizenry are mostly open. Every party tries to convince the public that their party is the one fit to govern. This holds equally true for

Key Term

anecdotal evidence Unconfirmable reports of interactions; journalism.

Key Concepts

The Politics of Social Cleavages

Most societies are split along one or more lines. Often these splits, or "cleavages," become the society's fault lines along which political views form. Here are some of the more politically relevant social cleavages.

Social Class

Karl Marx thought social class determined everything, that the split between the "bourgeoisie" and "proletariat" was the only important social cleavage. At times (the 1930s), this somewhat fit Europe, but in the Third World—which was preindustrial and precapitalist—it didn't fit at all. As the economy grows, however, we sometimes see the emergence of class differences.

Geographic Region

Most countries have regional differences, and often they are politically important. In the Third World, ethnic minorities often inhabit outlying regions and resent being ruled by the nation's capital. In China, Tibetans and Uygurs fight rule by Beijing. In Brazil, the southern states do not like being ruled by Brasília. In South Africa, Zulu leaders in KwaZulu/Natal do not like being ruled by Pretoria.

Religion

In some countries religious conflicts are still quite important. In Iran, religion dominates politics, but urban young people, secular in orientation, resent it. In China, a Buddhist offshoot was harshly repressed by a frightened government, which understood that two religion-based uprisings almost took power in the nineteenth century.

Urban-Rural

Urban dwellers are more educated, aware of politics, more participatory, and more open to modernization. This is especially true in the Third World, where the countryside remains backward while the cities modernize. China has a major urban-rural split in terms of living conditions, education, and political orientation.

There are other politically relevant social cleavages. In some cases, gender matters. In Iran, urban women are fed up with restrictions on their lives. Occupation, as distinct from social class, can also influence political attitudes; workers and farmers see things differently. Age can sometimes be an important political factor. Young people are usually more open to new ideas and more likely to embrace radical and even violent causes than are older citizens. China's Red Guards, South Africa's liberation fighters, and Iran's *hezbollahi* were all young.

Key Terms

interest group Association aimed at getting favorable policies.

corruption Use of public office for private gain.

globalization The world turning into one big capitalist market.

democratic and authoritarian systems. Do they succeed? Whom do the parties aim for, and how do they win them over? By ideology? Promises? Common interests? Or by convincing people the other party is worse?

The parties interact with each other, sometimes cooperatively but more often competitively. How do they denounce and discredit each other? Under what circumstances do they make deals? Is their competition murderous or moderate?

Parties also interact with the government. In China, the Party nearly is the government. In more politically open countries, parties try to capture and retain governmental power. How do parties form coalitions? Who gets the top cabinet jobs? Once in power, is the party able to act, or is it immobilized by contrary political forces? These are some questions to ask. Politics within the parties is an important point. We ask if a party has factions. Does the party have a traditionalist and a modernizing wing? How do its leaders hold it together? Do they pay off factions with key jobs or merely with lip service? Could the party split?

Parties also interact with **interest groups**. Some groups enjoy "structured access" to like-minded parties. In Brazil, labor unions are linked to the Workers party. In South Africa, Zulus tend to support the Inkatha Freedom party. Interest groups tend to grow in importance as the economy expands. One clear sign of interest-group activity is **corruption**: Groups paying money to politicians for favors, a strong characteristic of the Third World. All four of our countries have massive corruption.

What People Quarrel About

Here we move to current issues, the political struggles of the day. We start with economics, the universal and permanent quarrel over who gets what. Politics and economics are closely connected; one can make or break the other. (Political scientists should have a grounding in economics; take an economics course.)

First, we inquire if the economy of the country is growing. Rapidly or slowly? What is a good growth rate? In the West, 3 percent is decent annual GDP growth, but in the Third World 3 percent is slow, and for three reasons. First, there is the mathematical quirk that shows big percentage gains when you start with a small economy. If you start with $100 and make another dollar, you get only 1 percent growth. But if you start with $5 and add another dollar, you get 20 percent growth. Second, population growth in Third World countries is generally high, so 3 percent overall GDP growth becomes zero per capita if you have 3 percent annual population increases. Third, much of the Third World suffers from horrible poverty and unemployment, and rapid economic growth is the only way out.

We ask why some economies grow and others don't. Are workers lazy or energetic? Are managers inept or clever? How much of the economy is supervised and planned by government? Is government interference a hindrance to the economy? Would the economy be better off with a free market or some government supervision? How well-connected is the country's economy to **globalization**?

Other issues are the following: How strong are unions and what do they seek? Are wage settlements in line with productivity, or are they pricing the country out of the world market? China's low wages let it start climbing the economic ladder. South Africa's high wages contribute to massive (40 percent) unemployment. Does government try to

Comparison

The Importance of Being Comparative

"You can't be scientific if you're not comparing," UCLA's late, great James Coleman used to tell his students. Countries are not unique; they are comparable with other countries. When we say, for example, the parliament of country X has become a rubber stamp for the executive, this is not a very meaningful statement until we note it is also the tendency in countries Y and Z.

The "uniqueness trap" often catches commentators of the American scene off-guard. We hear statements such as: "The U.S. political system is breaking down." Compared to what? To Brazil in 1964? To China in 1989? Or to the United States itself in 1861? Compared to these other cases, the United States today is in great shape. Our thinking on politics will be greatly clarified if we put ourselves into a comparative mood by frequently asking, "Compared to what?"

influence wage increases? Pushing them up or holding them down? Do workers and management cooperate or battle each other?

There are, to be sure, noneconomic quarrels as well. Regionalism is persistent and even growing. What are a country's regions? Which of them are discontent? Over what? How does the discontent manifest itself? Does it include violence? Are there ideas to decentralize or devolve power to the regions?

Key Terms

absolutism (p. 5)
anecdotal evidence (p. 11)
autarchy (p. 9)
authoritarian (p. 5)
colonialism (p. 6)
constitution (p. 7)
corruption (p. 12)
cynicism (p. 8)
democracy (p. 1)
divide and rule (p. 6)
elites (p. 5)
GDP (p. 7)
generalization (p. 10)
globalization (p. 12)
ideology (p. 9)
institution (p. 7)
interest group (p. 12)
legitimacy (p. 8)
mass (p. 5)
Mongols (p. 5)
parliament (p. 7)
per capita (p. 7)
political culture (p. 8)
political geography (p. 5)
PPP (p. 7)
pragmatic (p. 9)
theory (p. 10)
totalitarian (p. 5)
tribalism (p. 6)

Further Reference

Diamond, Larry, ed. *Political Culture and Democracy in Developing Countries*. Boulder, CO: Lynne Rienner, 1994.

Gill, Graeme. *The Dynamics of Democratization: Elites, Civil Society, and the Transition Process*. New York: St. Martin's, 2000.

Harrison, Lawrence E., and Samuel P. Huntington, eds. *Culture Matters: How Values Shape Human Progress*. New York: Basic Books, 2000.

Huntington, Samuel P. *The Third Wave: Democratization in the Late Twentieth Century*. Norman, OK: University of Oklahoma Press, 1991.

Landes, David. *The Wealth and Poverty of Nations*. New York: Norton, 1998.

Lane, Ruth. *The Art of Comparative Politics*. Needham Heights, MA: Allyn & Bacon, 1997.

Peters, B. Guy. *Comparative Politics: Theory and Method*. New York: New York University Press, 1998.

Rapley, John. *Understanding Development: Theory and Practice in the Third World*. Boulder, CO: Lynne Rienner, 1996.

Sullivan, Michael J. *Comparing State Polities: A Framework for Analyzing 100 Governments*. Westport, CT: Greenwood, 1996.

CHAPTER 2

China

Questions to Consider

1. Why was it easy for Europeans to penetrate and derange China?
2. How did Mao and the Communists beat the Nationalists?
3. Why does Beijing inflict periodic upheavals on China? What were the big ones?
4. What is a "technocrat" in the Chinese context?
5. What is "voluntarism" and how did Mao exemplify it?
6. What forms of nationalism could dominate in China?
7. What goes wrong when you mix capitalism and socialism?
8. Explain second- and third-order consequences.
9. What should U.S. policy regarding China be? Why?

The Impact of the Past

China's population is some 1.3 billion and slowly growing, even though the regime promotes one-child families. Less than one-third of China's territory is arable—rice in the well-watered south and wheat in the drier north. China's **man-land ratio**—now only one-quarter acre of farmland for each Chinese—long imposed limits on politics, economics, and social thought.

With little new territory to expand into, Chinese society evolved **steady-state** structures to preserve stability and contentment among peasants rather than encourage them to pioneer and innovate. Labor-saving devices would render peasants jobless and were therefore not encouraged. China's achievements in science and technology—which put China far ahead of medieval Europe—remained curiosities instead of contributions to an industrial revolution.

Commercial expansion was also discouraged. Instead of encouraging reinvestment, growth, and risk taking, Chinese merchants sought a steady-state relationship with peasants and government officials; they depended heavily on government permits and monopolies.

Nor was there interest in overseas expansion. Once they had their Middle Kingdom perfected, the Chinese saw no use for anything foreign. All outlying countries were inhabited by barbarians who were permitted to **kow-tow** and pay tribute to the emperor. China had all the technology for overseas expansion but didn't bother. Expeditions brought back the news that there wasn't anything worthwhile beyond the seas. Thus, for centuries, China remained a stay-at-home country.

Key Terms

man-land ratio How much arable land per person.

steady-state A system that preserves itself with little change.

kow-tow Literally, head to the ground; to prostrate oneself.

The People's Republic of China

The solid black line shows the approximate route of the 1934–35 Long March.

A Traditional Political System

Politically, too, China was steady-state. China unified very early. Feudalism was replaced by a bureaucratic empire, complete with impartial civil-service exams to select the best talent. The resulting Mandarin class—schooled in the Confucian classics, which stressed obedience, authority, and hierarchy—was interested in perpetuating the system, not changing it. A gentry class of better-off people served as the literate intermediaries between the Mandarins and the 90 percent of the population that were peasants. The words of one peasant song are as follows:

> When the sun rises, I toil;
> When the sun sets, I rest;
> I dig wells for water;
> I till the fields for food;
> What has the Emperor's power to do with me?

Dynasties came and went every few hundred years in what is called the **dynastic cycle.** As the old dynasty became increasingly incompetent, water systems went unrepaired, famine broke out, wars and banditry appeared, and corruption grew. In the eyes of the people, it looked as if the emperor had lost the "Mandate of Heaven," that is, his legitimate right to rule. A conqueror, either Chinese or foreign (**Mongol** or **Manchu**), found it easy to take over a demoralized empire. By the very fact of his victory, the new ruler seemed to have gained the Mandate of Heaven. Under vigorous new emperors, things went well; the breakdowns were fixed. After some generations, though, the new dynasty fell prey to the same ills as the old, and people, especially the literate, began to think the emperor had lost his heavenly mandate. The cycle was ready to start over.

Two millennia of Chinese empire left an indelible mark on the China of today. Not a feudal system like Japan, China early became a unified and centralized system, with an emperor at the top setting the direction and tone, Mandarins carrying out Beijing's writ, gentry running local affairs, and peasants—the overwhelming majority of the population—toiling in the fields. New dynasties soon found themselves lulled into accepting the system and becoming part of it. Even the Communists were not able to totally eradicate the classic pattern of Chinese civilization.

Key Terms

dynastic cycle The rise, maturity, and fall of an imperial family.

Mongol Central Asian dynasty, founded by Genghis Khan, that ruled China in the thirteenth and fourteenth centuries.

Manchu Last imperial dynasty of China, also known as *Qing;* ruled from seventeenth century to 1911.

Middle Kingdom China's traditional name for itself, as if it were in the middle of the heavens.

The Long Collapse

For some 2,000 years the **Middle Kingdom** proved capable of absorbing the changes thrown at it in the form of invasions, famines, and new dynasties. The old pattern always reasserted itself. But as the modern epoch impinged on China, at least two new factors arose that the system could not handle: population growth and Western penetration.

In 1741, China's population was 143 million; just a century later, in 1851, it had become an amazing 432 million, the result of new crops (corn and sweet potatoes from the Americas), internal peace under the Manchu dynasty, some new farmland, and just plain harder work on

Geography

Bound China

China is bounded on the north by Russia, Mongolia, and Kazakhstan;

on the east by Korea and the Yellow, East China, and South China Seas;

on the south by Vietnam, Laos, Burma, India, Bhutan, and Nepal;

and on the west by Tajikistan, Afghanistan, and Pakistan.

If you know China's boundaries you can label most of mainland Asia. Only Cambodia, Thailand, and Bangladesh do not border China.

Geography

Rainfall

A focus on Europe may cause us to overlook one of the most basic physical determinants of a politico-economic system. Rainfall in Europe is generally sufficient and predictable, but in much of the world it is not. There is plenty of land in the world; water to grow crops is the limiting factor. An average Chinese has available only about 20 percent of the water of the global average. Irrigation can supplement rainfall, but this requires a high degree of human organization and governmental supervision. This may explain why high civilizations arose so early in China and Iran. Large desert or semi-desert areas of our four Third World examples—China, Brazil, South Africa, and Iran—will never be able to sustain much development.

the part of the peasants. Taxation and administration lagged behind the rapid population growth, which hit as the Manchus were going into the typical decline phase of their dynastic cycle in the nineteenth century.

At about the same time, the West was penetrating and disorienting China. It was a clash of two cultures—Western dynamism and greed versus Chinese stability—and the Chinese side was no match at all. In roughly a century of collapse, old China went into convulsions and breakdowns, which ended with the triumph of the Communists.

The first Westerners to reach China were Portuguese seamen in 1514. Gradually, they and other Europeans got permission to set up trading stations on the coast. For three centuries the Imperial government disdained the foreigners and their products and tried to keep their number to a minimum. In 1793, for example, in response to a British mission to Beijing, the emperor commended King George III for his "respectful spirit of submission" but pointed out that there could be little trade because "our celestial empire possesses all things in prolific abundance."

But the West, especially the British, pushed on, smelling enormous profits in the China trade. Matters came to a head with the Opium Wars of 1839 to 1842. The British found a product that Chinese would buy, opium from the poppy fields of British-held India. Opium smoking was illegal and unknown in China. The British, however, flouted the law and popularized opium smoking. When at last a zealous Imperial official tried to stop the opium trade, Britain went to war to keep the lucrative commerce open. Britain easily won, but the Chinese still refused to admit that the foreigners were superior. Moaned one Cantonese: "Except for your ships being solid, your gunfire fierce, and your rockets powerful, what good qualities do you have?" For the Chinese, war technology was not as important as moral quality, a view later adopted by Mao Zedong.

The 1842 Treaty of Nanjing (Nanking in the now-obsolete Wade-Giles transcription) wrested five **treaty ports** from the Chinese. Britain got Hong Kong as an outright possession. In the treaty ports the foreigners held sway, dominating the commerce and governance of the area. The Westerners enjoyed **extraterritoriality**, meaning they were not subject to Chinese law but had their own courts, a point deeply resented by both Chinese and Japanese. In the 1860s, nine more Chinese treaty ports were added.

Key Terms

treaty ports Areas of the China coast run by European powers.

extraterritoriality Privilege of Europeans in colonial situations to have separate laws and courts.

Around the treaty ports grew **spheres of influence**, understandings among the foreign powers as to who ran things there. The British, French, Germans, Russians, and Japanese in effect carved up the China coast with their spheres of influence, in which they dominated trade. The Americans, claiming to be above this sort of business, tagged along after the British. China was reduced to semicolonial status.

Key Terms

sphere of influence Semicolonial area under control of major power.

Taiping Major religion-based rebellion in nineteenth-century China.

Boxer Major Chinese antiforeigner rebellion in 1900.

From Empire to Republic

Internally, too, the Empire weakened. Rebellions broke out. From 1851 to 1864, the **Taipings**—espousing a mixture of Christianity (picked up from missionaries), Confucianism, and primitive communism—baptized millions in South China and nearly overthrew the Manchu (Qing) dynasty. In 1900, with the backing of some reactionary officials and the empress dowager, the antiforeign **Boxer** movement, based on traditional temple boxing-type exercises, killed missionaries and besieged Beijing's Legation Quarter for fifty-five days. An international expedition of British, French, German, Russian, American, and Japanese troops broke through and lifted the siege. The foreigners then demanded indemnities and additional concessions from the tottering Imperial government.

Could the Qing (pronounced "Ching") dynasty have adapted itself to the new Western pressures? The Japanese had; with the 1868 Meiji Restoration they preserved the form of empire but shifted to modernization and industrialization with spectacular success. Many young Chinese demanded reforms to strengthen China, especially after their humiliating defeat by Japan in 1895. In 1898 the young Emperor Guangxu gathered around him reformers and in the famous Hundred Days issued more than forty edicts, modernizing everything from education to the military. Conservative officials and the old empress dowager would have none of it; they carried out a coup, rescinded the changes, and put the emperor under house arrest for the rest of his short life. (He was probably poisoned.)

Key Concepts

Confucianism: Government by Right Thinking

The scholar Confucius (551–479 B.C.) advised rulers that the key to good, stable government lay in instilling correct, moral behavior in ruled and rulers alike. Each person must understand his or her role and perform it obediently. Sons were subservient to fathers, wives to husbands, younger brothers to elder brothers, and subjects to rulers. The ruler sets a moral example by purifying his spirit and perfecting his manners. In this way, goodness perpetuates the ruler in power. Other East Asian lands picked up Confucianism from China.

The Confucian system emphasized that good government starts with thinking good thoughts in utter sincerity. If things go wrong, it indicates rulers have been insincere. Mao Zedong hated everything old China stood for, but he couldn't help picking up the Confucian stress on right thinking. Adding a Marxist twist, Mao taught that one was a proletarian not because of blue-collar origin but because one had revolutionary, pure thoughts. Confucius would have been pleased.

Key Concepts

Cyclical versus Secular Change

China offers good illustrations of the two kinds of change that social scientists often deal with. Cyclical change is repetitive; certain familiar historical phases follow one another like a pendulum swing. China's dynastic cycles are examples of cyclical change; there is change, but the overall pattern is preserved.

Secular change means a long-term shift that does not revert to the old pattern. China's population growth, for example, was a secular change that helped break the stability of traditional China. One of the problems faced by historians, economists, and political scientists is whether a change they are examining is secular—a long-term, basic shift—or cyclical—something that comes and goes repeatedly.

A system that cannot reform is increasingly ripe for revolution. Younger people, especially army officers, grew fed up with China's weakness and became militant nationalists. Many Chinese studied in the West and were eager to westernize China. Under an idealistic, Western-trained doctor, San Yatsen (Sun Yat-sen in Wade-Giles), disgruntled provincial officials and military commanders overthrew the Manchus in 1911. It was the end of the last dynasty but not the beginning of stability. In the absence of central authority, so-called **warlords** in effect brought China into feudalism from 1916 to 1927.

Gradually overcoming the chaos was the **Nationalist** party, or Guomindang (in Wade-Giles, Kuomintang, KMT). Formed shortly after the Manchu's overthrow, the Nationalists were guided by intellectuals (many of them educated in the United States), army officers, and the modern business element. Their greatest strength was in the South, in Guangzhou (Canton), especially in the coastal cities where there was the most contact with the West. It was no accident that they made Nanjing their capital; the word in fact means "southern capital." (North-South tensions exist to this day in China.)

Power gravitated into the hands of General (later Generalissimo) Jiang Jieshi (Chiang Kai-shek), who by 1927 had succeeded in unifying most of China under the Nationalists. While Jiang was hailed as the founder and savior of the new China—Henry Luce, the son of a China missionary, put Jiang ten times on the cover of *Time*—in reality, the Nationalist rule was weak. The Western-oriented city people who staffed the Nationalists did not reform or develop the rural areas where most Chinese still lived, usually under the thumb of rapacious landlords. Administration became terribly corrupt. And the Nationalists offered no plausible ideology to rally the Chinese people.

Still, like Kerensky's provisional government in Russia, the Nationalists might have succeeded were it not for war. In 1931 the Japanese seized Manchuria and in 1937 began the conquest of the rest of China. By 1941 they had taken the entire coast, forcing the Nationalists to move their capital far up the Changjiang (Yangtze) River from Nanjing to Chongqing. The United States, in accordance with its long support of China, embargoed trade with Japan, a move that eventually led to Pearl Harbor. For the Americans in World War II, however, China was a sideshow. Jiang's forces preferred fighting Communists to Japanese, while waiting for a U.S. victory to return them to power.

Key Terms

warlord In 1920s China, a general who ran a province.

Nationalist Chiang Kai-shek's party that unified China in late 1920s, abbreviated KMT.

The Communist Triumph

One branch of Chinese nationalism, influenced by Marx and by the Bolshevik Revolution, decided that communism was the only effective basis for implementing a nationalist revolution. The Chinese Communists have always been first and foremost nationalists, and from its founding in 1921 the Chinese Communist party (CCP) worked with the Nationalists until Jiang, in 1927, decided to exterminate them as a threat. The fight between the KMT and CCP was a struggle between two versions of Chinese nationalism.

While Stalin advised the Chinese Communists to base themselves on the small proletariat of the coastal cities, Mao Zedong rose to leadership of the Party by developing a rural strategy called the "mass line." Mao concluded that the real revolutionary potential in China, which had little industry and hence few proletarians, was among the long-suffering peasants. It was a major revision of Marx, one that Marx probably would not recognize as Marxism.

In 1934, with KMT forces surrounding them, some 120,000 Chinese Communists began their incredible Long March of more than 6,000 miles (10,000 km) to the relative safety of Yan'an in the north. It lasted over a year and led across mountain ranges and rivers amidst hostile forces. Fewer than twenty thousand survived. The Long March became the epic of Chinese Communist history. Self-reliant and isolated from the Soviets, the Chinese Communists had to develop their own strategy for survival, including working with peasants and practicing guerrilla warfare.

While the war against Japan drained and demoralized the Nationalists, it strengthened and encouraged the Communists. Besides stocks of captured Japanese weapons from the Russian takeover of Manchuria in 1945, the Chinese Communists got little help from the Soviets and felt they never owed them much in return. Mao and his Communists came to power on their own, by perfecting their peasant and guerrilla strategies. This fact may have contributed to the later Sino-Soviet split.

After World War II, the Nationalist forces were much larger than the Communists', and they had many U.S. arms. Nationalist strength, however, melted away as hyperinflation

Chairman Mao Zedong proclaims the founding of the People's Republic of China on October 1, 1949. (Xinhua)

Key Concepts

Mao and Guerrilla War

In what became a model for would-be-revolutionaries the world over, the Chinese Communists swept to power in 1949 after a decade and a half of successful guerrilla warfare. During these years, Mao Zedong, often in his Yan'an cave, developed and taught what he called the **mass line**. His lessons included the following:

1. Take the countryside and surround the cities. While the enemy is stuck in the cities, able to venture out only in strength, you are mobilizing the masses.
2. Work very closely with the peasants, listen to their complaints, help them solve problems (for example, getting rid of a landlord or bringing in the harvest), propagandize them, and recruit them into the army and Party.
3. Don't engage the enemy's main forces but rather probe for his weak spots, harassing him and wearing him out.
4. Don't expect much help from the outside; be self-reliant. For weapons, take the enemies'.
5. Don't worry about the apparent superior numbers and firepower of the enemy and his imperialist allies; their strength is illusory because it is not based on the masses. Willpower and unity with the masses are more important than weaponry.
6. At certain stages guerrilla units come together to form larger units until at last, as the enemy stumbles, your forces become a regular army that takes the entire country.

destroyed the economy, corrupt officers sold their troops' weapons (often to the Communists), and war weariness paralyzed the population. The Nationalists had always neglected the rice roots of political strength: the common peasant. The Communists, by cultivating the peasantry (Mao himself was of peasant origin), won a new Mandate of Heaven. In 1949, the disintegrating Nationalists retreated to the island of Taiwan while the Communists restored Beijing ("northern capital") as the country's capital and proceeded to implement what is probably the world's most sweeping revolution. On that occasion, Mao, reflecting his deeply nationalistic sentiments, said: "Our nation will never again be an insulted nation. We have stood up."

The Key Institutions

The Soviet Parallel

The institutions of China's government are essentially what the Soviet Union had—interlocking state and Party hierarchies—but China adds a Third World twist: The army is also quite important, at times intervening directly into politics, as happens in other developing countries. China, no less than Brazil (see the next chapter), has experienced upheaval and chaos, which has led to army participation in politics. In this regard, the People's Republic of China (PRC) is still a Third World country.

Key Term

mass line Mao's theory of revolution for China.

As in the old Soviet model, each state and Party level ostensibly elects the one above it. In China, production and residential units elect local People's Congresses, which then elect county People's Congresses, which in turn choose provincial People's Congresses. China, organized on a unitary rather than federal pattern, has twenty-one provinces. The provincial People's Congresses then elect the National People's Congress (NPC) of nearly three thousand deputies for a five-year term.

As in the ex-Soviet Union, this parliament is too big to do much at its brief annual sessions. Recent NPC sessions, however, have featured some lively debate, contested committee elections, and negative votes—possibly indications that it may gradually turn into a real

Tandem Power: Mao and Zhou

For over a quarter of a century, until both died in 1976, power in Beijing was not concentrated in the hands of a single Stalin-like figure but divided between Party Chairman Mao Zedong and Premier Zhou Enlai. This Chinese pattern of tandem power may now be sufficiently deep to continue into the future.

Both men were of rural backgrounds, but Mao was born in 1893 into a better-off peasant family, while Zhou was born in 1898 into a gentry family. As young men, both were drawn to Chinese nationalism and then to its Marxist variation. Neither of them went much further than high school in formal education, although both studied, debated, and wrote in Chinese leftist circles. Zhou was in France from 1920 to 1924, ostensibly to study but actually to recruit Chinese students in Europe. Mao had no experience outside of China.

As instructed by the Soviets, the young Chinese Communist party worked closely with the Nationalists. Zhou, for example, was in charge of political education at the Nationalist military academy. In 1927, when Chiang Kai-shek turned on the Communists, both Mao and Zhou barely escaped with their lives. (Zhou was the model militant Chinese revolutionary for French writer André Malraux's novel *Man's Fate*, set in 1927 Shanghai.)

The next decade set their relationship. Mao concluded from his work with peasants that in them lay the path to China's revolution. Zhou, who briefly remained loyal to Moscow's proletarian line, by 1931 had changed his mind and joined Mao in his Jiangxi redoubt. From there, the two led the arduous Long March to the north. By the time they arrived in Yan'an, Mao was clearly the leader of the CCP, and his "mass line" of basing the revolution on the peasantry prevailed.

Mao dominated mainly by force of intellect. Other CCP leaders respected his ability to theorize in clear, blunt language. Mao became the Party chief and theoretician but did not concern himself with the day-to-day tasks of survival, warfare, and diplomacy. These became, in large part, Zhou's jobs. Zhou Enlai became the administrator of the revolution. Never bothering to theorize, Zhou was a master at shaping and controlling bureaucracies, smooth diplomacy, and political survival amidst changing lines.

Was there tension between the two? Probably, but Zhou never showed it. Publicly Zhou dedicated himself completely to fulfilling Mao's desires, although at times, in the shambles of the Great Leap Forward (1958–60) and the Cultural Revolution (1966–69), he seemed to be trying to hold things together and limit the damage.

Mao was the abstract thinker while Zhou was the pragmatic doer. This made Mao more radical and Zhou more conservative. Mao could spin out his utopian dreams, but Zhou had to make the bureaucracy, military, and economy function. Different roles require different personalities.

parliament with some checks on the executive. This, if it ever happens, would be a major step to democratization. A Standing Committee of about 155 is theoretically supreme, but it too does not have much power in overseeing the executive branch. The chairman of the Standing Committee is considered China's head of state or president, a largely honorific post currently held by Party Chairman Jiang Zemin.

The Invisible Puppeteer: Deng Xiaoping

Deng Xiaoping was a strange leader. He had been purged from Chinese politics twice before becoming "senior vice-premier" in 1977, a deliberately deceptive title to cover the fact he was China's undisputed boss. And Deng sought no fame or glory; unlike Mao, he built no personality cult. Deng seldom appeared in public or in the media but governed in the ancient Confucian tradition: quietly, behind the scenes, chiefly by picking the right personnel. MIT political scientist Lucian Pye called him the "invisible puppeteer." This former protégé of Zhou Enlai—who, like Zhou, was a pragmatic administrator rather than a theorizer—set China on its present course and gave China its current problems.

Deng was born in 1904 into a rural landlord family. Sent to study in France, Deng was recruited by Zhou Enlai and soon joined the Chinese Communists. As a political commissar and organizer of the People's Liberation Army, Deng forged strong military connections. Rising through major posts after 1949, Deng was named to the top of the Party—the Politburo's Standing Committee—in 1956.

Deng was not as adroit as Zhou and kept getting into political trouble. An outspoken pragmatist, Deng said after the Great Leap: "Private farming is alright as long as it raises production, just as it doesn't matter whether a cat is black or white as long as it catches mice." During the Cultural Revolution this utterance was used against Deng to show he was a "Capitalist Roader." Although not expelled from the Party, Deng dropped out of sight and lost his official position. His son was crippled by a mob during the Cultural Revolution.

But the little man—Deng was well under five feet tall—bounced back in 1973 when moderates regained control. In 1975, he seemed to be ready to take over; he spoke with visiting U.S. President Ford as one head of state to another. But just a month later Deng was again in disgrace, denounced by the radicals of the **Gang of Four** as anti-Mao. Again, he was stripped of his posts, but an old army buddy gave him sanctuary in an elite military resort.

But the adaptable Deng bounced back yet again. With the arrest of the Gang of Four in 1976, moderates came back out of the woodwork, among them Deng. In July 1977, he was reappointed to all his old posts. Many Chinese state, Party, and army leaders, badly shaken by the Cultural Revolution, felt that old comrade Deng was a man they could trust. In 1978 Deng, then already seventy-four, started China on its present course by splitting economics from politics. He in effect offered Chinese a new deal: Work and get rich in a semifree market but leave politics in the hands of the Communist party. This set the stage for China's amazing economic growth. But won't the massive economic changes eventually influence politics? Apparently, Deng never gave much thought to this problem, which is now China's chief problem.

Deng was no "liberal." He encouraged economic reform but blocked any moves toward democracy. In 1989, Deng brutally crushed the prodemocracy movement in Beijing's Tiananmen Square. Although weak and reclusive in the 1990s, Deng was still quietly in control of Beijing's top personnel and main policy lines until he died in 1997 at age ninety-two.

The top of the executive branch is the State Council, a cabinet of approximately forty ministers (specialized in economic branches) and a dozen vice-premiers led by a premier, China's head of government, since 1998 Zhu Rongji.

The formal structure of the executive does not always correspond to the real distribution of its power. In 1976, after the death of both Party Chairman Mao Zedong and Premier Zhou Enlai, a relative unknown, Hua Guofeng, was installed in both their offices. On paper, Hua appeared to be the most powerful figure in the land.

Key Terms

Gang of Four Mao's ultraradical helpers, arrested in 1976.

cadre French for "framework"; used by Asian Communists for local Party leaders.

But an elderly, twice-rehabilitated Party veteran, Deng Xiaoping, named to the modest post of senior vice-premier in 1977, was in fact more powerful than his nominal boss, Hua. When Deng toured the United States in 1979, he acted like a head of state. Deng's power grew out of his senior standing in the Party and the army. In 1980, he demoted Hua and assumed power himself, still without taking over the job titles, which he left to others. By 1982, Hua was out of the Politburo and out of sight.

The Party

Like the old Soviet Communist party (CPSU), the Chinese Communist party (CCP) is constitutionally and in practice the leading political element of the country. No other parties are allowed. With 61 million members, the CCP is large, but relative to China's population it is proportionately smaller than the CPSU was. In recent years, as China's economy has decentralized and shifted to markets, the CCP has lost some of its authority. Communist officials now use their positions for personal gain; massive corruption has set in.

In organization, the CCP parallels the defunct CPSU. Hierarchies of Party congresses at the local, county, provincial, and national levels feed into corresponding Party committees. At the top is the National Party Congress; composed of some 1,900 delegates and supposed to meet at least once in five years, this congress nominally chooses a Central Committee of about 200 members. Since both bodies are too big to run things, however, power ends up in the hands of a Politburo of about twenty Party chiefs. But this is not the last level. Within the Politburo is a Standing Committee of five to seven members who really decide things. Power is extremely concentrated in China.

The CCP's structure used to be a bit different from the classic Soviet model. Instead of a general secretary at its head, the CCP had a Party chairman, Mao's title, which he passed on to Hua Guofeng. By then, however, the office was robbed of meaning, and Hua was eclipsed by Senior Vice-Premier Deng Xiaoping, who, to be sure, also held important Party and army positions. In 1982, under Deng's guidance, the Party abolished the chairmanship—part of a repudiation of Mao's legacy—and upgraded the position of general secretary, so that now the CCP structure more closely matches that of the old CPSU. Deng arranged to have his protégé Hu Yaobang named general secretary. Hu, however, proved to be too liberal and a bit unpredictable. He also failed to win approval of the army (see next section) and was dropped in 1987. His place was taken by another Deng protégé, Zhao Ziyang, who in turn was ousted in 1989 for appearing to side with student demonstrators. Replacing him was the hard-line mayor of Shanghai, Jiang Zemin, who was also named head of state in 1993.

China's nervous system is its Party **cadres**. There are 30 million CCP cadres, and whoever controls them controls China. In 1979, Deng Xiaoping began the ticklish job of easing out both the incompetent old guard—whose only qualification, in many cases, was having been on the Long March—and the extreme leftists who wormed their way into the cadre structure during the tumultuous Cultural Revolution. Quietly, Deng brought in younger, better-educated cadres dedicated to his moderate, pragmatic line.

The Army

Until recently, the top figures in the Chinese elite held both high state and high Party offices, as in the old Soviet Union. In China, though, they also held high positions atop the military structure, through the important Military Affairs Commission, which interlocks with the CCP's Politburo. Mao, Hua, and Deng were all chairmen of the Military Affairs Commission. In addition, the CCP Standing Committee usually has at least one top general. Indeed, from the beginning, the People's Liberation Army (PLA), earlier known as the Chinese Red Army, has been so intertwined with the CCP that it's hard to separate them. Deng named an active-duty general to the elite Politburo Standing Committee, and nearly a quarter of the Central Committee is PLA. Fighting the Nationalists and the Japanese for at least a decade and a half, the CCP became a combination of Party and army. The pattern continues to this day. Political scientist Robert Tucker called the Chinese system "military communism."

Mao wrote "political power grows out of the barrel of a gun," but "the Party commands the gun, and the gun must never be allowed to command the Party." Where the two are nearly merged, however, it's hard to tell who's on top. As the Communists took over China in the 1940s, it was the PLA that first set up their power structures. Until recently, China's executive decision makers all had extensive military experience, often as political commissars in PLA units. Said Zhou Enlai: "We are all connected with the army." When the Cultural Revolution broke out in 1966, as we shall see, the army first facilitated, then dampened and finally crushed the Red Guards' rampages. By the time the Cultural Revolution sputtered out, the PLA was in de facto control of most provincial governments and most of the Politburo. In 1980, a third of the Politburo was still occupied by active military men. At various times during mobilization campaigns, the army is cited as a model for the rest of the country to follow, and heroic individual soldiers are celebrated in the media.

What does PLA influence mean for the governance of China? Armies, as guardians of their countries' security, define whatever is good for them as good for the country. Anyone who undermines their power earns their opposition. During the Cultural Revolution, for example, the army under Defense Minister Lin Biao supported Mao's program to shake up the Party and state bureaucracy. (The army was not touched.) As the chaos spread, however, military commanders worried that it was sapping China's strength and military preparedness. Lin became increasingly isolated within the military. In 1971 Peking released the amazing story that Lin had attempted a coup and fled to the Soviet Union in a plane that crashed. Outside observers suggest Lin died by other means. His supporters were purged from the military. The PLA thus helped tame Maoist radicalism.

China's leaders seem to have decided that the army is not a good way to control domestic unrest. (They are right.) The PLA did not like mowing down students in Tiananmen in 1989. To deal with such situations, Beijing built up the People's Armed Police (PAP), now over 1 million strong. This paramilitary police, resembling the French CRS, could also be used as a counterweight to the PLA in case there is political infighting.

Even before Deng died, China's leaders paid special attention to the PLA and increased

Tandem Power Continues

In 1989, when Deng Xiaoping at age eighty-five gave up his last formal post—as chairman of the powerful Military Affairs Commission—he made sure two protégés took over: Party General Secretary Jiang Zemin and Premier Li Peng. They were, respectively, sixty-three and sixty-one years old, the younger generation in Chinese politics. Although neither of the two had military experience, Jiang also took Deng's place on the Military Commission.

Jiang was born in Jiangsu province; little is known of his early years. He joined the Communist party in 1946 while a student at the Shanghai Technical University. He graduated as an electrical engineer and after the Communist takeover worked in several factories, finally becoming a top engineer at an automobile plant in the northeast of China. In 1980 Jiang arrived in Beijing as an export-import official and in 1982 was named minister for the electronics industry. As mayor of Shanghai from 1985 to 1988, Jiang was not well-liked and considered by some incompetent. He cracked down on prodemocracy Shanghai intellectuals.

Li Peng, born in Sichuan, was only two years old when his revolutionary father was executed. When he was eleven, Zhou Enlai's wife sent him for schooling to the Communist headquarters in Yan'an. From 1948 to 1954, Li studied at the Moscow Power Institute and then worked on power projects in China. Deng brought him onto the Politburo in 1985 and got him named education minister. Always considered a conservative, Li cracked down on student demands for more freedom and democracy. After two five-year terms, Li stepped down as premier in 1998 to become chairman of the National People's Congress.

The new premier is Zhu Rongji. Born poor in a poor province (Hunan) in 1928, Zhu studied electrical engineering and became an industrial planner. He was caught in Mao's Hundred Flowers campaign and demoted. Later, during the Cultural Revolution (see page 35) he was forced to work for years on farms. But Deng remembered him and, after twenty years as an outcast, promoted him rapidly. In 1992, Deng gave Zhu a "triple jump" right into the Standing Committee. Zhu became China's chief economic manager and cracked down on inefficiency and corruption. He cared only about the economy, not about democracy.

All three of these leaders were dedicated to keeping firm central control of politics while moving toward a partially market economy. All had experience silencing troublesome intellectuals. All were graduate engineers, and this gave their rule a technocratic bent. None were popular, nor did they seek to please the masses. None returned to the philosophy of Mao or to rapid change. With Jiang in charge of Party affairs and Zhu of the government, the two seem to continue the pattern of tandem rule.

its budget, but the PLA, with 2.8 million soldiers, is still poor and underequipped. Trying to supplement its meager budget, the PLA went massively into private industry, running some 15,000 businesses. Worried about the PLA's corruption, smuggling, and loss of mission, President Jiang ordered the army to get out of business and get back to soldiering. They complied, indicating that the Party still commands the gun. In general, the PLA has been a conservative force in Chinese politics, for almost axiomatically, an army stands for order and sees disorder as a security problem. In China, as will also be seen in Brazil, when chaos threatens, the army moves.

Chinese Political Culture

Traditional Culture

Mao used to say that his countrymen were "firstly poor, secondly blank," meaning that the Communists could start with a clean slate and create the Chinese citizens they wished. Mao was wrong. Plenty of traditional Chinese attitudes have carried over into the People's Republic. Indeed, even Mao's vision of perfecting human nature by thinking right thoughts is a deeply Confucian notion.

When the Communists restored Beijing as the capital in 1949, they were restoring an old symbol; Beijing had been the capital for centuries until Jiang's Nationalists moved it to Nanjing. Some government offices and elite living quarters now directly adjoin the old Forbidden City of the emperors, just as the Soviets made the Kremlin their home. Tiananmen ("Gate of Heavenly Peace") Square is still Beijing's parade and demonstration area, much like Red Square is in Moscow.

In some ways, the Communists' bureaucrats and cadres perform the same function as the old Mandarins and gentry. Reciting the latest Party line instead of Confucius, the new elites strive to place a gigantic population under central control and guidance. Their aim now, to be sure, is growth and modernization, but still under a central hand. Mao himself recognized the similarity of old and new when he denounced the bureaucrats as the "new Mandarins" during the Cultural Revolution. Deng Xiaoping governed in the old Confucian style, almost invisibly, as if he had reverted to the old pattern.

To become one of the new Mandarins, Chinese youths must undergo twelve and a half hours of grueling university entrance exams. Of the millions who take them, only about 10 percent of China's college-age youths pass and enter institutions of higher education (as opposed to some 40 percent in the United States). The three days of exams resemble nothing so much as the Imperial examination system of old China. The new exams, identical and kept secret, are given simultaneously throughout China. They include sections on Chinese literature, math, science, a foreign language, and politics.

Mao argued against the examinations and had them dropped during the Cultural Revolution; they were restored only in 1977. Mao thought the exams were elitist and unrevolutionary, that they created a class of new Mandarin bureaucrats. Mao was quite right, but without the brutally competitive exams, educational standards slid, and incompetents got into universities based on their political correctness. Inferior graduates retarded China's progress in industry and administration, so the post-Mao moderates restored the examinations. It was another example of a long-functional process reasserting itself.

In another carryover from Old China, age confers special qualities of wisdom and leadership in the People's Republic. Mao died at eighty-two and Zhou at seventy-eight, both in office. When he returned to power in 1977, Deng Xiaoping was seventy-three. In his early nineties he was still politically influential although weak and deaf. President Jiang and Prime Minister Zhu are both in their seventies.

Nationalism

Overlaying traditional Chinese values is a more recent one, the nationalism that has dominated China's intellectual life for more than a century. Chinese nationalism, like Third World nationalism generally, is the result of a proud and independent culture suffering penetration, disorientation, and humiliation at the hands of the West. This can induce explosive fury and the feeling that the native culture, although temporarily beaten by foreigners, is morally better and more enduring. In our day, Chinese, Russians, and Iranians still act out their resentment of the West, especially of America.

Key Term

voluntarism Belief that human will can change the world.

In Asia, Chinese and Japanese nationalists vowed to beat the West at its own game, building industry and weaponry but placing them at the service of the traditional culture. The Japanese were able to carry out their designs in the last century; the Chinese are still caught up in this process, which from time to time leaps out as bitter anti-Americanism. All of the founding generation of Chinese Communist leaders, including Mao and Zhou, began as young patriots urging their countrymen to revitalize China and stand up to the West and to Japan.

As in the old Soviet Union, one prevailing Chinese attitude is the nationalist drive to catch up with the West. During their good economic-growth years—the mid-1950s, and 1980s and 1990s—Chinese leaders were proud of their rapid progress. The Great Leap Forward and the Cultural Revolution ruined the economy. A pragmatic moderate such as Zhou or Deng always has a powerful argument against such disruptions: They harm growth and weaken the country. Basically, this is a nationalist argument, and one used by pragmatists today.

Chinese nationalism flared anew in the 1990s. Tension with the United States over Taiwan and American pressures against China over human rights and copyright violations sparked a government-approved anti-U.S. campaign. A popular book (modeled on an earlier Japanese book), *China Can Say No*, portrayed a vast conspiracy led by America to keep China down (the same line put out by extreme Russian nationalists). Well, America better watch out, the book said, because China will defend itself. Matters got worse when U.S. jets mistakenly bombed the Chinese embassy in Belgrade in 1999. There was genuine mass resentment, carefully orchestrated by Beijing, which did not permit publication of U.S. apologies. Observers suggest China's decaying regime is using nationalism to prolong its hold on power.

Maoism

Maoism, or Mao Zedong Thought, as Beijing calls it, is now fading into the background. It draws from both traditional and nationalistic values, despite its claim to be totally new and revolutionary. From traditional China, it takes the Confucian emphasis on thinking right thoughts, based on the idea that consciousness determines existence rather than the reverse: Willpower has primacy over weaponry in wars; willpower has primacy over technology in building China. The unleashed forces of the masses, guided by Mao Zedong Thought, can conquer anything. This extreme form of **voluntarism** is consonant with China's past.

From nationalism, Mao took the emphasis on strengthening and rebuilding China so that it could stand up to its old enemies and become a world power. The trouble is that these two stands are partly at odds with each other. Traditional values call for China to ignore the West and its technology, but nationalistic values call for China to learn and copy from the West. The continuing, unresolved conflict of these two streams of thought spell permanent trouble for China.

Maoism is an outgrowth of Mao thoughts on guerrilla warfare (see page 22). According to Maoist doctrine, what the PLA did to beat the Nationalists, China as a whole must do to advance and become a world leader: Work with the masses, be self-reliant, and put willpower on a higher plane than technology to overcome obstacles. Mao can be seen as a theorist of guerrilla warfare who continued to apply his principles to governance—with catastrophic results.

In the Great Leap Forward from 1958 to 1960, Mao tried guerrilla warfare tactics on the economy, using raw manual labor plus enthusiasm to build earthen dams and backyard blast furnaces. Engineers, experts, and administrators were bypassed. The Soviets warned Mao it wouldn't work and urged him to follow the Soviet model of building the economy by more conventional means; Mao refused to follow their lead. In 1960, the Soviets withdrew their substantial numbers of foreign-aid technicians, and the Sino-Soviet split came into the open.

For the Soviet Communists, the revolution was over; the proletariat triumphed in 1917 and moved Russia into the most advanced stage of history. For Mao, the revolution never ends. Mao held that at any stage there are conservative tendencies that block the path to socialism: bureaucratism, elitism, and opportunism. Mao resolved to combat these tendencies by means of "permanent revolution," periodic upheavals to let the force of the masses surge past the conservative bureaucrats.

Socialism and bureaucratism are closely connected—as Max Weber argued long ago—but Mao thought he could break the connection. He saw China settling into the bureaucratic patterns he hated and was determined to break them by instituting a permanent revolution before he died. The result was the Great Proletarian Cultural Revolution from 1966 to 1976, during which young people were encouraged to criticize, harass, and oust almost all authority except the army. Chaos spread through China, the economy slumped, and the army took over. Shortly after Mao's death, power returned to the bureaucrats; they won and Mao failed.

Mao refused to recognize the unhappy truth that if you want socialism you must accept the bureaucratism that comes with it. By trying to leap directly into some kind of guerrilla socialism without bureaucrats, Mao nearly wrecked China. On balance, Mao Zedong Thought is inherently inapplicable, and in post-Mao China, Mao is quoted infrequently.

Concealed Anger

As in Russia, wide sectors of China's population accord their regime less and less legitimacy. The Party, once respected as clean and competent, is now seen as corrupt and irrelevant. Even the peasants, at one time thought to be apathetic or even pleased at their increased

Slogans from the Cultural Revolution

- "Put destruction first, and in the process you have construction."
- "Destroy the four olds—old thought, old culture, old customs, old habits."
- "Once all struggle is grasped, miracles are possible."
- "Bombard the command post." (Attack established leaders if they are unrevolutionary.)
- "So long as it is revolutionary, no action is a crime."
- "Sweep the great renegade of the working class onto the garbage heap!" (Dump the moderate chief of state, Liu Shaoqi.)
- "Cadres step to the side." (Bypass established authorities.)
- "To rebel is justified."

GEOGRAPHY

REGION AND LANGUAGE

China illustrates the close connection—and problems—between a country's languages and its regions. All but small countries have regions, often based on language. In some cases, as between Serbs and Albanian-speaking Kosovars, the country splits apart. China is populated mostly by Han Chinese (there are important non-Han minorities in Tibet, Xinjiang, and elsewhere) but even Han do not all speak the same language.

Chinese rulers have always proclaimed the unity of China, but China has eight main language groups—mutually unintelligible—and hundreds of dialects, making it the world's most linguistically diverse country. The biggest by far is Mandarin, dialects of which are spoken by 800 million in a broad swath from north to south, but not in the important southern coastal provinces, where 90 million speak some form of the Wu language (including Shanghai) and 70 million speak Cantonese.

The regime has always feared that separate languages could lead to breakup. Since 1913 under the KMT, Beijing has tried to make Mandarin standard and universal, and the CCP carried this on, now pushing a largely Beijing dialect, *Putonghua* (common language), as the language of government and education. Most urban Chinese can now sort of speak it, but not country folk. The new prosperity in China's southern coastal provinces has actually boosted the use of their local dialects. Beijing is not pleased.

incomes from the "responsibility system," turned angry as corrupt local officials gouged them with fake taxes. Urban workers, Marx's "proletariat" that was supposed to be the backbone of communism, are trapped between uncertainty and inflation. Many sided with prodemocracy students and tried to start independent labor unions.

As ever, China's cities are the hotbeds of criticism and reform. Although a small minority, the urban educated classes have often taken the lead in changing China. Student protests in Beijing, for example, go back a century and contributed much to the overthrow of the Empire and the rise of first the Nationalists and then the Communists. The Communists under Mao in the 1930s, to be sure, had a peasant base, but many of the cadres were urban intellectuals. Accordingly, we probably get a better idea of where China is heading by focusing on city attitudes. In most countries, urban intellectuals are the spark plugs of political change.

During the twentieth century, educated Chinese have generally had a cause to believe in. At first it was building a new republic that would not be carved up by foreigners. Then it was in repelling the Japanese invaders. With the Communist takeover, many Chinese idealistically believed that Mao offered them a blueprint for a prosperous, socialist China. After Mao, Deng Xiaoping offered the encouraging image of a prosperous, semicapitalist China possibly moving to democracy. After the June 1989 massacre of prodemocracy students in Tiananmen Square, many Chinese fell into despair. Marx, Mao, and Deng have all been discredited, even among Party officials, although few say so openly. With nothing to believe in, a spiritual vacuum has opened up. What will fill it?

One classic answer is religion; both old (including Christianity) and new ones are growing rapidly despite harsh regime scrutiny and numerous arrests. What really got the regime nervous was a gathering in 1999 in central Beijing of over 10,000 practitioners of a new religion, *Falun Gong* (Buddhist Law), which attracts all kinds of Chinese with its belief in faith healing, traditional exercises, and the coming destruction of humankind (for the eighty-second time). Buddhism generates offshoots without limit. The cult's founder and leader now lives in New York City and claims tens of millions of adherents in China. The believers in China were calm and peaceful, but they remind some of the Taipings and Boxers in the nineteenth century. Beijing in 1999 denounced Falun Gong as superstition, outlawed it, and arrested thousands of its followers. This is the reaction of a nervous regime.

Over the decades, the Chinese have become politically numb. They had to mouth slogans and participate in mass campaigns—one year anti-Confucius, the next anticapitalist roaders, then anti-Gang of Four, then anti-"spiritual pollution," then anti-"bourgeois liberalization"—without end. Most Chinese are awfully fed up with this nonsense and mentally tune out.

The great hope for Chinese students is to go abroad. Many study English and dream of joining the 40,000 Chinese students already in the United States. Many, of course, do not return to China. The regime, aware of this brain drain, changed its relatively open policy on sending students abroad and sharply restricts their numbers. Chinese university graduates must first work five years before they can apply for graduate study overseas. The great prize: a graduate degree, often an MBA, from a prestigious U.S. university. Several high-ranking Chinese leaders had children in such programs.

The Chinese way of handling the latest government crackdown on freedom and democracy is called *biaotai*, "to express an attitude." Chinese know how to crank out the current line while concealing their true feelings. This leads to what Chinese call *nei jin, wai song*, "tranquility outside, repression within." Everything looks calm, but only because people know they are being carefully watched. Just below the surface, though, repressed anger waits to erupt. Some of this shows up in the constant flow of nasty rumors about repression, economic incompetence, and the corruption of high officials. This has been called a struggle between the Big Lie and Little Whisper: The government tries to fool people with big lies, but the people fight back with little whispers. Chinese at all levels, knowing that all foreigners are closely monitored, refuse to discuss anything political (or religious) with visitors.

Such a tightly controlled system is obviously unstable. A considerable fraction of China's population dislikes and distrusts the regime. This feeling is especially prevalent in the South, which has long resented rule by the North. They know that patience is a Chinese virtue, but they are also frustrated that China's progress is blocked by a Party elite that simply wants to cling to its power and good jobs. They know that in the coastal Special Economic Zones (mostly in the South), where capitalism and foreign investment are allowed, the economy is booming. Why then not just expand the Special Zones until they cover all of China? They also know that Taiwanese enjoy five times the per capita income and far more freedom than mainlanders. Some Chinese students speak with shame that they didn't have the guts to do what the Romanians did in 1989: stand up to the government's guns and overthrow the regime. In time, Chinese student frustration could boil over again.

In the right situation—for example, a split in Beijing leadership over the personnel and policies—China's peasants, workers, and students could quickly come together and overthrow the regime. Needless to say, the police work hard to prevent a Chinese equivalent of Poland's Solidarity. Political repression, of course, solves nothing; it merely postpones the day of reckoning. What happened in East Europe could happen in China.

Patterns of Interaction

Cycles of Upheaval

Since the Communists came to power in 1949 there have been three major upheavals plus several smaller ones. Among major upheavals are the "agrarian reforms" (that is, execution of landlords and redistribution of land) of the early 1950s, the Great Leap Forward from 1958 to 1960, and the Cultural Revolution from 1966 to 1976. Smaller upheavals include the brief Hundred Flowers liberalization of 1956, the antirightist campaigns of 1957 and the early 1970s, the crushing of the Gang of Four and their supporters in the late 1970s, and the repression of the alleged "counterrevolutionary rebellion" of prodemocracy students in 1989.

The big upheavals and most of the smaller ones can be traced to the same underlying problem: Beijing's leaders, having inherited a poor and backward land, want to make China rich, advanced, and socialistic. Mao Zedong Thought taught that everything is possible: China can leap into the modern age and even beyond it. But the old, stubborn, traditional China was unyielding; it frustrated the bold plans and tugged the system back toward the previous patterns and problems.

As long as China is not what its leaders wish it to be—modern, powerful, and respected—there is the possibility of another upheaval instituted from the top. Indeed, such upheavals seem to be inherent in the effort to modernize. Similar episodes occurred in Russia as leaders tried to force their country along: Peter the Great's Westernization, Stalin's industrialization, Khrushchev's experiments, and Gorbachev's reform attempts. The difference with China is that it is far more backward and hence the remedies put forward have been more extreme.

For China's periodic upheavals to cease, it will require the abandonment of the Communists' central tenet, namely, that communism delivers rapid progress. To admit that China is now making major economic progress—but only by the capitalist path of foreign investment, markets, and world trade—took a major psychological shift at the top of the CCP. Nothing has been announced publicly, but insiders report that under Deng's leadership China's elite

Radicals and Moderates in Chinese Politics

Radicals	*Moderates*
celebrate Mao Thought	selectively quote Mao
mass-oriented	elite-oriented
antiauthoritarian	hierarchical
demand purification	demand modernization
permanent revolution	stability
breakthrough growth	steady economic growth
politics in command	economics in command
learn from the people	follow the experts
wage equality	wage differentials
worker enthusiasm	material incentives
common sense	science and education
economically self-reliant	import technology
ideological	empirical

decided to have a largely capitalist economy but to call it "socialism with Chinese characteristics." We have to keep a careful lookout for a new round of revolutionary enthusiasm. The potential for extremism is still present, and there are no institutional mechanisms—competing parties, free elections, an independent judiciary—to block a new round of it. The limiting factors now are the weariness of the Chinese people after all the regime-sponsored disruptions and the success of the "capitalist road."

Radicals and Moderates

Outside observers used to label CCP figures as "radicals" or "moderates" according to their willingness to support the kind of upheavals previously described. This may oversimplify, for there were no distinct groups in China bearing these names. And many Party leaders demonstrated how they could play both sides of the field, depending on their career advantage.

China's moderates were and still are those high up in the Party, government, or army. Almost axiomatically, anyone who's part of the establishment will not be a radical. Mao was right: Bureaucrats are by nature conservative. China's radicals were drawn largely from those peripheral to power but ambitious for it: students, junior cadres, some provincial leaders.

One of the prime motivations for radicals, especially during the Cultural Revolution, was the scarcity of job openings in Party, state, army, industrial, and other offices. For the most part, positions until recently were staffed by aging Party comrades who go back to the 1949 liberation or even the Long March. They never retire, and their longevity in office breeds impatience and resentment among younger people with ambitions of their own. A further element fueling youthful discontent is the previously mentioned difficulty of getting into a university.

The Great Leap Forward: "Twenty Years in a Day"

In 1958 Mao Zedong launched one of the strangest efforts in the Third World's struggle to move ahead: the Great Leap Forward. Vowing to progress "twenty years in a day" and "catch up with Great Britain in fifteen years," all of China was urged to "walk on two legs" (use all possible means) to industrialize rapidly. Most peasants—and China is still mostly peasant—were herded into gigantic communes, some with as many as 100,000 people. Deprived of their private plots, they were ordered to eat in communal dining halls, leave their children in nurseries, and even sleep in large dormitories.

The communes were ordered to participate in engineering and industrial projects. Relying on "labor-intensive" methods to compensate for lack of capital, millions were turned out to move earth with baskets and carry poles to build dams and irrigation works. Backyard blast furnaces were ordered built so that every commune could produce its own iron.

Within a year the failure was plain for all to see. Even Mao had to admit it; he resigned as president of the PRC but kept his chairmanship of the CCP. Peasants—as in the Soviet Union—failed to produce without private incentives. Labor was wasted in foolish projects. A serious food shortage developed, and over 30 million Chinese died of malnutrition. To meet Party quotas, peasants melted down their good tools to produce implements of miserable quality. The communes were phased out, broken first into "production brigades" and then into "production teams," which were in fact the old villages. Private farming was again permitted. Mao lost; old China won.

The Great Proletarian Cultural Revolution

If the Great Leap Forward was strange, the Great Proletarian Cultural Revolution was downright bizarre. In it, an elderly Mao Zedong tried to make his revolution permanent by destroying the very structures his new China had created. Of the many slogans from the Cultural Revolution, "bombard the command post" perhaps best summarizes its character. Mao encouraged young people, who hastily grouped themselves into ragtag outfits called Red Guards, to destroy most authority, even the CCP. They did, and Chinese progress was set back years.

The Cultural Revolution began with a 1965 flap over a Shanghai play some radicals claimed criticized Mao by allegory. Mao turned what could have been a small literary debate into a mass criticism that led to the ouster of several Party officials. Then university and high school students were encouraged to air their grievances against teachers and school administrators. Behind their discontent was a shortage of the kind of jobs the students thought they deserved upon graduation.

By fall 1966, most schools closed as their students demonstrated, humiliated officials, wrote wall posters, and marched to and fro. China was in chaos. Hundreds of thousands of victims of the Red Guards committed suicide. A much larger number were "sent down" to the countryside to work with the peasants and "learn from the people." This included physical abuse and psychological humiliation. An unknown number were murdered outright. Worried officials set up their own Red Guard groups to protect themselves. Different Red Guard factions fought each other.

Even Mao became concerned, and in early 1967 he ordered the army to step in. By the end of 1967 the People's Liberation Army pretty much ran the country. To replace the broken governmental structures, the army set up "revolutionary committees" on which sat PLA officers, Red Guard leaders, and "repentant" officials. By 1969, the worst was over, although officially the Cultural Revolution did not end until 1976 when Mao died and the ultra-radical Gang of Four (headed by Mao's wife, Jiang Qing), was arrested.

The effects of the Cultural Revolution were all bad. Industry suffered. Education, when it resumed, was without standards, and students were chosen on the basis of political attitudes rather than ability. The more moderate and level-headed officials, whom the Red Guards sought to destroy, laid low and pretended to go along with the Cultural Revolution. When it was over, they reasserted themselves and made sure one of their own was in charge: Deng Xiaoping.

And what became of the Red Guards? Claiming their energy was needed on the farm, the army marched more than sixteen million young city people to rural communes for agricultural labor and forbade them to return to their cities. By hook or by crook, many of them managed to get back to their homes to try to continue their studies. Some, utterly disillusioned with the way they had been used, turned to petty crime or fled to the British colony of Hong Kong. Some eventually became capitalist millionaires in the burgeoning Special Economic Zones of the South.

These kinds of tensions underlay the radical outburst of the Cultural Revolution. Those who aspired to power enthusiastically attempted to carry out Mao's designs. Those who held power pretended to go along with it, often by mouthing the correct slogans and self-denunciations. In Mao's words, they "waved the red flag to oppose the red flag." When the campaign burned itself out, the bureaucrats and cadres took over again, and it appeared that the moderates had won.

Chinese Liberal and Conservative Politics

With the Maoist demon back in the bottle, a new conflict appeared in Chinese politics, a split between liberal and conservative forces, similar to what the Soviets went through before their system collapsed. The Chinese moderates who opposed the extremism of the Cultural Revolution essentially wanted to go back to the way things were before that upheaval. They earned the nickname the "seventeen-years-before people," because they thought the seventeen years (from 1949 to 1966) before the Cultural Revolution were pretty good. These tended to be older people, with secure positions in the Party, army, and bureaucracy, much like Soviet *apparatchiks*. They wanted socialism on the Soviet model, with centralized control over the economy, politics, and cultural life.

Facing them were liberalizers, usually younger people, who saw the unfairness and inefficiency of central control. They pointed to the amazing growth in output that came with the introduction of private and cooperative enterprises. In the Special Economic Zones, industrial growth set world records. "See, the market system works," they said in effect. They also wanted Western-style political democracy and cultural freedoms.

The Chinese conservatives, just like their old Soviet counterparts, feared that such a system would no longer be Communist and, even worse, that their jobs would be scrapped. Fumed one CCP member who supported reforms: "What do the conservatives want? They want to go back to the '50s. Who wants that? Nobody."

It was this split that caused Deng and his successors much grief. They were prepared to liberalize cautiously, hoping to confine it to the economic sector. But demands came bubbling up to go farther and faster. In the spring of 1989, tens of thousands of Chinese university students staged giant protests and hunger strikes in favor of democracy. Deng fired his handpicked and liberal-minded successor, Zhao Ziyang, and had the PLA mow down the students in Tiananmen

Anti-Western Campaigns

Every few years China is hit with a campaign aimed at making the Chinese pull away from the Western model of economic and political freedom. The work of conservatives within the CCP, these campaigns warned that decadent Western ideas such as free enterprise, open discussion, and a loosening of Party control would mean the end of socialism in China.

In late 1983, the catchword was "spiritual pollution," meaning that Western styles in clothes, music, and thought were ruining China. Deng, fearing the campaign was being used to block his economic liberalization, called it off after only four months.

In 1986, a somewhat longer lasting campaign against "bourgeois liberalization" appeared, ruling out any discussion of ending the CCP monopoly on power and replacing it with Western-style liberalism. After the 1989 Tiananmen Square massacre, conservatives charged that it was a "counterrevolutionary rebellion" inspired by Western influences, which had to be curbed.

In 1996, Beijing permitted publication of a book by a group of young, non-Party intellectuals denouncing U.S. high-handedness in telling China what to do in human rights and trade policy. In 1999, the regime whipped up anti-U.S. anger over the bombing of the Chinese embassy in Belgrade (but quickly forgot it). The regime tries to harness Chinese nationalism for its own ends. We have likely not seen the last anti-Western campaign.

The Tiananmen Massacre

During the early morning of June 4, 1989, more than 100,000 Chinese troops opened fire on young demonstrators camped out in Beijing's Tiananmen ("Gate of Heavenly Peace") Square, killing hundreds and injuring thousands. (The regime never released figures.) Much of the killing, including tanks crushing protesters and bicyclists shot at random, took place outside the Square, but the horror went down in history as "Tiananmen."

Tiananmen marked the point at which China's Communist chiefs choked over letting China's 1980s experiment with a partially free market economy spill over into political democracy. The economic results had been good, but they encouraged people to want democracy, never the intention of Beijing's rulers. The massacre illustrates the danger of halfway reform: It encourages people to want more.

Trouble began with the death of the liberal ex-Party chief Hu Yaobang in April 1989. Students began mourning him and protesting the current CCP leadership. On April 18, thousands began to occupy the Square. While the regime pondered how to handle the demonstration, the students organized, gave speeches, and built a Goddess of Democracy statue that resembled New York's Statue of Liberty. Around the country, many sympathized with the demonstrators, and criticism of the regime mounted.

If prodemocracy demonstrations had kept going, the regime would have been in trouble. The regime knew that and struck back. Zhao Ziyang, who succeeded Hu in 1987, went out to talk with the students. He was conciliatory and appeared to side with them. This gave Politburo hardliners the chance they had been looking for to oust Zhao. Deng Xiaoping, still the real power at age 84, wanted the army to crush the demonstrators. "We do not fear spilling blood," he said.

Troops and tanks poured into Beijing. The soldiers, mostly simple country boys, felt little in common with the urban students. In one memorable videotaped confrontation, a lone protester blocked a tank column; when the tanks tried to go around him, he quickly stepped in front of them again. It seemed to symbolize the individualism of democracy standing up to the coercion of dictatorship. After the bloodbath, thousands were arrested. The top protest figures received sentences of up to thirteen years, less for those who "repented." Hundreds were held for years without trial. China's elite decided to keep going with economic change but to keep the lid on political change. Some observers say the ingredients for a similar upheaval are again present.

Square. Several hundred died, and some ten thousand were imprisoned. A chill settled over Chinese life. Conservatives also launched anti-Western campaigns (see box on page 36). The conservatives had one serious drawback: Many were elderly. Time seemed to be on the side of the liberalizers, but not without rear-guard conservative actions.

The Underlying Problem

The earlier radical-moderate and current liberal-conservative struggles have some interesting points in common. First, the old "moderates" are basically today's "conservatives": older cadres who like bureaucratized socialism. They like it because they owe their jobs to it. Further, curious as it sounds, some of yesterday's "radicals"—the Red Guard punks who caused so much destruction in Mao's name—are now ardent "liberalizers," happy to discard Maoism.

Key Terms

yuan China's currency, worth about 12 U.S. cents.

deflation Overall decrease in prices; opposite of inflation.

devaluation Decreasing the worth of your currency in relation to others.

Both radicals and liberalizers shared the same impulse in trying to break up the bureaucratized socialist system, the former attacking from the left, the latter from the right.

How could they switch from left to right? Some of the switch can be attributed to young people realizing that they had been cynically used during the Cultural Revolution. Badly burned by the experience, they are now turned off by Mao Thought and open to Western-style reforms and liberalization.

But a more basic factor is that the young people—especially university students and recent graduates—who faced bleak job prospects then, face them still. They have been trained and expect higher-level jobs in the government and economy, but few are available. Why? Because those old conservatives never retire; both Chinese tradition and CCP practice grants lifetime tenure. They stay in office until they die. Making the job situation even worse is the fact that socialism does not spontaneously grow new firms to hire graduates. (Capitalism does.) The result, now as before, is frustration and resentment among young and better-educated Chinese.

Mao tapped this resentment for his Cultural Revolution. The unstated message of the Red Guards who shouted "Destroy the four olds!" was "Get rid of the old guys and give us their jobs!" Now, in a partially market economy, these same people (or their younger brothers and sisters) see their path to success in greater economic decentralization that will let the number of firms multiply and open up new job possibilities. Some of the young Chinese protesting in favor of democracy had little idea what it meant; they just wanted to make sure the old conservatives didn't reimpose their stranglehold. And the old conservatives, fearing for their jobs and status, fought back.

One of the great underlying problems of China is what to do with the younger generation. One solution would be to impose a mandatory retirement age, but this goes against Chinese tradition. Deng Xiaoping ordered many old comrades to retire but hardly set a good example himself. Youthful energy that is badly misdirected, as in the Cultural Revolution, can wreck China. Given productive outlets in a free economy, it could make China the growth wonder of the world.

Ideology is often a mask for self-interest. The people who have the cushy jobs warn that democracy and liberalization mean "abandoning socialism." In analyzing Communist (and many other) systems, take ideology with a grain of salt; follow the jobs. (Think the jobs explanation is an exaggeration? What motivates you?)

What Chinese Quarrel About

A Market Economy for China?

Starting in 1978, some amazing changes took place in the Chinese economy. China, like all Communist countries, faced the question of how centralized the economy should be and decided on decentralization while retaining centralized political control. This, as in other countries that tried it, is proving to be an unstable combination.

The earliest changes came in the countryside, where most of China's population still live. Collectivized agriculture was reduced and families were permitted to go on the "responsibility system," a euphemism for private enterprise. Peasants lease land from the state for up to fifteen years—still no private owners—and must deliver a certain quota to the state at set prices.

Beyond that, they can sell their produce on the free market for the best price they can get. They can choose their own crops and decide how to use fertilizer and farm machinery, which they buy at their own expense. Farm production soared, Chinese ate better, and farmers' incomes went up; some even got rich.

KEY CONCEPTS

THE TROUBLE WITH MARKETS

The trouble with a market economy when introduced piecemeal into Communist countries, such as Yugoslavia, Hungary, or China, is that it tends to run out of control. The country experiences improved economic performance but also develops problems that wreck the socialist system.

Unemployment appears: In Communist systems unemployment was disguised by gross labor inefficiency, but once firms have to compete in a market and make profits, they prune unnecessary workers. Chinese workers under Mao had an "iron rice bowl"—jobs for life. Deng broke the bowl and made millions unemployed. China had to permit small-scale private enterprise to soak up some of these unemployed. More than 100 million Chinese, most without permission, left rural inland areas to seek jobs in the cities and coastal Special Economic Zones. More are on their way. Under arbitrary "custody and repatriation" rules, several million internal Chinese migrants are placed in detention camps each year.

Income inequalities develop: With a market system, some Chinese farmers, entrepreneurs, and whole provinces get richer than others. The ones who don't do so well—the inland provinces with poorer soil and fewer natural resources—become jealous and complain to Beijing to redistribute some of the wealth. The richer provinces in the South and along the coast (home of the Special Economic Zones) object, arguing they work harder and produce more. Tensions between regions, especially between North and South, are growing.

Economic instability grows, usually in the form of inflation: Most of China's food, clothing, and consumer goods are now produced and sold on a free market, and at times too many **yuan** chased too few goods, producing inflation that reached 25 percent a year in the early 1990s. In the late 1990s, however, caught with too much production during a time of East Asian recession, **deflation** actually lowered Chinese prices. Many thought China would **devalue** its currency in order to fight recession, and that this would trigger potentially dangerous regional economic instability.

Corruption increases: Corruption grows at the interface of private and governmental sectors. Economic liberalization multiplies such interfaces as more and more entrepreneurs need raw materials and permits from government officials. Some Party officials have become outrageously corrupt, helping themselves to "taxes," kickbacks, and whole enterprises.

Crime rates soar: Putting together all the above and adding weakened social controls, crime becomes a serious problem. With this come repeated campaigns to crack down on crime, including many thousands executed by firing squad each year.

The problem of an economy that mixes socialism and capitalism is its instability. It cannot find a middle ground but tends to slide more and more toward full capitalism until blocked by central control. The result is a zigzag every few years as the government alternately tightens and relaxes supervision of the economy, never finding a stable balance. China is caught in this situation.

By the 1990s, things weren't going so well in the countryside, where 70 percent of Chinese still live. The government held down farm prices and paid peasants IOUs for their grain. Farm incomes declined as inflation soared. In many rural areas, peasants rioted and attacked local authorities, who extort illegal "taxes" from them. In a pattern very typical of the Third World, more than 100 million rural Chinese moved to the jobs and riches of the coastal cities where market economies were flourishing, a destabilizing tide the regime cannot control.

The partly free market spread to the cities. Faced with substantial unemployment, the regime let individuals open small stores, restaurants, repair shops, and even manufacturing facilities. It was even permissible to hire workers, something any Marxist would call capitalist exploitation. But it worked. The Chinese applied individual hustle to produce and sell more and better products than the indifferent state factories and stores ever could. Hole-in-the-wall "department stores" had customers waiting in line to buy the fashionable clothing and footwear Mao used to scorn. People swarmed to outdoor markets to buy home-produced chairs and sofas.

Starting with the area around Hong Kong, large regions of coastal China were declared "Special Economic Zones," open to private and foreign investors. Capital poured in (much of it from Taiwan and Hong Kong) to take advantage of low Chinese wages, and production soared. These firms compete in a world market to make profits. Because of these firms—which cover only part of the Chinese economy—China's GDP grew at an amazing 10 percent a year during the 1980s and into the 1990s to become the world's second largest overall economy (but not per capita). Imagine if all the Chinese economy shifted to capitalism. By comparison, one-third of the more than 100,000 state-run enterprises lose money and have to be propped up by subsidies. Of these, half are reckoned to be hopeless. Whether to close the losers (and create unemployment) is one of the great questions facing Beijing.

While most Chinese liked their taste of the free market, many cadres did not. If you really go to a market system, what do you do with the cadres who make a good living by supervising a controlled economy? They dig in their heels and try to block major change. Deng purged or retired the old guard and replaced them with young technocrats who pursue capitalist-style economic growth and call it "socialism with Chinese characteristics."

But market economies produce problems of their own (see box on page 39) and awaken resentments and jealousies. Some suggest the Chinese economy is careening out of control at a time when political authority is weakening. Political reform has been deliberately blocked, for China is still very much a one-Party dictatorship. What will happen when the free-market economy gets totally out of kilter with the dictatorial political system?

A Middle Way for the Middle Kingdom?

The basic supposition of Deng Xiaoping and his successors was that there is a middle way between capitalism and communism, between a controlled and a free-market economy, between the Soviet and American models. (Russian President Putin entertained similar notions.) By bringing in elements of a market economy while retaining a large state sector, they sought a middle way. Is there one? Not really, and many observers now think the Chinese elite has quietly admitted it, at least among themselves.

When a Communist country introduces a bit of market economics—supply and demand, competing producers, profits, family farming, prices finding their own level—the first few years are usually good. Farm output especially grows, and everyone eats well. Consumer goods become far more available, and people live and dress better. New industries produce clothing and consumer electronics for the world market. Statistically, growth rates shoot up. It looks like they've found the happy balance: a market economy at the "micro" level to provide for consumer needs under the benevolent guidance of a state-run economy at the "macro" level. The farmers, shoemakers, and tailors are mostly private; many big industries, as well as banking and planning systems, are state-owned and under Party control.

But after a few years things start to go wrong. Shortages, distortions, and bottlenecks stall economic growth. Indeed, China's growth slowed in the late 1990s. The private sector keeps bumping into the state sector. Every time it does, there is a "crisis" that can only be resolved by expanding the private sector and shrinking the state sector. After some years of this, there is little socialism left, and this Beijing's rulers do not like.

Key Concepts

Second- and Third-Order Effects

China's fierce program to limit population growth shows what can go wrong with coercing society into what the government has decided is desirable. It also illustrates the problem of second- and third-order consequences, that is, how hard it is to predict the longer-term effects of a policy.

In the early 1980s China carried out a ferocious program to curb births. Urban women were ordered to have only one child and were fined and lost benefits if they had more. Many women were forced to have abortions. The first-order consequence, as might be expected, was to bring down China's rate of population increase to 1.3 percent a year, low for the Third World, much of which grows at 3 percent; only Europe shows less than 1 percent increase.

A second-order effect, however, was a large excess of boy over girl babies, both by abortion and female infanticide. About 5 percent of the girls expected to be born from 1979 to 1995 are missing, 10 percent in the 1990s. Like many Third World cultures, Chinese value boys above girls, both to work on the farm and to support the parents in old age. So, if they are allowed only one child, many Chinese strongly prefer a son. Bodies of newborn girls are frequently found floating in rural canals, a pattern that goes back centuries in crowded China.

Third-order effects flow from the second. The surplus of males over females mean that millions of Chinese men will never find brides. Further, the drastic restriction in fertility rates—to below the replacement rate of 2.1 births per average woman—means that China's retired generation—now much bigger and living much longer thanks to improved nutrition and health care—will not have enough working Chinese to support it. China, still a poor country, will thus face exactly the same problem as the rich countries. China's State Family Planning Commission, which now emphasizes education and contraception, never considered the second- and third-order consequences.

How then to handle the serious Third World problem of too-rapid population growth? Economic growth solves the problem without coercion. As the economy grows, more people become urban and middle class and decide for themselves to limit their number of children, as Japanese have done. As more women are educated they postpone marriage in favor of work and have fewer children. No rich country has a problem of too many babies (in fact, it's just the opposite), and newly industrializing lands show a dramatic falloff in births. China's demographic debacle is one example of Mao's (and, earlier, Stalin's) thinking that society can be forced into any shape the Party decrees.

The Chinese—like the Yugoslavs and Hungarians—found that a little bit of capitalism is like being a little bit pregnant. The choice Communist countries faced was difficult. If they went part of the way with a market economy, they experienced a few years of growth followed by dangerous distortions. If they called off the liberal experiment, they returned to the centralized, Stalinist system that was slowly running down, leaving them further and further behind the capitalist world. If they went all the way to a market system, they admitted they had been wrong all these decades.

Another problem cropped up with the financial problems that hit other East Asian lands in 1997: China's banks had also loaned recklessly and sometimes crookedly and faced insolvency. Some of their loans were under government orders, to prop up money-losing state industries. The central government itself was deeply in debt from subsidizing too much and collecting too little in taxes. With a faulty and foolish financial system, China's growth slowed.

Some observers argue that China's reforms were far more clever than the Soviet Union's and have a much better chance to succeed. First, China permitted private farming. The Soviet Union was still debating private farming when it collapsed. Then China permitted small businesses. China designated Special Economic Zones for foreign investment. Missing in China was the political liberalization that blew up in Gorbachev's face. None of Beijing's rulers wanted to be China's Gorbachev, hence they tolerated no democracy, competing parties, or free press, precisely the reforms that Gorbachev did first. Did the Chinese do it right, sequencing their reforms so as to build an economic basis for democracy before reforming their political system?

Other observers fear that China could collapse, that its partial economic reforms without political reforms could blow up.

With an increase in corruption, inflation, and inequality (see box on page 39) there is increasing mass unrest. So far, the only successful transitions from communism to free-market capitalism have come in Central Europe—Poland, the Czech Republic, and Hungary—where anticommunists completely threw out the Communist regimes. No controlled, middle-way transition has worked.

Do Markets Lead to Democracy?

Economic liberalization tends to encourage political participation. You can't reform the economy alone, for economic reform generates demands for political reform, namely, democracy. Amidst economic improvement, the Chinese find they have plenty to complain about: rampant corruption, terrible medical care, rising prices, and continued economic controls and restrictions. Immediate and specific grievances turn into general criticism of the entire regime. Student complaints about wretched college conditions—no heat or toilets, incompetent teachers, food fit for hogs, no job prospects—underlay the 1989 student demonstrations, which turned into calls for full-blown democracy.

Many observers agree with political scientist Peter Berger: "When market economies are successful over a period of time, pressure for democratization inevitably ensues." A market economy generates a large, educated middle class and interest groups. People start resenting a corrupt government treating them like small children. They want democracy. If the regime is intelligent and flexible, it gradually opens up, usually by permitting a critical press, then opposition parties, and finally free and fair elections.

Taiwan is the textbook example of this transition from authoritarianism to democracy. Some thinkers argue that China will follow a similar path, but there are differences. Taiwan's elite, many of them educated in the United States, led the way to democracy in the late 1970s.

One of their motives: Show the Americans they are a democracy in order to win U.S. support against Beijing's demands to take over Taiwan. We must be careful in supposing the Taiwan model fits mainland China.

China's elite is still firmly Communist, has no desire for democracy, and is not trying to please the Americans. They have deliberately tried to prevent the formation of an autonomous middle class. Calls for democracy are ruthlessly crushed. Do not count on China moving to democracy automatically or peacefully.

Rather than achieve stable democracy, China could explode. Consider China's problems: a huge country hard to govern in good times, with up-and-down economic growth, corruption out of control, restive minorities, major splits within the Party, central authority weakening, and many Chinese unhappy with the regime. China could break up into the "warlord" pattern of the 1920s, some observers feared. Others feared Beijing would try to deflect unrest onto other lands by promoting expansionist nationalism, a common practice of nervous regimes.

Which Is the Real China?

As the millennium changes, we face two very different images of China. The first one, supported by many journalists and academics, is that China is having a difficult transition but will eventually turn into a free-market democracy. Beijing itself argues that amid all these changes China needs "stability," and this justifies keeping politics out of mass hands. Modernization theory predicts that economic growth leads to democracy. If China occasionally snarls at us, we must forebear. Just give them time.

The other image is not as optimistic. Some observers argue that Beijing craves economic growth, not to make its people prosperous but for national power and respect. It has no intention of letting itself be turned into a democracy. Dissidents who publicly argue for democracy serve many years in prison; some of the more troublesome dissidents are shipped off to the United States. Under tight surveillance, few Chinese discuss politics with foreigners. These policies betray the regime's extreme nervousness and fear of being ousted.

Beijing also aims to become the number-one military power of East Asia, eclipsing Japan. Said Party chief Jiang: "There will only be two superpowers by around 2020—China and the United States." Unlikely, no matter how many nuclear secrets they steal. One of China's priorities is its navy, with which it has claimed and fortified islets far from its shores in the East and South China Seas. This angers other countries in the region—Japan, the Philippines, Malaysia, Indonesia, and Vietnam. And Beijing proclaims the right to seize Taiwan, which it regards as a renegade province, any time. By a 1979 law, the United States is committed to a peaceful, voluntary reunification. But if Beijing applies force or intimidation, how should we react?

These optimistic and pessimistic images reflect the power struggle between reformist and conservative wings of the CCP. Beijing is clearly trying to keep a lid on political challenges, but will it be able to in the long run? Beijing is happy to join the World Trade Organization (WTO), but how can it control the flow of goods, money, and ideas that come with world trade? How will China control the Internet—widely used among educated Chinese—with its ability to communicate and inform instantly? Can any country now run without it? China clearly wishes to develop its military power, but its army is still poorly equipped and has little mobility. Underlying everything is a deep craving for dignity and respect for what was once the world's greatest civilization but one that was brought low by Western and Japanese imperialists. How China achieves this recognition will be one of the great chapters of twenty-first century history.

GEOGRAPHY

THE HONG KONG EXAMPLE

In mid-1997 the British colony of Hong Kong reverted back to China. Most of Hong Kong actually consisted of leased territory on the mainland—the source of the colony's water supplies—and the lease was up in 1997. The British decided to give the whole package back to Beijing. Many prosperous and hardworking Hong Kongese didn't want to be part of China, although Beijing guaranteed, under the formula "one nation, two systems," that Hong Kong can keep its autonomy for fifty years.

In 1999, China took over the even-smaller Portuguese colony of Macao near Hong Kong and also gave it autonomy. Beijing's intention, many believed, is to demonstrate to Taiwan that it could rejoin the mainland and still keep its political and economic system. Few Taiwanese are buying.

Beijing did not openly break its word, but slowly Hong Kong lost its autonomy and capitalistic vitality. Beijing court decisions eroded Hong Kong's special status. Critical Hong Kong editors lost their jobs. Corruption appeared, as certain cooperative Hong Kongese got special deals. Beijing seemed to favor Shanghai as China's financial hub, as it once was before World War II. Prime Minister Zhu—like President Jiang, a former mayor of Shanghai—said in 1999, "Shanghai will be China's New York." Hong Kong will be its "Toronto." Hong Kong, one of the world's great financial centers, did more and more business with mainland China and less and less with other Pacific Rim countries. As Hong Kong lost its glitter, Singapore tried to move into its place as the great trading post of the Pacific Rim.

Key Terms

Boxer (p. 19)
cadre (p. 25)
deflation (p. 38)
devaluation (p. 38)
dynastic cycle (p. 17)
extraterritoriality (p. 18)
Gang of Four (p. 25)
kow-tow (p. 15)
Manchu (p. 17)
man-land ratio (p. 15)
mass line (p. 22)
Middle Kingdom (p. 17)
Mongol (p. 17)
Nationalist (p. 20)
sphere of influence (p. 19)
steady-state (p. 15)
Taiping (p. 19)
treaty ports (p. 18)
voluntarism (p. 29)
warlord (p. 20)
yuan (p. 38)

Further Reference

Chinoy, Mike. *China Live: Two Decades in the Heart of the Dragon*, updated ed. Lanham, MD: Rowman & Littlefield, 1999.

Dreyer, June Teufel. *China's Political System: Modernization and Tradition*, 2nd ed. Needham, MA: Allyn & Bacon, 1996.

Evans, Richard. *Deng Xiaoping and the Making of Modern China*. New York: Viking, 1994.

Fairbank, John King. *China: A New History*. Cambridge, MA: Harvard University Press, 1994.

Gilley, Bruce. *Tiger on the Brink: Jiang Zemin and China's New Elite*. Berkeley, CA: University of California Press, 1999.

Gore, Lance L. P. *Market Communism: The Institutional Foundation of China's Post-Mao Hyper-Growth*. New York: Oxford University Press, 1999.

Hunter, Alan, and John Sexton. *Contemporary China*. New York: St. Martin's, 1999.

Kwong, Julia. *The Political Economy of Corruption in China*. Armonk, NY: M. E. Sharpe, 1997.

Lam, Willy. *The Era of Jaing Zemin*. Upper Saddle River, NJ: Prentice Hall, 1999.

Li, Cheng. *Rediscovering China: Dynamics and Dilemmas of Reform*. Lanham, MD: Rowman & Littlefield, 1997.

MacFarquhar, Roderick, ed. *The Politics of China: The Eras of Mao and Deng*. New York: Cambridge University Press, 1997.

Nathan, Andrew J. *China's Transition*. New York: Columbia University Press, 1998.

Walder, Andrew G., ed. *The Waning of the Communist State: Economic Origins of Political Decline in China and Hungary*. Berkeley, CA: University of California Press, 1995.

Wei Jingsheng. *The Courage to Stand Alone: Letters from Prison and Other Writings*. New York: Viking, 1997.

Winckler, Edwin A., ed. *Transition from Communism in China: Institutional and Comparative Analyses*. Boulder, CO: L. Rienner, 1999.

Yang, Benjamin. *Deng: A Political Biography*. Armonk, NY: M. E. Sharpe, 1998.

Zhu, Fang. *Gun Barrel Politics: Party-Army Relations in Mao's China*. Boulder, CO: Westview, 1998.

CHAPTER 3

Brazil

Questions to Consider

1. How did Spanish and Portuguese colonialism differ?
2. How did the Old Republic typify "whig democracy"?
3. What did Vargas attempt to do with his "New State"?
4. Why did Brazil's generals take over in 1964? Why did they leave?
5. What are Brazil's institutional weaknesses?
6. Explain the role of inflation in Brazilian politics.
7. Compare Brazilian and South African racism.
8. What factors made Brazil democratic? Will it last?
9. How does Brazil illustrate "praetorianism"?
10. What are Brazil's economic problems?

The Impact of the Past

Portugal had a claim to Brazil even before its explorers arrived there. In 1494 the Treaty of Tordesillas gave Portugal lands in the yet-unexplored New World. The treaty drew a line 370 leagues (some 1,100 miles) west of the Cape Verde Islands; land to the east of the line went to Portugal, and land to the west of the line went to Spain. This arrangement sliced off the easternmost bulge of present-day Brazil; subsequent Portuguese settlements pushed their control further westward to give Brazil its present borders. The first Portuguese arrived in 1500, when Pedro Alvares Cabral, claiming he was blown off course, took formal possession of the land for the king of Portugal.

The Portuguese Influence

Portugal did not administer its new colony the way Spain did. The Spanish charged quickly into Latin America for "gold, God, and glory." The Portuguese did nothing for thirty years, partly because they were busy with the rich trade route around Africa to India and partly because Brazil seemed to offer little gold. About the only Portuguese interest in the new land was in its red wood that could be used to make dye. From the brazed color of brazilwood came the name Brazil (*Brasil* in Portuguese).

It was when the French started to settle there in 1530 that the Portuguese crown began to take an interest. Ordering the French expelled, Dom João (King John) III parceled out the coastline into fifteen *capitanías* or royal grants which he gave to wealthy Portuguese willing to finance settlement. The original *capitanías*, like the thirteen English colonies in North America, gave initial shape to Brazil's present-day states and laid the foundation for its federalism. Growth in the *capitanías*, however, was slow and spotty. Portugal's population at that time was only around one million, and there were not many people eager to become colonists. Compared to the Spanish colonies, there were no quick and easy mineral riches to be found in Brazil.

Economic life centered on sugar, for which Europe had recently acquired a taste. Sugar farming requires lots of labor, however. The Indians of Brazil were relatively few in number and made poor slaves; used to a life of casual hunting, many refused to work. With many trading posts down the African coast, though, the Portuguese found their answer in black slaves. From the 1530s to the 1850s, at least three million Africans (perhaps six times the number that were brought to the United States) were brought to Brazil and sold, chiefly to work in the sugar-cane fields. Interbreeding among the three population groups—Indians, blacks, and Portuguese—was rife, producing Brazil's complex racial mixture. The Portuguese always prided themselves on being nonracist, and this attitude, in public anyway, carries over into present-day Brazil.

Other Portuguese attitudes distinguish Brazil from the former Spanish colonies of Latin America. Portuguese have been less inclined to violence than Spaniards. As many Portuguese point out: "In a Portuguese bullfight, we don't kill the bull." Flexibility and compromise are more valued in Brazilian politics than in the politics of its Spanish-speaking neighbors.

A Painless Independence

Brazil's independence from Portugal is also in marked contrast to the long struggles waged by the Spanish colonies. Slowly, Brazil grew in population and importance. When the Netherlands made Pernambuco (now Recife) a Dutch colony in the mid-seventeenth century,

Black, white, and Indian blood flow together freely in Brazil, producing a complex racial mixture. (Michael Roskin)

GEOGRAPHY

BOUND BRAZIL

Brazil is bounded on the north by Venezuela, Guyana, Suriname, and French Guiana;

on the east by the Atlantic Ocean;

on the south by Uruguay;

and on the west by Argentina, Paraguay, Bolivia, Peru, and Colombia.

Bounding Brazil allows you to label most of South America. Only Chile and Ecuador do not border Brazil. What is the difference between South America and Latin America? South America is everything south of Panama. Latin America is everything south of the U.S. border with Mexico.

VENEZUELA
GUYANA
SURINAME
FRENCH GUIANA
COLOMBIA
RORAIMA
AMAPÁ
Amazon R.
AMAZONAS
PARÁ
MARANHÃO
CEARÁ
RIO GRANDE DO NORTE
PARAÍBA
Recife
PIAUI
PERNAMBUCO
ALAGÔAS
SERGIPE
ACRE
PERU
RONDÔNIA
B R A Z I L
GOIÁS
BAHIA
BOLIVIA
MATO GROSSO
Brazilia
MINAS GERAIS
ESPÉRITO SANTO
SÃO PAULO
São Paulo
RIO DE JANEIRO
Rio de Janeiro
PARAGUAY
PACIFIC OCEAN
PARANÁ
ATLANTIC OCEAN
SANTA CATARINA
CHILE
ARGENTINA
RIO GRANDE DO SUL
URUGUAY
0 250 500 Miles
0 250 500 Kilometers
0°
10°
20°
30°
80°
50°
40°
30°

Portuguese, blacks, and Indians together struggled to expel them and, in the process, began to think of themselves as Brazilians. In the 1690s, gold was discovered in what became the state of Minas Gerais (General Mines). A gold rush and later a diamond rush boosted Brazil's population. Economic activity shifted from the sugar-growing region of the Northeast to the South and stayed there. To this day, the growth area has been in the more temperate climes of the South, while the Northeast, impoverished and drought-stricken, has become a problem area.

By the late eighteenth century, Brazil had become more important economically than Portugal, and thoughts of independence began to flicker in the growing Brazilian consciousness, inspired, as throughout Latin America, by the U.S. and French revolutionary examples. Brazilian independence, curiously, came about partly because of Napoleon.

In trying to seal off the European continent from Britain, Napoleon sent an army to take Portugal in 1807. The royal court in Lisbon—some fifteen thousand people in all—at British prodding, boarded ships and sailed for Brazil. Dom João VI was at first wildly welcomed in Brazil, but the royal court was horrified at conditions in Rio and irritated leading residents by requisitioning their houses. Dom João ordered Rio cleaned, beautified, and turned into a true capital. In 1815, Brazil was raised in rank from colony to kingdom within the Portuguese empire.

In 1821, the British advised Dom João to return to Lisbon to make sure Portuguese liberals didn't get out of hand. He left his son, Dom Pedro, then age twenty-three, as regent in Brazil and gave him some parting advice: If Brazilian independence became inevitable, he should make sure he led it. It was a pragmatic, level-headed idea, an example of Portuguese flexibility in contrast to Spanish obduracy. In this way the Portuguese royal house served as a bridge between colonial and independent status. In 1822 Dom Pedro proclaimed Brazil independent, and Portugal did not resist.

From Empire to Republic

Monarchy is rare in the Western Hemisphere; it appeared only briefly in Haiti and Mexico (Maximilian). Brazil, however, was a true monarchy from 1822 to 1889, another point of contrast with the rest of Latin America. Dom Pedro I proved an inept ruler, and when the army turned against him he abdicated in 1831 while his Brazilian-born son was still a child. Under a regency—a council that runs affairs until a king comes of age—power was dispersed among the various states; an 1834 act set up states' rights and introduced de facto federalism. Politics became a series of quarrels among the states and the rich landowning families that ran them. The instability was so serious that it led finally to widespread agreement in 1840 to declare Dom Pedro II—only fourteen years old—of age to rule.

Dom Pedro II was beloved for his calm, tolerant manner and his concern for his nation. But he did not do much of anything. Basing his rule on big plantation owners (*fazendeiros*), Pedro let things drift while he exercised the "moderating power" of the liberal 1824 constitution in appointing and dismissing ministers. But the Brazilian economy changed. The large landowners mattered less while vigorous businessmen and bankers gained in importance. The growing modern element came to resent the conservative monarchy and to favor a republic. One big question Dom Pedro II couldn't handle was slavery. Under British pressure, the importation of new slaves ended during the 1850s, but slavery continued, deemed humane and necessary by Pedro's landowning supporters. Various formulas for phasing out slavery were considered, but Pedro let the question drift until his daughter, Princess Isabel, acting as regent while he was in Europe, signed an abolition bill in 1888. Brazil was the last Western country to emancipate its slaves.

Key Concepts

"Order and Progress"

French philosopher Auguste Comte (1798–1857) developed a doctrine known as **Positivism**. With its slogan of "Order and Progress," this optimistic philosophy held that mankind can and will progress by turning away from theology and abstract speculation and toward the scientific study of nature and of society. By applying the natural-science methods of empirical observation and data gathering, society can be analyzed, predicted, and then improved, not in a revolutionary way, but gradually and under the supervision of humanitarian specialists. Said Comte: "Progress is the development of order."

Comte's Positivism launched modern social science (and still holds sway in psychology) and took root especially in Brazil. By the 1880s many Brazilian army officers had been instructed in Positivism by the mathematics professor Benjamin Constant Magalhães, who taught in the national military academy. With the 1889 republic, Positivists put their motto into the Brazilian flag, where it remains to this day: *Ordem e Progresso.*

By now, wide sectors of the Brazilian population were disgusted with monarchy. Intellectuals, businesspeople, and army officers, imbued with Positivist philosophy (see box, above), wanted modernization. Deprived of their slaves, even the plantation owners turned against Dom Pedro. In 1889, a military coup ended the monarchy and introduced a republic without firing a shot.

The Old Republic

The relative stability conferred by Brazil's Portuguese heritage (bloodless independence and nineteenth-century monarchy) wore off during the **Old Republic**, and Brazil came to resemble its Hispanic neighbors. Revolts, rigged elections, and military intervention marked this period. The 1891 constitution was modeled after that of the United States, but power gravitated into the hands of **coronéis** and the military. For most of the Old Republic, the presidency alternated between the political bosses of two of the most important states, São Paulo and Minas Gerais.

Grumbling increased during the life of the Old Republic. New sectors of the population became aware that their interests were unheeded by the conservative political bosses. Idealistic army officers revolted in 1922 and 1924, believing they could save the republic. The Brazilian army at this time was by no means conservative. Many officers were imbued with Positivism and hated conservative politicians, who seemed to block progress. To this day, the Brazilian military sees itself as a progressive rather than as a conservative force.

What finally destroyed the Old Republic was the worldwide depression and the collapse of the price of coffee, a crop that Brazil depended upon heavily for export earnings. Further, in 1930 a split developed in the old Paulista-Mineiro combination, and a crafty politician from Rio Grande do Sul—the home of many maverick politicians—took advantage of it to run for the presidency. Getúlio Vargas claimed the election results had been rigged

Key Terms

Positivism Philosophy of applying scientific method to social problems and gradually improving society.

Old Republic Brazil's first republic, 1889–1930; a rigged democracy.

coronéis "Colonels"; Brazilian state-level political bosses.

against him (entirely plausible) and, with help from the military and amid great popular acclaim, took over the presidency in Rio in October 1930.

Vargas's "New State"

Latin American populist strongmen (*caudillos* in Spanish, *caudilhos* in Portuguese) are hard to label, for they appear to be both leftist and rightist. They expand the economy by statist means (see box on page 52). They claim to be for the people and are proud of the many welfare measures they institute. Often they create a labor movement and give it a privileged status that is long remembered among the working class. But they are no more democratic than the old political bosses they overthrew and often support the interests of existing elites, such as keeping coffee prices high. And they are very much for "order."

Key Terms

mobilize To bring new sectors of the population into political participation.

corporatism Representation by a branch of industry; a device of Mussolini.

autogolpe "Self-coup"; a top executive seizes more power.

Estado Nôvo "New State"; Vargas's corporatistic welfare state.

Some called such figures as Vargas of Brazil and Perón of Argentina fascists, but they probably were not. Rather than building a party along ideological lines, these populist dictators **mobilized** the masses with their personal appeal. During the 1930s and 1940s, however, when fascism in Europe was having its day, they threw in some fascistic rhetoric.

Vargas, like Perón, looked after the working class. Under Vargas, Brazil instituted an eight-hour work day, minimum wages, paid vacations, and collective bargaining. Labor did not fight and win its rights; Vargas handed them over long before there was an organized labor movement to make demands. The result, as in much of Latin America, is a weak labor movement that constantly seeks the protection of a paternalistic state.

Vargas's 1934 constitution brought in a **corporatist** element—one-fifth of the legislature directly represented professional and trade groups—on the pattern of Italy and Portugal. The constitution also limited the president to a single four-year term. By 1937, however, Vargas decided he wanted to stay president and carried out a coup against his own regime, what is called in Latin America an **autogolpe**. Vargas proclaimed himself president, but this time there was no legislature to limit his powers. Vargas called his regime the **Estado Nôvo**. His critics called it "fascism with sugar." There was material progress—industry, highways, public health, social welfare—but there was also a loss of freedom. The United States got along well with Vargas, for he did not curb U.S. investments. In 1942, Brazil declared war on the Axis powers (but sent few troops).

Vargas discovered the power of the urban working class and mobilized them to his cause by setting up labor unions and the *Partido Trabalhista Brasileiro* (Brazilian Labor party, PTB for short). The military, however, became alarmed at his populistic dictatorship and forced him to resign in 1945. By then Vargas had become a hero to many Brazilians, who continued to support his PTB. In both Brazil and Argentina, the working masses longed for the return of their respective dictators and reelected them to office, Vargas in 1950 and Perón in 1946 and 1973. Once mobilized by a populistic dictator, the masses may prefer such rulers and their statism to democracy and free markets.

The Rise and Fall of Jango Goulart

The reelected Vargas was a poor president; corruption and inflation soared. Many Brazilians, including top military officers, demanded he resign in 1954. Instead, he committed suicide, blaming reactionary international (that is, U.S.) and domestic forces for blocking his good

Key Concepts

The Addiction of Statism

The Old Regime in France started the tradition of "statism," the idea that the government should supervise the economy and own much industry, and it spread throughout much of the world. Regimes intent on rapid change—the Bolsheviks in Russia, Ataturk in Turkey, Perón in Argentina, and Vargas in Brazil—embraced statism as a seemingly logical solution to their problems of backwardness. Statism caught on like an addiction in Latin America: Once you had a little state supervision, you soon wanted more. Have a social or economic problem? A new government program, industry, or regulation can solve it.

Statism's basic premises have long been examined and found wanting. Adam Smith, for example, concluded that state intervention gets in the way of economic growth. State-owned industries often become monopolistic, uncompetitive, graft-ridden, and inefficient. Many have to be propped up with state subsidies, money that comes from citizens' pockets. But once established, statist structures defy reform. Politicians, fearful of unemployment and of appearing pro-American or pro-capitalist, hesitate to privatize inefficient and crooked state enterprises. Once addicted, an economy tends to stay statist. Only in our day have wide areas of Latin America begun to kick the habit and turn to the free market. Privatizing Brazil's state-owned industry has been one of its great steps forward.

works. One of Vargas's appointments had particularly angered the military. Vargas named a neighbor from Rio Grande do Sul, the radical João (Jango) Goulart, as labor minister, but the military forced him to resign in 1954.

Goulart, however, continued to head the PTB and in 1955 helped moderate Juscelino Kubitschek win the presidency with Goulart as vice president. Kubitschek mobilized into his Social Democratic party (PSD) the old political class of state and local elites who had dominated Brazil before Vargas. Kubitschek tried to focus Brazilians' energies on developing the interior; he pushed construction of Brasilia, which became the capital in 1960. Heedless of economic problems, Kubitschek promoted industrialization and allowed inflation to skyrocket.

Brazil's working masses were still responsive to populist appeals. In 1960 a Paulista populist, Jânio Quadros, won the presidency in a landslide with reformist promises; Goulart was vice president. An unstable alcoholic, Quadros resigned after just seven months, leaving a quixotic note reminiscent of Vargas's. Now Goulart, the very man the military forced out in 1954, was in line for the presidency.

The Brazilian army started talking about a coup, but a compromise was worked out: Goulart could be president but with the powers of that office greatly curtailed. Goulart accepted but played a waiting game. As the economy got worse—inflation climbed to 100 percent a year by 1964—he knew the Brazilian masses, by now mobilized and seething with demands for radical change, would support him in a leftward course. Goulart's strategy worked: In a January 1963 plebiscite Brazilians voted five-to-one to restore full powers to the president so he could deal with the economic chaos.

Goulart now veered further left and called for "Basic Reforms": land redistribution, nationalizing the oil industry, enfranchising illiterates, legalizing the Communist party, and turning the legislature, which had blocked his schemes, into a "congress composed of peasants, workers, sergeants, and nationalist officers."

From northwest to southeast, the countries of Central America are: Belize, Guatemala, Honduras, El Salvador, Nicaragua, Costa Rica, and Panama. Mexico is considered part of North America.

Key Terms

statute An ordinary law, usually for a specific problem.

fiscal Related to taxes and public spending.

Brazilian society—like France and Germany in earlier decades—split into leftist and conservative wings with little middle ground. Conservatives, including most middle-class Brazilians, were horrified at Goulart and his appointment of Marxists to high positions. The United States saw Goulart as another Castro, cut off financial aid, and stepped up covert activity to destabilize the Goulart government. Brazil seemed to be on the edge of a revolution.

What finally brought Goulart down was his challenge to the armed forces. Goulart publicly supported some mutinous sailors, which Brazil's generals saw as undermining their military discipline and command structure. On March 31, 1964, with scarcely a shot, the armed forces put an end to Brazil's tumultuous democracy.

The Key Institutions

Flawed Structure

Brazil illustrates what can go wrong if a country's basic institutions are defective: The best intentions and good will are stymied, and the country gets stuck in patterns of the past. The past is alive and well in Brazil's 1988 constitution. The Old Republic echoes today in the freespending powers of Brazil's states and their governors. Vargas's New State echoes in the state-owned industries and employee protections. Overcoming these roadblocks is much on the mind of reformist Brazilians, including President Fernando Henrique Cardoso.

Criticism focuses on Brazil's 1988 constitution, the country's seventh since independence. Its aims and general structure are fine, but its details seem designed to trip up needed reforms. Like most modern constitutions, Brazil's includes numerous social and economic rights—a forty-hour work week, medical and retirement plans, minimum wages, a 12-percent interest ceiling on loans, the right to strike, Indian rights, and environmental protection. Such details have no place in a constitution. But the writers of new constitutions, especially in the Third World, are often idealistic and think they can right all wrongs by mandating fixes in the constitution.

The problem with guaranteeing such rights is that they create expectations and demands that cannot possibly be met by a struggling economy, and this deepens popular discontent. Such details also fail to distinguish between a constitution and **statutes**. Even worse, it built in referendums—called "popular vetoes" and "popular initiatives"—to voice these discontents. California, with its myriad initiatives on each ballot, can get away with such hyperdemocratic nonsense; in Brazil it fosters instability. Another potentially disruptive feature of Brazil's constitution: Voting age now starts at sixteen.

Brazilian states and municipalities are more independent and less responsible than their U.S. counterparts. They raise some of their own taxes but are entitled to big chunks of federal revenue and run up big debts. (U.S. states have to stand nearly on their own **fiscally** and cannot run deficit budgets.) Brazilian states and cities are overstaffed with patronage civil servants who retire young on good pensions, one of the problems of Brazilian public-sector overspending. Trimming bureaucrats' pensions is a major reform effort, one that the bureaucrats resist.

Congress and the Presidency

The 1988 Brazilian constitution is basically presidential—a powerful president is directly elected. But the Congress is fragmented into many weak parties, often making it difficult to pass badly needed reforms. Until changed in 1997, Brazilian presidents could be elected for just one

Comparison

Spain Turns Democratic

In 1975, when Franco died, Spain was an authoritarian system with a hand-picked parliament, curbs on the press, and no legal political parties. Just two years later, Spain was a full-fledged democracy with a freely elected parliament, a lively and critical press, and a complete party system. The Franco system had become history. Spain has had free and fair elections ever since.

Dictators kid themselves that they have built lastingly. Their immediate successors like to think they can give a few tokens of democracy but preserve the authoritarian system. They can't. A little bit of democracy just whets people's appetites for more, and the system tends to slide all the way into full democracy. There are several points of comparison between Spain's rapid shift to democracy and Brazil's, with one important difference. Spain has a mostly middle-class population, and this tends to make for centrist politics. Brazil has a large class of extremely poor people, and this can still make for unstable politics.

five-year term; now they can be elected to two four-year terms. In 1993, a plebiscite decided to keep the presidential system—Brazil's tradition since 1889 and the pattern throughout Latin America—rather than go to a parliamentary system with a prime minister as chief executive.

Brazil's parliament, the National Congress, is bicameral. It is also utterly fragmented, undisciplined, and uncooperative, almost designed to block reforms (like Russia's Duma). The upper house, the Senate, consists of eighty-one members who are elected for eight-year terms. Each of Brazil's twenty-six states gets three senators. The lower house, the Chamber of Deputies, has 513 members, each elected for four-year terms based on a type of proportional representation that begs for trouble. Brazil's twenty-six states (plus the Federal District of Brasilia) have from eight to seventy deputies, depending on population. This overrepresents the rural, less-populous states and is unfair to the populous, economic-powerhouse states such as São Paulo.

Each state is a multimember PR district. Voters can pick either a party or write in the names of their preferred candidates. This system, known technically as "open-list proportional representation," means that candidates of the same party compete against each other, one of the flaws of the old Japanese electoral system. It also means that party matters little; candidates run on personality, contributing to the weakness of Brazil's parties.

The military presidents of Brazil were extremely powerful, their civilian successors much less so. Their power to initiate needed reforms is restricted by Congress on one side and state governors on the other. Members of Brazil's Congress, essentially the representatives of their states and its powerful interest groups, generally want to spend more, especially on their clients. They pay little attention to the budget deficits this creates, which in turn lead quickly to inflation. All their incentives push them to spend.

Brazil's presidents, especially Cardoso, understand what causes inflation and try to curb government spending. A series of reforms to do this, however, have rough going in the fragmented Congress. Few think of the good of the whole, only of their favored interest group. Some state governors have simply ignored Brasilia's decrees to balance their budgets, trim the bureaucracy, and stop borrowing. Brazilian politicians—like those of the French Fourth Republic—are good at blocking but not at building.

Democracy

The Inflation Connection

Brazil's presidential elections of 1994 and 1998 were quite similar. The two top candidates were the same. Both times, Brazilians voted against inflation by electing Fernando Henrique Cardoso of the centrist Social Democratic party and against fiery Workers party leader "Lula." Just before the 1994 election, as finance minister, Cardoso had authored the "Real Plan" that introduced a new currency, the **real**, and drastically reduced Brazil's runaway inflation. (One real was worth 2.75×10^{15} of the *cruzeiros* of 30 years earlier.) Lula had been leading in the polls, but Cardoso beat him 54 to 27 percent in the first round. In 1998, Carodoso again beat Lula 53 to 32 percent in the first round. Lula was seen as a destabilizing radical, Cardoso as a realistic reformer.

Cardoso had himself been a radical, a sociology professor and promoter of **dependency theory**, a Marxist-type theory popular throughout Latin America, that the United States keeps Latin America poor (see box on page 64). Under the generals, Cardoso was arrested, barred from teaching, and forced into exile. Over the years, like many Latin American radicals, Cardoso abandoned dependency theory in favor of the free market and international trade as the way out of poverty. By the time he ran for president in 1994, Cardoso was pledging to rid Brazil of its state-owned and protected industries (the same promise Collor de Mello had made).

The taming of inflation is what won both times for Cardoso. Cardoso's Real Plan dropped inflation from a monthly rate of 45 percent in June to 1.5 percent in just three months. Economic stabilization gave Brazilians hope. Lula, on the other hand, spoke of socialist programs for the poor. Such programs are inflationary, something that even poor Brazilians don't want any more. Said one Rio *favelado*, "I'm voting for Fernando Henrique. He invented the Real Plan."

Cardoso's popularity went down after the 1998 election because he had to devalue the real, and this induced a **recession**. He did this to head off inflation. As the financial world held its breath, it worked. Carodoso's popularity **varied inversely** with the fear of inflation: when it went up, his popularity went down. Cardoso was able to form a four-party coalition and continue, with difficulty and setbacks, his reform agenda. With Brazil's recent economic growth, Brazil seems to have entered the ranks of stable democracies whose citizens do not fall for populist **demagoguery**.

Brazilian President Fernando Henrique Cardoso. (Embassy of Brazil)

An Inchoate Party System

Under the military, Brazil had essentially fake parties, one a total creature of the regime, the Renovating Alliance (*Aliança Renovadora Nacional*, ARENA), the other a tame opposition, the Brazilian Democratic Movement (*Movimento Democrático Brasileiro*, MDB). With the opening up (*abertura*) of the 1980s, the MDB turned itself into the Party of the MDB (PMDB), a moderate center party.

Several socialist or workers' parties sprang up. The main party of the left, the Workers party (*Partido dos Trabalhadores*, PT), is led by a charismatic union organizer, Luis Inácio da Silva, nicknamed "Lula," the PT's habitual candidate for president. Leonel Brizola, a radical intellectual and Goulart's brother-in-law, set up a center-left Democratic Labor party (*Partido Democrático Trabalhista*, PDT) and ran as Lula's vice presidential candidate in 1998.

At center-left (but more to the center), Cardoso's Brazilian Social Democratic party (*Partido da Social Democracia Brasileira*, PSDB) was formed in 1988 from a variety of centrist and reformist deputies. Cardoso won the presidential elections in 1994 and 1998. The Liberal Front party (*Partido da Frente Liberal*, PFL), a conservative party led by former President José Sarney, worked with the PSDB in congress. The populist former São Paulo mayor Paulo Maluf used his (conservative) Brazilian Progressive party to position him for presidential runs.

Brazil's parties and their members change like quicksilver. Like Russia's, they are founded, merge, and split so fast it's hard to keep up with them. Brazilians do not trust their parties; they see them as corrupt and irresponsible. In the 1990s, Brazil's Congress had nineteen parties. In the 1994–98 Congress, 230 representatives in the lower house (out of 513) switched parties, some more than once. These are the marks of an **inchoate** party system in which the poorly institutionalized parties are simply personalistic vehicles to get politicians elected.

Few parties articulate a clear program or implement coherent policies. Rather, once elected, leaders use government resources (jobs, contracts, loans, kickbacks) to keep themselves in power and get rich. Fernando Alfonso Collor de Mello, for example, created his own National Reconstruction party to win the presidency in 1989, but his party soon faded. He did not care, for he was then able to enrich himself and his friends. (Under impeachment for corruption, he resigned in 1992 and lives well in Miami.) Settling down into a stable, meaningful party system is one of the best things Brazilian democracy could do for itself. But such an evolution will take reforms, several elections, and patient organizational work, something Brazilians have not been good at.

Key Terms

real plural *reís*; Brazil's currency, worth about $0.50.

dependency theory Radical theory that rich countries keep poor countries poor by siphoning off their wealth.

recession An economy going downward.

vary inversely As one thing goes up, another goes down.

demagoguery Crowd-pleasing promises that cannot be fulfilled.

inchoate Not yet organized; incoherent.

The Military as Political Institution

As in much of the Third World, Brazil's political institutions are weak. Unlike Europe, with its well-established parliaments, parties, and bureaucracies, Brazil's political institutions are barely capable of handling the demands of mass politics in an orderly way. When the political system gets stuck or chaotic, the army is often the only institution capable of governing. Direct military participation ended in 1985, but if things get tumultuous again, another military takeover is possible.

The Brazilian military has intervened in politics many times: at the birth and through the life of the Old Republic, at first in support of Vargas and then against him, at the establishment of reasonably democratic regimes at the end of the two Vargas periods, and in 1964. Prior to 1964, however, the Brazilian military never tried to stay in power. They saw themselves in much the same way as Dom Pedro II had seen his role, that of a "moderating power" to restrain politicians from excesses. Step in when need be, set things right, then step out, was the Brazilian military pattern.

By 1964, both the Brazilian military attitude and the nation's situation had changed. Brazilian officers, partly thanks to U.S. guidance, had redefined their mission from defending Brazil against external enemies to guarding it against internal threats, especially communism. In the Superior War College, the ESG (see box, below), top officers studied politics, economics, psychology, and counterinsurgency.

Thus the Brazilian military, technically highly trained and newly motivated toward a more active role in their country's politics, was ready to upset a long-held view (especially by Americans) that truly professional military officers do not engage in coups. Looking around, the Brazilian officers found—almost like a case study—a Brazil that was sliding rapidly to the left. The Brazilian army chose to intervene, and it did so precisely because it was professionally trained to prevent revolution. This time the officers were determined to stay in power, block the return of divisive politics, and modernize their potentially rich country in an organized, rational manner.

Comparison

Brazil's Powerful Military School

A school facing a luxurious Rio beach does not seem a likely spot for a powerful political institution, but in Brazil virtually an entire ruling class emerged from the Superior War College (*Escola Superior da Guerra*, ESG). Founded in 1949 on the model of the U.S. National War College (which trains midcareer officers for higher command), by the 1960s the ESG had shifted its emphasis from external to internal security. Still influenced by the old Positivism—which, in fact, had been spread in the last century through Brazil's military academy—ESG students came to the conclusion that only Brazil's rapid economic development would save it from chaos and communism.

The ESG trained not only the best colonels, but top civilians as well. Government administrators, private industrialists, and leading professional people tended to outnumber ESG's military students. The ESG drew its ninety students a year from key areas of the political and economic power structure: banking, mass communications, education, and industry. ESG's graduates returned to their branches imbued with the authoritarian developmentalist doctrines they learned at the school. In civilian-ruled Brazil, ESG graduates are not so influential, although many are still in high positions. They still form a cadre of technocrats the military could rely on again should they return to power.

The ESG actually resembles a French *grande école*, such as the Polytechnique or ENA, except that ESG students are generally older and already established in careers. In both cases, however, the schools put their stamp on bright, carefully selected people, training them to think and act the same way and to maintain close ties with each other. This is what gave French and Brazilian policy making its cohesion and continuity. "We don't actually make government policy," said a senior Brazilian officer on the ESG staff. "The great contribution of the school has been to establish an elite of people who can think in the same language and who have learned the team approach to planning here." The French couldn't have said it better.

For two decades, Brazil was governed by a succession of generals, each chosen by a small group of generals. The Brazilian military did not rule the country directly, as if it were an army camp. Rather, they structured the political system so that only a military officer or a civilian who worked closely and cooperatively with the military could attain executive office. Once named president, a Brazilian general usually retired from active service and seldom wore his uniform.

Brazil's military regime was not just military, and that may be why it lasted so long. The Brazilian military had close ties to civilian bankers, educators, industrialists, and governmental administrators, many of whom trained together in the Superior War College in Rio. The weakness of most military regimes is their isolation and lack of contact with civilian elites. Unable to run the complexities of economy, society, and diplomacy without skilled civilians, military regimes frequently blunder so badly that they decide to give up power and responsibility.

Brazil's generals avoided this kind of isolation by partially integrating themselves with conservative civilian elites who held views and values close to the military's. Brazil's "military" regime was actually a civilian-military network of authoritarian developmentalists who controlled most of Brazil's economic, political, and military structures. In public, the government looked civilian. Most executive positions were occupied by civilian technocrats.

Can an army be a political institution? Historically, the evidence is against the military holding power permanently. Armies are clumsy tools to govern with. After some years, military regimes tend to return power to civilians, or turn into civilian regimes themselves, or get overthrown in a new military coup. The first is what happened in Brazil in the early 1980s.

A Lack of Institutions

The underlying reason that Brazil got its military governments was the lack of sturdy institutions that could handle the influx of newly mobilized sectors of the population and their demands. In the absence of firm, well-established parties and parliaments, demagogic populists aroused both the masses and the military. The military won, and, as we shall see, the masses lost. The trouble was that the Brazilian military did not really found durable institutions either.

One of the principal functions of political institutions is winning and channeling mass loyalty to the system. The chief mechanism for doing this is political parties. Without loyalty, mere technical arrangements, even if they work well in promoting economic growth, become more and more isolated from the population they rule. Franco's Spain supervised an economic boom, but there was little positive feeling among Spaniards for the Franco institutions. After his death in 1975, those institutions were dismantled with scarcely a protest.

By stunting the growth of political institutions, the Brazilian military did great harm to the country. We are now watching to see if Brazil can escape from its cycle of weak civilian institutions overthrown by clumsy military regimes, which in turn give way to weak civilian administrations again. Could there be another coup? From time to time, one hears muttering from top officers, but Brazil's economic growth has now moved it into the ranks of the middle-income countries (over $6,000 per capita GDP), and they tend to be stable democracies. Unless there is a terrible crisis, we are not likely to see military rule again in Brazil.

Brazilian Political Culture

The Easygoing Image

Both Brazilians and resident foreigners tend to describe Brazilians as easygoing people, seldom angry or violent, largely indifferent to politics, and unlikely to rise in revolt. There's a lot of truth to this image. In most of Brazil for most of the year it's too hot to make a revolution. People would rather go to the beach.

Brazilians have better things to do with their energies than take them out in politics. Brazilians are emotional; they laugh, joke, and embrace in public. They love children—possibly, some suggest, because the infant mortality rate is so high—and tend to spoil their offspring, especially the boys. This creates a male-centered society in which the men are expected to indulge themselves but not the women.

Many of the Portuguese who settled Brazil either were minor noblemen or pretended they were. They brought with them antiwork attitudes and looked down on tawdry moneymaking. Until fairly recently this attitude was still present in the Brazilian middle and upper classes, limiting their entrepreneurial energy. Many of the more vigorous business and government people have been of non-Portuguese origin (German, Italian, Japanese, and East European). Avoidance of work is common throughout the middle and upper classes in Latin America; people would rather attach themselves to the state bureaucracy than develop private industry. The elements of hustle and vigor are missing from much of Latin American capitalism, a point sometimes offered as an explanation of both backwardness and penetration by U.S. capital.

The image of Brazilians as lazy and laid-back amidst tropical languor, however, may have been overdone. An economy can't expand at several percentage points a year without people working hard. The "tropical languor" theory may have been deliberately cultivated in Brazil, for it serves as a rationalization for keeping the broad mass of Brazilians apolitical while leaving elites free to run the country as they wish. Brazilian elites tell themselves that the poor are content in their ignorance and are apathetic by nature. They, the elites, must shoulder the arduous tasks of running government and the business sector, both of which mostly benefit the elites.

Furthermore, there wasn't anything easygoing about Brazilian attitudes as the country has approached the brink of social collapse. Desperate people, some of them reduced from middle-class jobs to street peddling, turned angry. About 30 percent of Brazilians live in **absolute poverty**, and Brazil has practically no unemployment compensation, welfare benefits, or food stamps. When Brazilians have no more money for food, they are forced to starve or steal. Traditionally, Brazilians shrugged off their impoverished class as a normal thing that could not be helped. With the prospect of social breakdown and violence, however, some have begun to take notice and try to do something about it.

Key Term

absolute poverty Extremely low income; defined by World Bank as living on under $1 a day.

Brazilian Racism

One area where the easygoing Brazilian attitude has helped to keep society calm and stable is their proclaimed indifference to race. At least one-third of Brazilians have African ancestors, giving Brazil the largest African-descended population outside of Africa. Precise classification is impossible, however, because of both racial mixing and the Latin American tendency to let culture decide race. Throughout the continent, a person with the right education, manners, and money is considered "European" with little regard to skin color. Brazilians have dozens of words to distinguish among the combinations that make up the country's racial spectrum: *branco*, *alvo*, and *claro* for the lighter skinned, *moreno* and *mulato* for the middle shades, and *negro*, *preto*, *cabo verde*, and *escuro* for the darker. In theory and in most public places, there is no discrimination in Brazil. Walking down the street, one Brazilian feels as good as another.

Key Terms

personalismo Politics by strong, showoff personalities.

machismo Strutting, exaggerated masculinity.

Brazil's dirty little secret, however, is that in fact it is a racist society, one that adheres to the old American song: "If you're white you're all right, and if you're brown stick around, but if you're black get back." Career chances are strongly related to skin color in Brazil. If you're white, your chances of going to a university, entering a profession, making lots of money, and living in a nice house are much, much higher. If you're black, you run a high risk of infant death, malnutrition, rural poverty, and the lowest jobs or unemployment.

The Brazilian economic and political elite is white, whether the government is civilian or military. A small number of blacks have moved upward, but their way is often blocked by job requirements specifying "good appearance" (that is, white or near-white). Individual blacks can succeed in entertainment and sports, but they are a handful. The world's greatest (and highest-paid) soccer star, Pelé, is black. Even he encountered discrimination early in his career. When he served as Cardoso's minister of sports, he was the only black in an all-white cabinet. Intermarriage is perfectly legal but seldom takes place. Problems of race are rarely discussed in Brazil's mass media. Increasingly, Brazil's blacks resent this.

Brazil's Poor: Passive or Explosive?

Do poor people turn naturally to social revolution, or are they too busy trying to stay alive to bother with political questions? In Brazil, we have a laboratory to test some of the longstanding debates about why people revolt. The answers depend not just on people being poor—

POLITICAL CULTURE

PERSONALISMO AND *MACHISMO*

Latin American politicians often rely on **personalismo** in politics rather than on clear thinking, party programs, or organizing. Many Latin Americans like to be perceived as strong, the men especially as macho, leading to **machismo**. Latin American leaders, civilian or military, traditionally combine personalismo and machismo in varying degrees. They figure it's the only way to gain mass respect.

The Brazilian generals, given the way in which they were selected for power, tended to downplay these qualities. With the return of civilian politics, however, personalismo and machismo reappeared in Brazilian politics. Both Collor de Mello in 1989 and Lula in 1994 exuded personalismo. A sign of Brazilians' maturity was the election and reelection of Cardoso, Brazil's first nonclownish civilian president.

Key Term

favela Brazilian shantytown, found around most cities.

most Brazilians through history have been poor—but on the context in which poor people find themselves.

In the dry, overpopulated Northeast, some people starve. Many rural poor, hoping to improve their condition, flood to the **favelas** surrounding the cities, where some do find work while others eke out a precarious living from peddling or crime. Rich Brazilians, on the other hand, live sumptuously. For most of the military era, there was little open class resentment. First and most important, the Brazilian underclass was deprived of its leadership and organizational alternatives. The radical parties and leaders of the Goulart period were, respectively, outlawed and exiled or had their political rights annulled, *cassado* in Portuguese. Anyone caught trying to form a radical opposition got into bad trouble—"disappeared" to torture or death.

The strong economic growth of the 1970s gave people hope and thus dampened protests, but with the economic downturns of the 1980s and 1990s hope dimmed. "I tell you frankly I'm desperate," said one sidewalk peddler whose pregnant wife stood nearby. "They keep telling us that things will get better, but who can afford to wait? Hunger doesn't wait. Yesterday I sold nothing. Our food is ending. When it ends, what do I do?" The answer for some Brazilians was

Comparison

Apartheid, Brazilian-Style

Until *apartheid* ended in the early 1990s, South Africa classified population groups and then used elaborate laws to discriminate against nonwhites. From the Brazilian perspective this was not only unjust but expensive and stupid as well. The Brazilian system, while claiming that all are equal, assigns people to social roles on the basis of race as the South African system did, but without the obvious unfairness, the many laws, or the social tension that the apartheid system brought. By pretending to be color-blind, Brazilian society dampens the black resentment that could lead to rage and revolt.

Curiously, tacitly racist breakaway movements in Brazil's southernmost provinces, where the population is 85 percent European, parallel South Africa's apartheid. People in the clean, prosperous states of Rio Grande do Sul, Santa Catarina, and Parana, upset by the influx of impoverished darker Brazilians from further north, talk about setting up a new country, the Republic of the Pampas. It would be the size of France and have 22 million mostly white citizens. German and Italian would be coequal languages with Portuguese.

One spokesman for this republic is businessman Irton Marx, the blond son of German immigrants, who argues Brazil is too big, too statist, and too corrupt. "Our culture and economy are different here in the south. We are part of the First World. We are subsidizing the whole country and getting nothing back." Denying he or his movement is racist, Marx contends his tidy region is threatened by the mass migration of poor northeastern Brazilians, who do not have the local "Teutonic" attitude toward work.

Some municipalities in the south of Brazil already make it difficult for poor nonwhites to settle. They deny them permits or even put them on buses back to where they came from. Chances are the breakaway movement will get nowhere, but it does illustrate (1) there is racism in Brazil, (2) Brazil is in a shaky condition, and (3) the crux of apartheid, whether in South Africa, Brazil, or U.S. suburbia, is influx control.

Marginals in Brazil's Favelas

Brazil's poor are sometimes called **marginals**. Many of them huddle in favelas. Some favelados hold regular jobs, others sell pop on the beach, and some steal. Brazil's crime rates are astronomical. There is no place for the marginals to go, and no one cares about them.

Politically they are on the margin, too. Unorganized and too busy just trying to get food, they riot only when faced with starvation. Brazilian sociologists point out that however wretched life seems in the favelas, it's worse in the countryside. Moving to a favela for many is a step up, for there they have access to some education and health services and may even find a job.

"Keep Your Distance," says this Rio road sign, but it could also serve as a warning about the favelas that nestle between Rio's peaks. (Michael Roskin)

to raid food stores. Everything from corner grocery shops to supermarkets were smashed open by hungry crowds and quickly looted. Brazil's food riots sent chilling warning signs throughout the Third World.

Especially ominous is that this arousal of Brazil's poor, from passive to active, comes at the time Brazil has democratized and formed parties, some of them with radical leadership. Even more explosive is the fact that many middle-class Brazilians find themselves getting pushed down into the lower classes, and middle-class people are far more likely to rise in revolt than those who have always been downtrodden. Sectors of the middle class, desperate to hold on to their tenuous positions, could serve as the spark plug for major unrest.

In sum, the poor are not automatically passive or active but can become either, depending on the situation. If Brazilian radicals attempt once again to mobilize mass discontent, the military might decide to intervene again.

Uneven Democratic Attitudes

Most Brazilians respect democracy in the abstract, but a 2000 poll found that only 18 percent were satisfied with the way Brazil's democracy works in practice. Twenty-five percent said authoritarianism might be better; 28 percent didn't care. Some Brazilians, especially

Key Term

marginal Poor person on the edge of society and the economy.

among elites, are convinced democrats. Others, especially poorer and working-class people, are interested in little besides jobs and are willing to support whatever will put some food on the table, democratic or not. This is typical of the Third World—and even much of the First. Commitment to democratic values is stronger among those higher up on the socioeconomic ladder, people who don't have to worry about eating.

Researchers in Brazil and other Third World lands often find that poorer and less-educated people are more interested in law-and-order and bread-and-butter issues than in civil rights and democracy. Many actually prefer an authoritarian populist in command. One survey had found 63 percent of Brazilian illiterates named the dictatorial Vargas as the best president. Those with high school or college education favored Médici, the toughest of Brazil's military presidents. Their reasons? Poor people liked the way Vargas raised wages and looked after the poor; middle-class people pointed to industrialization under Médici.

The strong vote for Cardoso in 1994 and 1998 was not necessarily a vote for democracy; it was a vote for bread on the table. Only among better-educated and better-off Brazilians do we find an interest in democracy for its own sake, and even here it is not overwhelming. And these Brazilian findings are not unique. In many countries—including the United States—commitment to democratic values falls off as one moves down the socioeconomic ladder. The irony here is that democracy—a system that's supposed to be based on the broad masses of people—receives its strongest support from elites.

Key Concepts

Latin America's Changing Leftists

During much of the Cold War, Latin American intellectuals subscribed to fashionable leftist views that their region's poverty was the result of exploitation by wicked capitalists, especially by *Norteamericanos*. Some worked this into a Marxist type of theory called "dependency" that was accepted as an article of faith throughout much of the Western Hemisphere. Only by getting out from under U.S. corporations—who dictated what Latin American lands would produce (bananas and coffee) and what they would consume (Chevrolets and Coca Cola)—would Latins find prosperity. Accordingly, revolutionary regimes such as Cuba and Nicaragua were not bad, because they broke the Yankee connection.

In recent decades the Latin left has had to rethink its Marxist and dependency theories. The demise of Communist regimes in the Soviet Union and East Europe made many wonder if "socialism" really worked. The economic success of Chile, where a military dictator enforced capitalism, made many appreciate the vigor of market systems, especially those connected to the world economy. Argentina's restructuring in the early 1990s had a similar impact. And intellectually, many were persuaded by the arguments of Peruvian economist Hernando de Soto that the only effective and dynamic sector of Latin economies is the black market. Why? Every other sector is choked into stagnation by government controls.

The result of all this was that many Latin intellectuals, including Cardoso, abandoned statism and socialism. Free markets, international trade, and foreign investment no longer looked bad; maybe they were even good. The new attitude spread unevenly in Latin America, though. It was most pronounced in Mexico, Chile, and Argentina but weaker in Brazil and Uruguay.

This doesn't mean that democracy is impossible in Brazil, but it's an uphill struggle. Part of the impulse for Brazil's democratization comes from the educated upper-middle class, a group that's relatively small but strategically positioned to make its voice heard. Brazil makes us aware that democracy—or indeed any kind of political system—is usually the work of the few mobilizing the many.

Key Term

whig democracy Democracy with limited participation, typical of democracy's initial phases.

Patterns of Interaction

An Elite Game

Politics in Brazil has been largely a game for elites: big landowners, bankers and industrialists, and top bureaucrats and military people. Many do not welcome mass participation in politics. The stakes of the game are political power, the patronage jobs, and the control of funds that come with it. The rules of the game are that none of the players gets seriously hurt or threatened and that nobody mobilizes the Brazilian masses in an angry way, for that would destroy the game's fragile balance and hurt them all.

Accordingly, Vargas, himself a wealthy rancher, was an acceptable player when he supported coffee prices for the growers, but when he started to mobilize poor Brazilians he had to be ousted. Kubitschek was a good player who looked after his elite friends and deflected potential discontent with his grandiose plans to open Brazil's interior. Goulart, also a wealthy rancher, was a very bad player: He threatened all the elites and mobilized the masses at a furious rate. The PT's Lula, an antielite labor-union radical, mobilized Brazil's working class in a way that frightened most of Brazil's elites. If he had won, the military might have been inclined to move again.

Until recently, Brazil's political history has been the same elite game: Dom Pedro with his fazendeiro friends, the Old Republic with its Paulista-Mineiro alternation, and the military technocracy with its industrial and bureaucratic clientele. Since Vargas, however, the political mobilization of the masses has been a recurring threat to the game. Periodically, a politician who doesn't like the elite's fixed rules is tempted to reach out to Brazil's masses, both to secure his own power and to help the downtrodden. Seeing the threat, Brazil's elites, through the military, remove it and try to demobilize the masses. Mobilization and demobilization can be seen as a cycle.

The Mobilization-Demobilization Cycle

Scholars of the Third World in general and Brazil in particular often focus on "political mobilization." Mobilization means the masses waking up, becoming aware, and often becoming angry. Prior to the beginning of mass political mobilization in a country, few participate in politics, and decisions are made by traditional elites, such as Brazil's big landowners and political bosses. Some call this **whig democracy**, and it is standard in the opening decades of democratic development. Democracies typically start with participation limited to the better off (even in the United States). Some social stimulus, such as economic growth, brings new sectors of the population (in Brazil, the urban working class) to political awareness; they are "mobilized" and start participating in politics with new demands.

The problem with Brazil—and many other Third World countries—is that the existing institutions haven't been able to handle this influx of new participants and their demands. Well-organized, strong political parties can channel, moderate, and calm mass demands in a constructive way. But Brazilian parties are weak, little more than personalistic vehicles to get their chiefs into power. The chiefs, such as Vargas and Goulart, use their parties in a demagogic way, to whip up support among the newly mobilized and politically unsophisticated masses by promising them instant economic improvement. The more conservative elements in society—the wealthy, who often have close ties to the military—view this process with horror. The military sees it as "leftist chaos" and may end it by a military coup, the story of many Latin American countries. Thus mobilization, which could be the start of democratization, often leads to authoritarian takeovers.

The 1964 military takeover in Brazil ended one phase of what might be termed a mobilization-demobilization cycle. The generals had grown to hate civilian politics, especially political parties and their demagogic leaders. We can to a degree understand their hatred. As guardians of Brazil's unity and security, they witnessed their beloved republic falling into the hands of irresponsible crowd-pleasers.

Typically, the military tries the only solution they know: demobilization. Believing that the solution lies in an end to disruptive political activity, they ban most parties, handpick

Democracy

Political Mobilization, Brazilian-Style

The turnouts in Brazilian elections provide a graphic indicator of political mobilization.

Even in 1962, the figure was rather small compared to the total Brazilian population, then about 76 million. But a literacy requirement held down the size of the electorate and eliminated the poorest from voting. Conservative, better-off Brazilians and the military were horrified at the prospect of Goulart's dropping the literacy test and letting lower-class Brazilians into the election booth with their potentially radical demands. Now there is no literacy requirement, the voting age is sixteen, and voting is compulsory (but not enforced). The 1998 election indicates the growth of apathy, as Brazilians discover that politics can't solve everything.

Year	Turnout
1930 and earlier	never more than .25 million
1933	1.25 million
1945	6.2 million
1950	7.9 million
1955	8.6 million
1960	11.6 million
1962	14.7 million
1989	63.0 million
1994	93.0 million
1998	84.0 million

Key Concepts

The Praetorian Tendency

As the Roman Empire ossified and crumbled, the emperor's bodyguard, the Praetorian Guard, came to play a powerful role, making and unmaking emperors. Political scientists now use **praetorianism** to indicate a situation where the military feels driven to take over the government.

Praetorianism is not just a problem of a power-hungry army but reflects deep conflict in the whole society. In praetorian societies, it's not only the army that wants to take power, but many other groups as well: students, labor unions, revolutionaries, and politicians would like to seize the state machinery. Institutional constraints and balances have broken down; nobody plays by the rules. In such situations of chaos and breakdown, it is the army among the many power contenders that is best equipped to seize power, so praetorianism usually means military takeover.

political leaders, and permit only rigged elections. Initially, things do calm down. Some people are thankful the army has stepped in to put an end to extremist politics and empty promises. Mass rallies, loud demands, and radical leaders disappear—the latter sometimes physically.

But the problems aren't solved. The demands—although no longer whipped up by politicians—are still there and growing. Indeed, as the economy grows, more people come to live in cities, and the pent-up demands for change increase. To repress such demands, the regime turns to the police-state brutality of arbitrary arrests and torture. Once people are awakened or mobilized they can never be fully demobilized, even by massive doses of coercion.

The Inflation Connection

Inflation is a political problem the world over, especially in Latin America, where regimes may fall over the rate of inflation. Inflation may also be seen as part of the mobilization-demobilization cycle. In Brazil, inflation in currency corresponds to the inflation in promises made by politicians seeking mass support.

Controlling inflation is an unhappy task. By restricting credit and cutting the amount of money being printed, an austerity policy can lower the inflation rate, but at a cost of unemployment and slow economic growth. Latin American inflation cutters are often conservative authoritarians, usually military men, who can pursue disinflationary measures without regard to mass desires. As in much of Latin America, the Brazilian military in effect says to its citizenry: "We don't care how much it hurts, the sooner inflation ends the better we'll all be. Take the bitter medicine now before inflation wrecks the entire economy." When Cardoso made Brazilians swallow this bitter medicine just after his reelection in late 1998, his popularity fell.

Encouraging inflation, on the other hand, is easy; regimes can almost do it in a fit of absentmindedness. Politicians, wanting to make everybody happy, let the national mint's printing presses run to finance government projects. This is the way Kubitschek built Brasilia. Inflation tends to feed on itself and get out of hand, and soon people can't

Key Term

praetorianism Tendency for military takeovers.

make ends meet. Conservative industrialists and bankers become convinced that the politicians have gone insane. The military, whose fixed salaries are eroded by the galloping inflation, seethes in jealous rage and starts planning a coup to save both the republic and their incomes.

When the military does take power, their disinflationary measures correspond to the political demobilization they also try to enforce. Under the military, this consisted of controls on wages but not on prices, with the result that lower-class Brazilians have to work like dogs to keep up with food prices while some speculators enjoy an economic boom. Civilian regimes may try to do the opposite, with equally bad results (see box below).

Although the Brazilian generals had excellent economic planners, they did not end inflation, which by 1984 reached 223 percent, double what it was in 1964 when the military seized power. This extremely embarrassing fact undermined regime support among the businessmen and bankers who had welcomed the 1964 takeover. One reason Brazil turned democratic was that the military proved as inept as civilians in controlling inflation.

The Corruption Connection

One of the standard characteristics of the Third World is its massive corruption. Throughout Latin America, officials expect *la mordida* ("the bite") to issue contracts and licenses. Some argue that corruption is simply a part of Latin American political culture. Perhaps, but corruption tends to flourish under certain institutional arrangements; namely, it grows at the interface of the public and private sectors. Latin America, with its large state sectors and regulated economies, is thus especially fertile ground for corruption. The solution? Cut the state sector back. Where this was done, in Chile, corruption also diminished.

Brazil's Struggle against Inflation

Until recently, Brazil suffered seemingly incurable inflation, sometimes at more than 50 percent a month. At times the government froze wages and prices and took other drastic steps. "Prices, starting tomorrow, are halted," said the economy minister in 1991.

But the prices disobeyed. The 1991 effort was the fifth plan to control wages and prices in five years. Five years earlier, Brazilians saw how President Sarney's plan to do the same thing ended in disaster, with prices going up after a short pause and many producers driven out of business. Sarney's popularity plunged lower than ever, unions struck, crowds took to the streets, and the military glowered angrily, as if awaiting their turn to take over.

The real problem, one about which both Collor de Mello and Cardoso campaigned, is Brazil's overlarge state sector that has to be propped up with big subsidies, which are provided by simply printing more money. In the early 1990s, Brazil's Central Bank increased the nation's money supply severalfold each year, producing hyperinflation, which hit 1,149 percent in 1992, 2,489 percent in 1993, and 5,154 percent in early 1994. To turn off the printing presses, though, would mean shutting down a large part of the Brazilian economy, resulting in even more unemployment. Unions warned they wouldn't stand for it. Wage-and-price freezes, experience from many countries shows, simply do not work for more than a few months. They are instituted in desperation when the real cures would hurt too many politically influential groups.

The Brazilian Political Cycle

With some oversimplification, Brazilian politics over the decades can be seen as a cycle or progression of phases that repeat themselves. If we were to sketch out our discussion of the last few pages, it would look like the diagram below:

The cycle could start all over with the mobilized masses falling under the sway of demagogic politicians. That's the way Brazilian politics worked earlier—for example, during the two "Vargas cycles."

Mobilization → Demagoguery → Military Takeover → Demobilization → Liberalization → Democratization
(inflation) (disinflation)

The interesting thing about Brazil (and some other Latin American countries) is that the public is increasingly fed up with corruption, especially in high places. The presidents of Brazil and Venezuela were hounded from office when the media uncovered the extent of their corruption. Dozens of Brazilian Congresspersons (most in the PMDB) enriched themselves through fake projects (such as pretend help for the poor). The chairman of the budget committee got $51 million over five years. (He said he was very lucky in the lottery.) As in Russia, parliamentary immunity shields such crooks.

This new public concern is a very good sign, an indication of growing political maturity. Stealing from the starving is no longer acceptable. Brazilian politicians have looted their country long enough; let them now face angry citizens. The danger here is that when Brazilians start to think that democracy equals corruption, the way is open for a coup. Brazil's top general warned Congress to clean up its act: "Beware the anger of the legions," the exact words once used by Rome's Praetorian Guard.

Resurgent Interest Groups

For most of the life of the military regime, the Brazilian government continued the corporatist model that Vargas had borrowed from Italy and Portugal. Under corporatism, interest groups are controlled or coordinated by the government. With the *abertura* of the 1980s, Brazil's interest groups emerged with a life of their own once again.

After the 1964 takeover, the military abolished the big union that had been fostered by Goulart and placed all labor unions under direct government control. Particularly drastic was the control of rural unions, whose impoverished and militant farm workers threatened the property of the conservative landowning allies of the military government. Union leaders were henceforth handpicked to make sure they would cooperate with the new order and not lead workers in excessive wage demands or strikes.

While this arrangement held down wages, prices rose until workers could stand it no more. New unions and leaders outside government control emerged as a major force. The largest and most radical Brazilian union, the United Confederation of Workers (CUT), is tied to Lula's Workers party. CUT is especially strong in São Paulo and has struck against many big industries there. The military does not like CUT. The tamer General Confederation of Workers (CGT) is tied to the large but corrupt PMBD.

Many businessmen had welcomed the 1964 coup only to find that the military technocrats would sometimes ride roughshod over their interests in the name of economic rationality. The theory of **constructive bankruptcy** let weak Brazilian firms go under rather than subsidize them with tariff protection against foreign competition. Now businesses generally want sound money and an end to government economic controls and restrictions. Other groups, such as students and farmers, also voice their discontent. Opposition to the rule of the generals developed across a broad front of conservative and radical Brazilians. The most interesting group, however, was the Catholic church, a force to be reckoned with in the world's largest Catholic country.

The Church as Opposition

The Roman Catholic church was the only large Brazilian group that maintained its autonomy and was in a position to criticize the military regime. Typically in Catholic countries the Church has been conservative and has favored conservative regimes. In France, the long fight between clericalism and anticlericalism split society into two camps. The same thing happened in Spain and Italy.

Brazil never had this kind of split. With the 1891 republican constitution, modeled after the U.S. constitution, the Brazilian church consented to disestablishment, that is, to losing its special privileges as church and state were separated. Brazil settled this important and divisive issue quickly and early, leaving the church as an independent force.

Still, in social and economic outlook the Brazilian Catholic church was pretty conservative, urging the faithful to save their souls rather than to reform and improve society. With the **Second Vatican Council** of 1962–65, this conservative attitude changed, and many churchmen, especially younger ones, adopted the "theology of liberation" that put the church on the side of the poor and oppressed. In some Latin American countries, young priests actually became guerrilla fighters trying to overthrow what they regarded as wicked and reactionary regimes.

In the late 1960s, Brazilian church leaders denounced the regime for "fascist doctrines" and for arresting and torturing priests and nuns accused of harboring political fugitives. During the 1970s, the Brazilian church developed a strong stand for human rights and against Brazil's terrible poverty. When strikes flared in the 1980s, strikers often held meetings and sought refuge from police clubs in churches. As a whole, the Brazilian Catholic church was the most activist in Latin America, usually to the chagrin of the Vatican, which ordered priests out of direct political actions.

In 1980, John Paul II visited Brazil. He was visibly moved by what he saw in the favelas. In one, he removed the ring given him by Pope Paul VI when he became a cardinal and gave it to a local priest as a donation. John Paul seemed to be turning into an activist himself. In a Rio slum he called to Brazil's rich: "Look around a bit. Does it not wound your heart? Do you not feel remorse of conscience because of your riches and abundance?" But he stopped short of endorsing active church involvement in politics. Church people should guide spiritually but not politically. In Brazil, this middle road is hard to tread because concern for the poor tends to radicalize people.

Under the democratic regime, the Brazilian church continued its critical attitudes in support of the poor. Some Brazilian churchmen pretended not to hear the Vatican's order to steer clear of radical politics. Their argument is that in order to reach people to save their souls, the church must also help feed them. In poverty-stricken northeast Brazil, therefore, priests keep

Key Terms

constructive bankruptcy Economic theory that weak firms should fold to make way for new enterprises.

Second Vatican Council Series of meetings that modernized the Roman Catholic Church and turned it to problems of poverty; also called Vatican II.

Chico Mendes: Another Death in the Amazon

To Americans the murder of Chico Mendes in 1988 seemed to be part of an environmental outrage concerning the destruction of Brazil's Amazonian rain forest. Less noticed is the murder every year of dozens of leaders of the rural poor in land conflicts with farmers and ranchers intent on keeping their large holdings.

Mendes, who lived in Brazil's westernmost state of Acre, was national leader of rubber tappers who made common cause with environmentalists and Indians in trying to halt the destruction by ranchers and farmers of the lush jungle. The rubber tappers simply use existing trees and have no interest in burning down the forest. The ranchers and farmers, encouraged for decades by Brazil's government to develop the interior, cut and burn tens of millions of acres a year, contributing to global warming and to a shrinking of the earth's capacity to produce oxygen.

Mendes led major protests and legal actions to stop the developers. They in turn detested and frequently threatened him. In 1990, a rancher's son stunned an Acre court by admitting, "I killed Chico Mendes." He probably confessed to protect his father, who was charged with the murder of other peasant leaders. Guns for hire are cheap in the Amazon region, where some two thousand union leaders, small farmers, lawyers, priests, and nuns have been slain. (The Brazilian Catholic Church has taken a leading role in speaking for the rural poor.)

For most Brazilians, poverty is a bigger issue than the environment; people are more important than trees. The question is how and for whom the Amazon will be developed: for the masses of rural poor or for big ranchers who claim thousands of acres as their cattle pasture?

reminding the government of its land-reform program while they support the militant *Movimento Sem Terra* (Movement of Those Without Land). Conservative landlords charge that priests and nuns encourage the poor to illegally occupy private farms. Many are threatened with death.

Especially troublesome were radical French, Dutch, and other West European priests working in land reform. When the Brasilia government tried to keep them out, Brazil's bishops protested. The federal police chief said, "It's necessary to talk to them and pray, to pray above all that priests return to praying."

What Brazilians Quarrel About

How to Make a Second Brazilian Miracle

After the 1964 military takeover, the Brazilian economy improved. From 1968 to 1974 the annual growth rate averaged 10 percent, equal to Japanese rates at the time. A series of very bright economic technocrats used state-owned banks and industries to make a Brazilian miracle. The miracle had problems, however. It was based on foreign rather than Brazilian capital investment and on cheap imported oil. Brazilian capitalists, instead of reinvesting their money in industrial growth, preferred to spend it, speculate with it, or stash it abroad.

Key Term

capital flight Tendency of businesspersons in countries with shaky economies to send their money out of the country.

Capital flight is common in Latin America and more recently in Russia. For new capital investment they got government or foreign loans. This was one of the reasons Brazil accumulated one of the Third World's largest foreign debts, over $200 billion.

In the 1980s the cheap foreign loans and oil dried up, turning the boom into a declining GDP a decade later. From 1980 to 1993 Brazil's GDP grew at an annual average of only 1.5 percent. Per capita GDP (which takes into account population growth) declined an average of half a percent a year. Brazilians grew poorer. Some say this shows the limits of technocratic, state-led economic development, which can produce quick, one-time growth, but not for long.

How to turn this around? At this same time (as discussed in boxes on pages 56 and 64), Latin American intellectuals were starting to think that state-owned industries and government supervision of the economy might be mistaken paths. Cardoso made such a shift and privatized (by auction) state-owned telecommunication, electricity, mines, railroads, banking, and other industries. (Collor had begun the job by selling off steel and petroleum industries.) Cardoso also cut Brazil's nationalistic restrictions on foreign ownership, drastically trimmed the number of Brazil's bureaucrats and their pensions, and reined in state-level banks, who loan recklessly to friends of governors. Cardoso faced strong opposition every step of the way, for every one of these measures meant rich, powerful interests giving up their cushy deals. Brazil's congress represents these interests—some in Cardoso's own party—and often fought him.

The freeing up of Brazil's red-tape economy is analogous to the economic reforms undertaken in Russia and Japan. Many people see what needs to be done for the long-term good of the country, but those who will be hurt by the reforms do everything they can to block them. Cardoso, to his credit, made progress in freeing Brazil's economy and selling state-owned companies, but much work remains. By 1996, Brazil started registering growth rates of 2 percent a year, not great but a lot better than negative growth. With the currency collapse of late 1998 (triggered by the Russian collapse), growth again slumped.

They Got an Awful Lot of Everything in Brazil

Brazil has economic problems, but these should not overshadow its amazing achievements. In recent decades Brazil has developed rapidly to become the

- eighth largest economy of the world,
- fifth biggest food exporter in the world,
- third biggest shoe producer in the world,
- seventh biggest steel producer of the world,
- ninth largest producer of cars in the world,
- second largest producer of iron ore,
- eighth largest producer of aluminum,
- fifth biggest arms exporter, and
- of course, world's biggest coffee producer.

With a burgeoning economy that still has great growth potential, one can see why foreign banks put an awful lot of money into Brazil. If Brazil ever achieves economic stability, it could be a growth wonder. One Brazilian wisecrack: "Brazil is the country of the future and always will be."

GEOGRAPHY

MERCOSUR: A REGIONAL TRADE BLOC

One stimulus to Brazil's growth was **Mercosur** (*Mercosul* in Portuguese), a free-trade area formed in 1991 by Argentina, Brazil, Paraguay, and Uruguay. (Chile and Bolivia are associate members.) Just as West Europe's Common Market pushed its economy into greater competition, efficiency, and prosperity, Mercosur seems to be doing the same. Trade among members shot up. In time, Mercosur could expand to include all of South America and eventually even merge with our North American Free Trade Agreement (NAFTA) to form a common market for the whole Western Hemisphere.

Brazil's State Capitalism

While leftists point to foreign dependency as the root of Brazil's problems, many businessmen and economists point to Brazil's large state sector and red-tape controls on the economy. Brazil, they emphasize, has not really been a free-market country relying on private initiative. Until recent privatization, some 60 percent of Brazil's industry was in government hands—including mines, petroleum production, and electric companies. In addition, the majority of loans came from government banks, giving the state the power to determine what got built and where. Collor de Mello started to dismantle this statist empire, and Cardoso continued the task.

Statism—where the government is the number-one capitalist—can both accomplish big projects and make big mistakes. Some projects that Brazil poured money into were prestigious but money losers. For example, the government invested heavily in nuclear power in a country where hydroelectricity had scarcely been tapped. The nuclear program was a foolish waste—although it made Brazil look like an advanced country—and by 1980 it was greatly curtailed.

Government loans were sometimes extended foolishly, too. The interest on these loans was so low, and Brazil's inflation so high, that the credits amounted to free money, which the borrower could immediately loan out at high interest. Why work for a living when you can just shift some paper around? The subsidized loans from the government, however, ultimately came from working Brazilians in the form of inflation. Brazil's cheap government loans were another reason the rich got richer and the poor got poorer.

State control produces other distortions in the economy. There are so many laws and regulations that businesses have to employ red-tape specialists called *despachantes* (expediters) to jog the bureaucracy into giving a license or allowing a price change. Many despachantes are related to the bureaucrats they deal with; some are former bureaucrats themselves. The Brazilian word for getting around a regulation is *jeito*, literally "knack," meaning having someone who can fix it for you. The whole system feeds corruption.

Another problem area is minimum wages, a holdover from Vargas's populist paternalism. As in other countries, minimum wages dissuade employers from hiring unskilled workers. Many poor people then cannot find entry-level jobs. Minimum wages, aimed at helping the working poor, simply mean more unemployed marginals in the favelas.

Key Term

Mercosur "Southern market"; free-trade area covering southern part of South America.

HEADED FOR EXTINCTION: BRAZIL'S INDIANS

With Brazil's expansion into the vast Amazon frontier has come the pushing back of its Indians until they may be facing extinction. Brazil's constitution guarantees Indians rights to traditional rain-forest lands, but in practice the need of ranchers and miners for ever more territory has made enforcement spotty at best. Of the 270 tribes of Brazilian Indians found at the beginning of the twentieth century, ninety have disappeared altogether and others are slipping fast. Particularly vicious have been gold miners, who readily invade Indian reserves and kill them by guns and dynamite or by poisoning the water with the mercury they use to isolate gold particles. More intent on development and jobs, few Brazilians worry much about the plight of the Indians.

Even worse, many of Brazil's grandiose projects have been capital-intensive (using lots of machinery) rather than labor-intensive (using lots of workers). Brazil is short of capital but has lots of labor. More labor-intensive projects would kill two birds with one stone, alleviating both the capital shortage and tremendous unemployment. But such projects were not to the taste of Brazil's technocrats, probably because they were less prestigious than mammoth capital investments.

Who's right—the leftists, who point to dependency, or the businesspeople, who point to state strangulation? Actually, the two views complement each other. State control does stunt domestic capital formation, and this makes Brazil chronically dependent on foreign capital. Instead of a vigorous private sector of local businesses, the Brazilian economy is divided between the foreign multinationals and the state. Brazilians tend to attach themselves to one of the two. The cure for statism is privatization, which Brazil undertook during the 1990s. Most of the purchasers were foreign (especially U.S.) multinationals. Leftists objected, claiming that Brazil was giving foreign capitalists its wealth. Promarketeers cheered, arguing that the sales bring new investment, competition, and economic growth. Finally, with much hesitation, Brazil is moving away from statism.

Growth for Whom?

Another weakness of the Brazilian economy is that Brazil has one of the most unequal income distributions in the world. The richest 20 percent of Brazilians rake in 65 percent of all income, while the poorest 20 percent get 2 percent. The rich get richer and the poor poorer. Half of Brazilians are reckoned as poor, and many are destitute. Per capita income in the Northeast is lower than in Bangladesh. The "Brazilian miracle" overlooked these people.

Critics on the left argue that the miracle, because it was controlled by U.S. multinationals and Brazilian technocrats, produced semiluxury goods and grandiose projects that benefited the better off. It made cars and swanky apartments rather than public transportation and basic housing. The leftists would redistribute income to the poor.

Those defending the system point out that Brazil contains two economies, a First World economy that is modern and productive and a Third World one that is traditional and unproductive. Actually, most Third World countries have First World sectors within them. In

For poor urban dwellers, streetcorner or beach hawking may be the only way to eke out a living. Here, a Rio woman and her children sell candles to light in the church behind them. (Michael Roskin)

Brazil the contrast is stark. But, argue the defenders, the gap cannot be bridged overnight. Brazil must first build up its modern sector until it gradually takes over the whole country. To simply redistribute income to marginals, who produce little or nothing, would be economic folly. The trick is to keep the economy growing so as to absorb the marginals and turn them into producers and consumers. This is known as the developmentalist solution to Brazilian poverty.

The critic on the left rejoins that Brazilian development, because it is capital-intensive, can't begin to create the 1.3 million new jobs needed every year.

The Population Problem

Brazil, like most of the Third World, has seen a hefty population increase. The Catholic church, of course, forbids any artificial method of birth control, and the military regime thought a high birth rate contributed to economic growth. Accordingly, in Brazil, until the 1970s, there was no emphasis on slowing population growth, and Brazil's population is now 168 million. The good news is that Brazil's fertility rate, like much of the Third World, has plummeted since 1970, when a Brazilian woman had an average of 5.8 children, to 2.1 in 1997, not much above First World levels. This showed the impact of birth control, television, and economic downturn. Brazil's popular TV soaps show small, affluent families with only one or two children, and this has become a national norm.

It is poor people, especially peasants, who have the most children. The poverty-stricken Northeast, where people have especially large families, is an inexhaustible reservoir of marginal Brazilians. However many millions of them pour into the cities of the South, there are millions more still coming. The result is **hyperurbanization**, common throughout the Third World, where cities are usually surrounded by huge slum belts created by peasants who can no longer live off the land. Two-thirds of Brazilians live in cities, an absurd situation for a big, empty country. São Paulo with 18 million inhabitants is the third largest city in the world (after Tokyo and Mexico City).

The rural immigrants to the cities settle in favelas. With no education—a majority of Brazilians haven't finished primary school—or job skills, many do not find regular work. Those that do usually

Key Term

hyperurbanization Overconcentration of populations in cities.

must travel hours to and from their jobs. With prices rising, most discover themselves getting poorer. If they cannot feed their numerous children, they are forced to abandon them. Millions of "nobody's children" live on the streets, usually by stealing.

Some of Brazil's urban poor, caught at the bottom of a worsening economic situation, turn to crime. With widespread gun ownership, Brazilian murder rates are among the world's highest. Brazilian citizens and police, fed up with crime, turn to extralegal remedies. Unofficial "death squads" of off-duty policemen execute thousands of criminal suspects a year in the favelas or streets. Sometimes shopkeepers pay them to clean up the sidewalks. Young purse and wallet snatchers are sometimes beaten to death on the street. Police shoot street kids as they sleep on the assumption they are petty criminals. And the police may be worse than the criminals. Some police set up roadblocks to shake down and even shoot motorists. Some gun down landless peasants. Policemen are rarely convicted of anything.

Is Democracy Here to Stay?

In the 1970s, almost all of Latin America was some form of dictatorship, but since then almost all of Latin America has returned to democratic, civilian rule (except Cuba). Democracy may be contagious. But will Brazil's democracy, or any of the others, last? The problems of all of Latin America's nations are incredible: severe economic difficulties, bloated state sectors, growing populations, military establishments accustomed to intervening in politics, and a lack of seasoned political institutions such as parties and parliaments. The good news is the bad news is wrong, or at least exaggerated. Democracy has been reasonably sturdy in Latin America, despite some economic hard times, and these hard times, widely trumpeted in the media, always pass.

What has changed? The region as a whole is richer and has a bigger middle class, the bearers of democracy. Better educated and informed, they no longer swallow demagogic promises. Many are now aware of the dangers of statism and inflation. Markets work, and trade between countries benefits all. Even Cuba may soon give way to the democratic tide. For another country with great potential also struggling toward stable democracy, let us now turn to South Africa.

Key Terms

absolute poverty (p. 60)
autogolpe (p. 51)
capital flight (p. 72)
constructive bankruptcy (p. 70)
coroneís (p. 50)
corporatism (p. 51)
demagoguery (p. 57)
dependency theory (p. 57)
Estado Nôvo (p. 51)
favela (p. 62)
fiscal (p. 54)
hyperurbanization (p. 75)
inchoate (p. 57)
machismo (p. 61)
marginal (p. 63)
Mercosur (p. 73)
mobilize (p. 51)
Old Republic (p. 50)
personalismo (p. 61)
positivism (p. 50)

praetorianism (p. 67)
real (p. 57)
recession (p. 57)
Second Vatican Council (p. 70)
statute (p. 54)
vary inversely (p. 57)
whig democracy (p. 65)

Further Reference

Abers, Rebecca Neaera. *Inventing Local Democracy: Grassroots Politics in Brazil.* Boulder, CO: Lynne Rienner, 2000.

Baaklini, Abdo I. *The Brazilian Legislature and Political System.* Westport, CT: Greenwood, 1992.

Bresser Pereira, Luiz Carlos. *Economic Crisis and State Reform in Brazil: Toward a New Interpretation of Latin America.* Boulder, CO: Lynne Rienner, 1996.

Diamond, Larry, Jonathan Hartlyn, Juan J. Linz, and Seymour Martin Lipset, eds. *Democracy in Developing Countries: Latin America,* 2nd ed. Boulder, CO: Lynne Rienner, 1999.

Eakin, Marshall C. *Brazil: The Once and Future Country.* New York: St. Martin's Press, 1997.

Goertzel, Ted G. *Fernando Henrique Cardoso: Reinventing Democracy in Brazil.* Boulder, CO: Lynne Rienner, 1999.

Hagopian, Frances. *Traditional Politics and Regime Change in Brazil.* New York: Cambridge University Press, 1996.

Hall, Anthony. *Sustaining Amazonia: Grassroots Action for Productive Conservation.* New York: St. Martin's, 1998.

Hunter, Wendy. *Eroding Military Influence in Brazil: Politicians Against Soldiers.* Chapel Hill, NC: University of North Carolina Press, 1997.

Kingstone, Peter R., and Timothy J. Powers, eds. *Democratic Brazil: Actors, Institutions, and Processes.* Pittsburgh, PA: University of Pittsburgh Press, 2000.

Levine, Robert M. *Brazilian Legacies.* Armonk, NY: M. E. Sharpe, 1997.

Mainwaring, Scott. *Rethinking Party Systems in the Third Wave of Democratization: The Case of Brazil.* Stanford, CA: Stanford University Press, 1999.

Purcell, Susan Kaufman, and Riordan Roett, eds. *Brazil Under Cardoso.* Boulder, CO: Lynne Rienner, 1997.

Roberts, Paul Craig, and Karen LaFollete Araujo. *The Capitalist Revolution in Latin America.* New York: Oxford University Press, 1997.

Rosenn, Keith S., and Richard Downes, eds. *Corruption and Political Reform in Brazil: The Impact of Collor's Impeachment.* Boulder, CO: Lynne Rienner, 1999.

Schneider, Ronald M. *Brazil: Culture and Politics in a New Industrial Power.* Boulder, CO: Westview, 1996.

Skidmore, Thomas F. *The Politics of Military Rule in Brazil, 1964–1985.* New York: Oxford University Press, 1988.

Weyland, Kurt. *Democracy without Equity: Failures of Reform in Brazil.* Pittsburgh, PA: University of Pittsburgh Press, 1996.

CHAPTER 4

South Africa

Questions to Consider

1. Explain South Africa's population groups.
2. What did the Boer War do to South Africa's politics?
3. What and when was *apartheid*?
4. Why was Nelson Mandela important to South Africa's transformation?
5. How did South Africa escape revolution?
6. What are South Africa's parties and what do they stand for?
7. What is "consociation" and how did South Africa attempt it?
8. How does Inkatha illustrate the tribal nature of African politics?
9. What could go wrong in South Africa?

The Impact of the Past

South Africa began as a colony and continued until recently to have a **colonialist** structure and mentality, the elimination of which is not complete. It began when the Dutch East India Company sent Jan van Riebeeck with two hundred men to start a "refreshment station" at the Cape of Good Hope in 1652. They encountered the native Khoi Khoi, whom they enslaved, impregnated, and eventually killed off with smallpox. Needing more slaves, they imported them chiefly from the Indies and Madagascar. The resulting mixture—Khoi Khoi, Dutch, Malay, and other—produced the so-called Cape Coloureds. This process is reminiscent of the early settlement of Brazil, which also produced a racial mixture. The difference in South Africa was that the whites developed exclusivist attitudes about race and classified the Coloureds as an inferior group. As in the United States, racism started early and lasted.

As the Cape colony expanded, mostly Dutch farmers (*boers*) pushed outward, taking the land they wanted. When the soil was exhausted, they moved on. Their constant movement earned them the name *trekboers*, or farmers on the move. Farther inland, they met the primitive San people, whom they shot as "pests." Very early, Afrikaners had the attitude that the land was exclusively theirs and that the natives were to be either enslaved or exterminated.

The Dutch didn't pay much attention to the Cape colony, but it grew, aided by the arrival of French Huguenots and Germans, who brought the French

Key Term

colonialism A system in which a few Europeans rule many "natives."

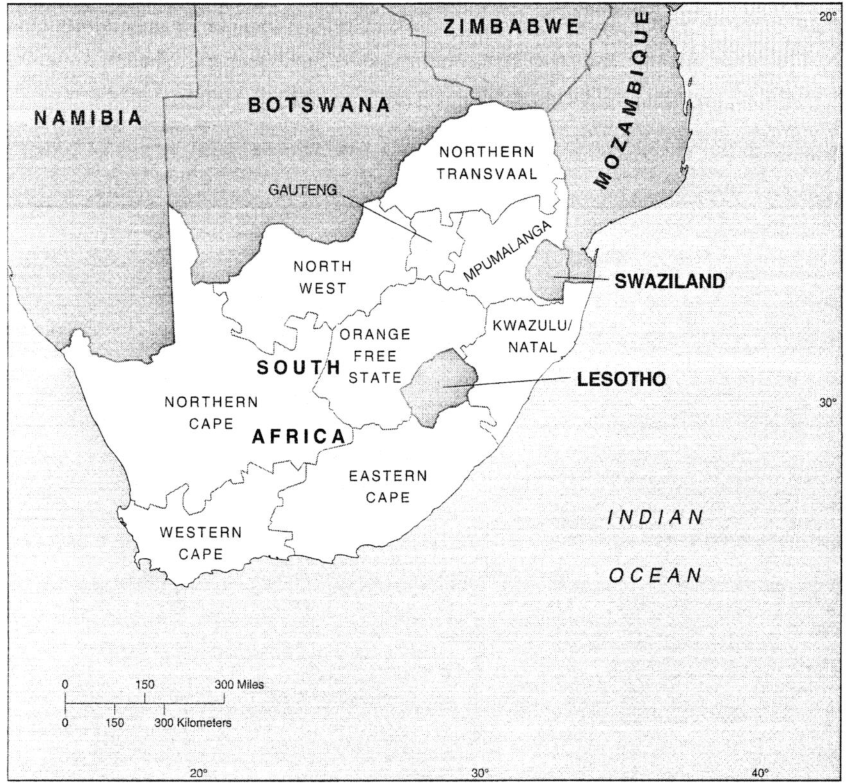

South Africa's New Territorial Organization

and German names found today among Afrikaners as well as wine-making skills. As the trekboers pushed along the Indian Ocean coast in the late eighteenth century, they met African Negroes, bigger, stronger, much better organized, and more warlike than Khoi Khoi or San. These Africans were moving south, away from population pressure, tribal wars, and slave raids. In a series of battles over a century, the so-called Kaffir Wars, the Boers subdued the Africans and again took the land they wanted.

Napoleon indirectly triggered the rise of both modern Brazil and South Africa. When a French revolutionary army occupied the Netherlands in 1795, the Dutch let the British take over the Cape to keep Table Bay—around which Cape Town is built—out of French hands. The British stayed as welcome guests until 1803 but returned in 1806, this time for good. In 1814, the Netherlands officially turned over the Cape to Britain, and the English moved to remake it into a British colony.

The Great Trek

Many Boers bristled at British rule. Not only did the British want everybody to speak English, they wanted everybody to be equal before the law. Even Coloured servants could bear witness against their masters. In 1834, to the outrage of many Boers, slavery was abolished.

Key Term

Zulu Largest South African population group, living chiefly in KwaZulu/Natal.

The Boers became convinced that the English were destroying their language, institutions, way of life, and freedom.

Between 1836 and 1838, an estimated twelve thousand Boer men, women, and children—about one-quarter of the Cape's Dutch population—loaded up ox carts and, like American pioneers, moved into the interior seeking land and freedom. The epic is known as the Great Trek and is celebrated by Afrikaners today as a symbol of their toughness, courage, and go-it-alone attitude. At times the *voortrekkers* (pioneers) had to disassemble their wagons to get them over roadless escarpments. Some columns fought battles with Africans, drawing their wagons into a circle called a *laager*. One column disappeared without a trace, another was slaughtered by **Zulus**.

The voortrekkers' dealings with Africans paralleled the Americans' with Indians. Sometimes by force and sometimes by persuasion, the voortrekkers made treaties with chiefs to obtain land. The Africans, who had no concept of owning land, thought they were letting the Boers use the land for a while. Disputes were settled by the pioneers crushing the natives.

The rich soil and adequate rainfall of Natal, fronting the Indian Ocean, was the initial goal of most voortrekkers. But the British also took an interest in this lush province and annexed it in 1843. The British claimed it was to prevent further bloodshed between voortrekkers and Africans; the Boers retorted that it was to rob them of their land once again. In disgust, many voortrekkers repacked their ox wagons and moved back inland where, they thought, they would be forever free of the hated British.

The voortrekkers consolidated their inland settlements into two small republics, the Transvaal (meaning on the far side of the Vaal River) and the Orange Free State. Here, the Boers were at home. The language, religion (Dutch Reformed), governmental institutions, and way of life were all theirs. The Boer republics lived in uneasy peace with the British in the Cape and Natal until diamonds and gold were discovered.

The Boer War

With the discovery of diamonds in 1870 and gold in 1886, Europeans and even some Americans poured into the Cape and Transvaal. There, on the Witwatersrand (literally, "white-water ridge"), gold was mined in such quantities that a new city, Johannesburg, was built atop the waste rock. It soon became South Africa's largest city—and it was mostly English-speaking.

For the Boers, it looked as if the English were pursuing them and destroying their way of life. By 1895, the English-speaking *uitlanders* ("outlanders" or foreigners) outnumbered the Boers more than two to one. The Transvaal government under Paul Kruger, worried that it would be swamped by uitlanders, made life difficult for them, denied them the vote, and ignored their petitions. Disenfranchising other groups became an Afrikaner tactic to preserve dominance.

Meanwhile, to the south in the Cape, the British were plotting to add the Transvaal and Orange Free State to the British Empire. Sir Cecil Rhodes, the Cape millionaire who set up the Rhodes scholarships to Oxford, wanted the mineral wealth of the Boer republics. He had already sent a column around the Boers to the north to found Rhodesia. Said Rhodes: "Expansion is everything." With him was the British high commissioner in the Cape, Alfred (later Lord) Milner, who wanted a British-ruled swath of Africa from Cairo to the Cape. Using the issue of uitlander rights in the Transvaal, Rhodes and Milner provoked Kruger into declaring war in 1899.

The Boers fought tenaciously. Good riders and marksmen—and equipped with modern arms from a sympathetic Germany—the Boers at first set the British reeling back and laid siege to British-held cities. Wrote Kipling: "We have had a jolly good lesson, and it serves us jolly well

GEOGRAPHY

BOUNDARIES IN AFRICA

The boundaries of Africa are especially artificial. Many of them were settled at a conference in Berlin in 1885, the great "carve-up" of Africa to suit the imperialists. Many African boundaries cut through tribes and force together unworkable combinations of tribes. A river in Africa is a poor border because typically people of the same tribe live on both sides of it.

In 1963, with most of Africa independent, the new Organization of African Unity decided, however, not to change the Berlin borders and even put them in its charter. The new leaders were both afraid of unleashing chaos and of losing their governing jobs. Best to leave these artificial borders alone, they figured. Notice how several of Africa's borders are straight lines, the sure sign that a border is artificial. In Africa, the imperialists' land grabs became permanent boundaries.

right." Ultimately, Britain needed 450,000 soldiers to subdue 88,000 Boer fighters, who were reduced to guerrilla bands. To isolate the Boer "commandos" from food and supplies, the British resorted to rounding up Boer families and placing them in "concentration camps." Typhoid broke out and some 26,000 died in the camps. Even today, every **Afrikaner** family has the memory of losing at least one relative in a camp; they never forgave the English and depict themselves as the century's first concentration-camp victims.

Finally, in 1902, the Boers capitulated and signed a treaty ending the war, but the British, guilty over the misery they had inflicted, failed to follow up on their victory. Instead of suppressing the defeated foe, they gave them full political rights, and, over time, the Afrikaners used their legal powers ultimately to take over all South Africa. After half a century, the Boers won.

From Defeat to Victory

The defeated Boer republics were made British crown colonies but were soon given internal self-government. In 1908, a National Convention met in Durban to draw up plans for making the four colonies one country, and, in 1910, the Union of South Africa was proclaimed. Politically, the English and the Afrikaners, as they now called themselves, managed to cooperate and even form parties that included members of both language groups. Some of South Africa's leading statesmen, such as the famed General Jan Christiaan Smuts, had earlier fought the British. A spirit of good feeling and forgiveness seemed to reign.

But many Afrikaners opposed the alliance: First, it tied them to British foreign policy because South Africa was now a British dominion, and most Afrikaners didn't wish to fight for Britain. When South Africa entered World War I, many Afrikaners rebelled rather than help take over the neighboring German colony of South-West Africa. In 1939 when parliament voted to enter World War II, an Afrikaner fascist movement, the *Ossewa-Brandwag* (ox wagon torch guard), sprang up to oppose South African help for a traditional enemy against a traditional friend.

Key Term

Afrikaners White South Africans of mostly Dutch descent, who speak *Afrikaans.*

South Africa's Population (in Millions)

South Africa's white population increases at a modest 1.7 percent a year (high compared to Europe). The nonwhite population, however, increases at Third World rates, 2.5 percent for Africans, 2.2 percent for Coloureds (mixed descent), and 2.1 percent for Asians (chiefly Indians). Every year, whites become a smaller minority. Take these figures with caution; they may have undercounted the Africans.

This sign on a bus for blacks in Soweto shows what is on white minds: a rapidly growing black population. (Michael Roskin)

	1960	*1998*
Africans	12.0 (70%)	32.0 (78%)
Whites	3.1 (18%)	5.0 (11%)
Coloureds	1.5 (9%)	3.5 (8%)
Asians	.5 (3%)	1.0 (3%)

Second, and of equal importance, the Afrikaners were economic underdogs to the English, who nearly monopolized industry and commerce. The Afrikaners were largely farmers, and when farm prices collapsed worldwide between the two wars, many Afrikaners were reduced to poverty. Afrikaners streamed to the cities looking for work. Jobs for poor whites became their rallying cry.

Their path to salvation was "ethnic mobilization," organizing themselves to promote Afrikaners in business and politics. They built cultural associations, insurance companies, schools and universities, and, above all, the National party. The National party was founded in 1914 for Afrikaners, but its moderate leaders believed in cooperation with the English. When the party split in 1934, the militant Daniel F. Malan remade the Nationalists into the party of Afrikaner power. Malan stood not only for white supremacy but for making sure every Afrikaner had a job, a pseudo-socialist component that survived for decades.

Key Term

apartheid Literally, "apartness"; a system of strict racial segregation in South Africa from 1948 to early 1990s.

Slowly, the Nationalists built their strength. A well-organized party, the Nationalists indoctrinated Afrikaners with the idea that anyone not supporting the party had broken the laager and betrayed his brothers. By 1948, they had sufficiently mobilized Afrikaners, who were and still are a majority of the country's whites, to win the general election. Now at last the country was restored to them. No longer would the British push them around. They proceeded to build precisely the system they wished, **apartheid**, which ended only in the early 1990s.

The Key Institutions

Key Term

African National Congress South Africa's largest and oldest party, formerly a vehicle for black liberation.

System in Flux

Until recently, South African institutions were designed to keep blacks powerless. Beginning with the release of Nelson Mandela from prison in early 1990, however, breathtaking changes occurred that culminated in Mandela's election as president in 1994. In 1993 and 1994, an advisory committee representing all the population groups hammered out an interim constitution that went into effect with the first multiracial elections of 1994.

The new parliament completed a permanent constitution in 1996 that was basically the same as the 1994 constitution. One interesting point: A two-thirds majority of the new South African parliament is needed to modify the constitution, and the largest party, the **African National Congress (ANC)**, is just short of that. Accordingly, the ANC must debate and bargain for constitutional changes with other parties, and that's good, for it helps build consensus and a gradual approach to change.

From 1910 to 1984, South Africa had been structured along British lines—"the Westminster model"—with a prime minister chosen by an all-white parliament. When South Africa broke away from the British Commonwealth in 1961 (it returned in 1994), it instituted a figurehead president as honorific head of state of the new Republic of South Africa (RSA).

A Quasi-Presidential System

In 1990 South Africa switched from a parliamentary to a quasi-presidential system. We say "quasi" (almost) because South Africa's president is elected not by the population directly but by the National Assembly, now for a maximum of two five-year terms. The president may also be ousted by a parliamentary vote of no-confidence. This makes South Africa's "president" more like a prime minister. The president, however, still has a lot of power, and this gave reform-minded Presidents P. W. Botha and F. W. de Klerk the ability to institute reforms without being blocked at every turn by a conservative majority in the whites-only House of Assembly. As de Gaulle concluded in France, a presidential system is more effective in instituting changes. South Africa has three deputy presidents, black, white, and brown.

GEOGRAPHY

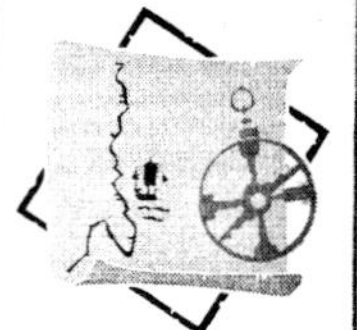

BOUND SOUTH AFRICA

South Africa is bounded on the north by Botswana and Zimbabwe;

on the east by Mozambique and Swaziland;

on the south by the Indian Ocean;

and on the west by the Atlantic Ocean and Namibia.

Lesotho, a residue of British colonialism, is totally surrounded by South Africa, a rare situation.

Democracy

Why Did Apartheid End?

With supreme self-confidence, the National party built its apartheid system. But starting in the mid-1970s the Afrikaner regime started to lose its nerve, which gave democracy a chance. Some of the key dates:

- 1975—Portugal, after years of fighting, pulls out of its colonies of Angola and Mozambique, where black Communists sympathetic to the ANC take power. A South African military incursion into Angola is mauled by Cubans and pulls out.
- 1976—Young Africans riot in Soweto and cannot be quickly controlled. Some sneak out to join ANC guerrilla forces.
- 1978—P. W. Botha is elected prime minister and soon promises a "new dispensation." He does little but heighten expectations.
- 1980—White-ruled Rhodesia turns into black-ruled Zimbabwe, and South Africa loses the last buffer zone on its north.
- 1985—Major international banks start doubting South Africa's creditworthiness and refuse new loans, jolting the South African business community.
- late 1980s—Pretoria government concludes black homelands are economically inviable and require too many subsidies.
- 1989—Soviet power collapses, and the Cold War ends. The ANC loses its Soviet support, and the Pretoria regime loses its U.S. support. Both sides realize they no longer have outside backers.
- 1990—F. W. de Klerk is elected, frees Nelson Mandela, rolls back the apartheid system, and negotiates an end to white rule.

This transition to democracy was not forced on the white regime, which suffered no military defeats or serious threats and could have stayed in power years longer. It was chiefly the product of sufficient Nationalist leaders coming to realize that the longer they delayed, the worse would be the revolution. They could clearly see the trend: no more protective belt of white-ruled colonies to their north, no more U.S. interest in stopping communism in Africa, and a black population that grew bigger and angrier every year. The Afrikaners split into liberal and conservative wings, and the liberals won. What we have witnessed is a "negotiated revolution" based on the power of human reason.

South Africa's capital moves twice a year. The parliament buildings are in Cape Town rather than in Pretoria, the administrative capital. When the president comes to Cape Town to officially open a parliamentary session, the capital comes with him. This means that every year hundreds of ministers, bureaucrats, journalists, and diplomats decamp to Cape Town and then trek back to Pretoria when parliament is over.

In response to demands from many groups (Zulus, some whites), South Africa shifted from a unitary to a federal system. The old colonies (the Cape, Natal, the Transvaal, and the Orange Free State) had been the country's four provinces. In 1994 the country was divided into nine provinces, and the "black homelands" were abolished, ending the fiction of independent black republics. Each province now has its own legislature concerned with local affairs such as police, education, health services, highways, and fish and game; it also elects a premier for the province. The provinces, which depend mostly on Pretoria for their revenues, became money pits of mismanagement and corruption that require repeated federal bailouts.

A Bicameral Parliament

In 1984 the all-white South African regime instituted a curious parliament consisting of three houses: a big one for whites and two smaller ones for Coloureds and Indians. White supremacy was effectively preserved. Blacks, three-quarters of the population, got no representation on the theory that they were represented in their tribal homelands.

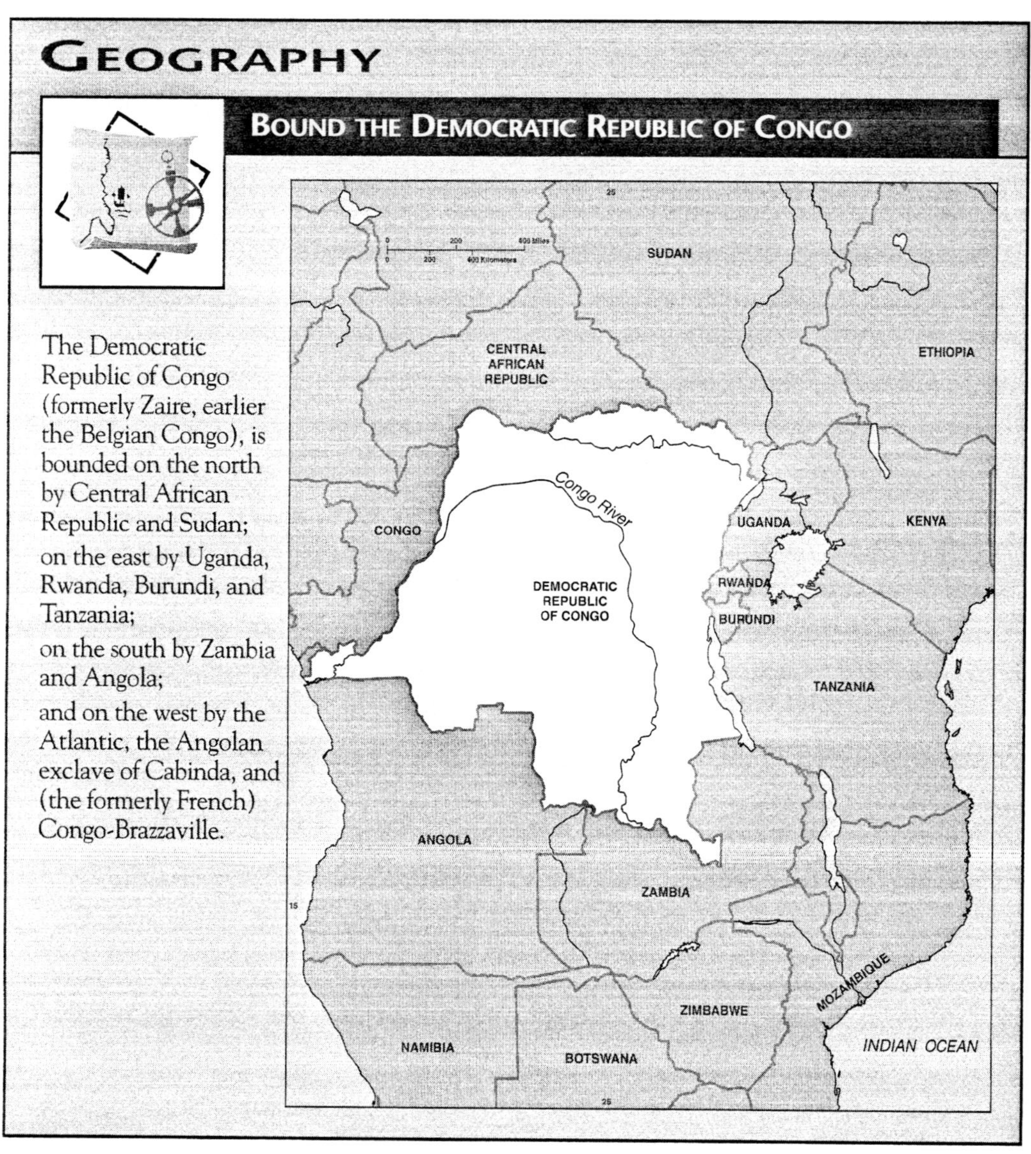

GEOGRAPHY

BOUND THE DEMOCRATIC REPUBLIC OF CONGO

The Democratic Republic of Congo (formerly Zaire, earlier the Belgian Congo), is bounded on the north by Central African Republic and Sudan;

on the east by Uganda, Rwanda, Burundi, and Tanzania;

on the south by Zambia and Angola;

and on the west by the Atlantic, the Angolan exclave of Cabinda, and (the formerly French) Congo-Brazzaville.

A President for All South Africans

For a man who spent twenty-seven years in prison for opposing apartheid, Nelson Mandela was extremely calm, showing no sign of hatred. He wanted to get on with building a prosperous and just South Africa where no one is penalized because of skin color, origin, or gender. He eschewed theories and focused on pragmatism and consensus-building.

Born into a chiefly clan of the Xhosa tribe in a village in the Eastern Cape in 1918, Mandela went to missionary boarding school and then to Fort Hare University, where he studied law (but got suspended for leading a student protest). His chiefly lineage showed in his calm self-confidence and ability to lead.

Mandela rejected an arranged marriage in his village in favor of the excitement of Johannesburg, where he opened his law practice and joined the African National Congress. Mandela learned to ignore ethnic differences and multiculturalism. "I no longer attach any value to any kind of ethnicity," he said.

With the Afrikaners building apartheid, Mandela and other young ANC members saw that mere petitions would get them nowhere. They organized a militant ANC Youth League and used it to take over the ANC leadership.

The 1960 Sharpeville massacre, where police gunned down sixty-nine peaceful protesters, persuaded the ANC leadership to turn to armed struggle. Mandela became founder and commander of a guerrilla group, *Umkhonto we Sizwe* (Spear of the Nation). The whites-only government banned the ANC and arrested ANC leaders. For plotting revolution, Mandela, then forty-four, was sentenced to life on Robben Island off Cape Town.

Prison did not break Mandela, and every year he grew more legendary, especially among young black South Africans. In 1982, Mandela was moved to comfortable quarters on the mainland and treated like a VIP. By 1986, the white regime knew it had to talk with Mandela, and secret meetings began.

Not long after F. W. de Klerk won election, in February 1990, he ordered Mandela released from prison. Here at last was a sign that major change was underway. In four laborious years of talks among all population groups, South Africa's first free and fair elections were held. Mandela, at age seventy-five, became president unopposed and by unanimous consent of the National Assembly. Even white conservatives knew there was no other possible choice. Mandela served only one term but set a standard of good sense and moderation.

In 1999 Mandela, then age eighty, was succeeded by his first deputy president, brainy Thabo Mbeki, then fifty-six, and like Mandela a Xhosa. Mbeki, a British-educated, multilingual economist, lived thirty years in exile. His father, a Communist, served decades in jail with Mandela. Mbeki's only son and a younger brother vanished, presumably killed by security forces. For a time, Mbeki was a socialist but more recently discovered markets. Mbeki did much of the daily work of governance while Mandela served as a calming and unifying symbolic figure.

What kind of a president will Mbeki make? A reserved person, he has none of Mandela's charisma but is a good backroom deal-maker. A no-nonsense administrator, he fired several incompetent officials. Mbeki demanded the opening of executive and managerial positions to blacks, a stronger version of U.S. affirmative action. Mbeki doesn't like rivals or criticism. Some see ruthlessness in Mbeki and the potential for a corrupt ANC dictatorship.

South Africa's President Thabo Mbeki (South African Embassy)

In general, parliaments with more than two chambers (Yugoslavia had a five-chambered legislature from 1963 to 1974) have been short-lived experiments. In the South African case, the tricameral parliament showed how desperate the Afrikaners' National party was getting.

Key Term

lingua franca In a multilingual situation, the one language used overall.

The current parliament is fairly conventional: two houses, one representing population, the other provinces. As in Britain, elections must come every five years but can sometimes come sooner. The lower house, the National Assembly, consists of four hundred members elected by proportional representation but on two levels, one national, the other provincial. Two hundred are chosen from nationwide party lists, the other two hundred from the nine provinces with seats proportional to population. The large but arid and sparsely inhabited Northern Cape gets only four seats; the small but industrial and thickly settled Rand (now called Gauteng province) gets forty-four seats. Thus South Africa's new lower house represents the country as a whole as well as regional perspectives.

The upper house, the Council of Provinces, consists of ninety members, ten from each province, elected by provincial legislatures. The Council has less power than the lower chamber, the norm for all upper houses except the U.S. Senate. In 1994, voters also cast ballots for their provincial legislatures. Members of parliament are entitled to speak in any of South Africa's eleven official languages, but, mercifully, most use English, the country's **lingua franca**.

No population groups are directly represented. Zulus do not automatically get a certain number of seats; they are represented by being able to vote for whom they wish. In KwaZulu/Natal province, Zulus divide their votes between the Zulu-based Inkatha Freedom party and the African National Congress, both of whom run Zulu candidates locally. Tswanas, who live mostly in the Northwest province, generally vote for the ANC, whose local candidates tend to be Tswanas. The effort is to keep any one population group from identifying too closely with just one party, for that is the path of tribalism and civil conflict that has bedeviled much of Africa.

In 1999 the African National Congress again took most of these seats, 266 out of 400, but still short of the two-thirds needed to change the constitution. The ANC must earn the cooperation of other parties for such changes. This tends to inhibit the dictatorial and corrupting tendencies that arise when one party gains complete power. Early drafts of South Africa's electoral law contemplated a German-style 5-percent threshold, but numerous small groups protested, so the threshold was abolished. Theoretically, a party that wins as little as 0.25 percent could get a seat in parliament.

The Cabinet

The new South African cabinet has about twenty-seven ministers. Under the interim constitution, each party that won 5 percent of the popular vote was entitled to a share of cabinet ministers roughly proportional to its vote. Thus, in the national-unity government of 1994–96, the ANC, with 63 percent of the vote, got twelve ministries; the Nats (the Afrikaners' National party), with 20 percent, got six; and Inkatha, with 10 percent, got three. This "consociational" (see box on page 99) provision was designed to make sure no major population group felt left out. This provision was dropped in the 1996 constitution.

The Parties

Theoretically, there are no longer "black" parties and "white" parties in South Africa. All citizens over eighteen years of age receive common ballots and may, in the secrecy of the voting booth, mark an X by whichever party they wish. Each party is identified on the ballot by name, symbol, and photo of its leader to help illiterates vote. Further, it is highly desirable in a democracy that some voters cross the color line and vote for parties not closely related to their own group. Most South African blacks, however, vote for black parties, and most nonblacks vote for traditionally white parties.

DEMOCRACY

HOW TO REFORM AN UNJUST SYSTEM

Since 1985 the South African government has repealed or liberalized almost all of the more than 350 apartheid laws. Some of these laws went back to 1913, but the Nationalists, starting in 1949, introduced far more specific, detailed legislation to keep blacks assigned to separate and inferior lands, housing, jobs, education, buses, beaches, rest rooms, and, ultimately, countries. The culmination of apartheid, in the Bantu Homelands Citizenship Act of 1970, was to make all Africans citizens of their tribal homelands and deprive them of South African citizenship. In all this, black South Africans had not one word of input, and protest was illegal.

The crux of apartheid was "influx control," keeping blacks from flocking to the cities. As we considered in Brazil, flight from the poor countryside to better opportunities in the cities is universal in the Third World. The white regime in South Africa tried to fight this by an elaborate system of passbooks that had to be carried by all blacks; these had to be officially "endorsed" to live in an urban area. Only long-term black residents and people with guaranteed jobs were entitled to remain; others could be "endorsed out" to some impoverished homeland with the thump of a police stamp. The single things blacks hated most were the passbooks, accompanied by the policeman's gruff demand, "Where's your pass, boy?"

P. W. Botha came to power in 1978 and spoke of a "new dispensation" that would give blacks a better deal. Just two years before, Soweto had erupted. "Apartheid is dead," proclaimed his government. A positive, almost joyous feeling began to emerge that major reforms would make South Africa a just and happy land. But the reforms came too little and too late. Fearful of backlash from white voters, Botha hesitated for years.

In 1985, the Immorality and Mixed Marriages Acts, prohibiting contact across the color line, were repealed. In 1986, the pass laws, influx controls, and citizenship laws were reformed to make it easier for blacks to live in cities and obtain citizenship in their own country. Some of the reforms were word games that left the system intact. Influx control became "orderly urbanization"; passbooks became "identity documents"; apartheid became "separate development." Blacks, now sensing they had the regime on the defensive, became angrier than ever. Halfway reforms can be worse than no reforms.

President de Klerk picked up in 1990 where Botha had chickened out. De Klerk's reforms went much further and faster than Botha's. For example, in 1990 and 1991 de Klerk had parliament repeal the segregationist Separate Amenities Act, Group Areas Act, Land Acts, and Population Registration Act, virtually ending the legal basis of apartheid.

Notice how the zig-zag of South Africa's reforms resemble those of Gorbachev in the Soviet Union. In both cases, leaders knew the system had to change but were terrified of losing power and unleashing chaos, so they alternated between promises and stalling. When an unjust, inefficient system is overripe for reform, hesitation can push the structure toward collapse.

A Constitutional Court for South Africa

A first for South Africa (and rare worldwide), the constitution set up a Constitutional Court whose eleven members are appointed for seven-year terms by the president after consultation with political parties, current members of the court, and a judicial review commission. Theoretically above the political fray, like the U.S. and German high courts, South Africa's Constitutional Court interprets the constitution and settles disputes between levels of government. Included in the new constitution are U.S.-style guarantees of freedom of speech and assembly, equality of race and gender, and rights to hold property, join a union and strike, and receive a fair trial. The death penalty, amply applied by the old regime, is effectively banned.

Although it proceeds on the basis of cases brought before it, South Africa has moved away from the Common Law, which is what gives enormous power to the U.S. Supreme Court. Instead of the power of precedent, which is the heart of the Common Law, South Africa uses old Dutch-Roman law, based more on codes and statutes and less on precedent. Accordingly, the powers of South Africa's Constitutional Court may be less sweeping than those of the U.S. Supreme Court.

In 1990 black political parties were legalized in South Africa. They had existed over the decades, either labeled as cultural associations or underground and in exile. The oldest and most important black party is the African National Congress, not to be confused with the Afrikaners' National party ("the Nats"). The ANC was founded in 1912 by Africans educated in missionary schools. The ANC still likes to call itself "the world's oldest liberation movement." For half a century the ANC practiced nonviolent protest; its leader during the 1950s, the great and gentle Chief Albert Luthuli, won the 1961 Nobel Peace Prize. He was, nonetheless, banished to a remote village. The ANC was banned in 1960 and, as the regime brutally implemented its apartheid structure, came to the conclusion that violence was necessary to communicate its message. In 1964, the ANC's leaders were convicted of plotting revolution and sentenced to life imprisonment.

But the ANC did not die. Operating in exile, it gave young blacks weapons training (with Soviet-bloc help) and had them infiltrate the Republic for sabotage and attacks on police stations. Its leader, Nelson Mandela, grew more legendary with every year he spent in prison. When he was released, along with many other black leaders in 1990, mass rejoicing broke out. "He is the symbol of our struggle," said a black high school student. "To me, he is like Jesus Christ." As expected, the ANC won the 1994 and 1999 national elections.

The ANC's leadership is heavily Xhosa, but it defines itself as a multiracial party, and some of its leaders were white (e.g., the late Joe Slovo, a Communist). Decades ago, the tiny South African Communist party (SACP) joined the ANC and came to be well represented in its leadership. In 1994 and 1999, the SACP did not run a separate slate but stayed under the wing of the ANC. Slovo (now deceased) became minister of housing and welfare. In 1992, five parliamentarians from the liberal white Democratic party moved to the ANC. Whites in the ANC, although few in number, do two things: They help educate ANC members away from revolution and toward liberalism, and they help calm white fears that the ANC is extremist and out for revenge against whites. A few percent of South Africa's whites vote for the ANC.

To the left of the ANC, the smaller Pan-Africanist Congress (PAC) originally was radical and violent. PAC broke away from the ANC in 1958 over the question of building a black society as opposed to a multiracial one. PAC's chilling slogan until 1994: "One settler, one bullet." It was PAC militants who slashed to death American Fulbright student Amy Biehl in 1993, not knowing or caring that she was proliberation. PAC did poorly in 1994 and 1999. Since then, PAC has moderated under the leadership of a Methodist bishop but still seeks return of lands taken by settlers generations ago. The even smaller Azanian People's Organization (AZAPO), wins almost no seats.

Meanwhile, to the right of the ANC, the Zulu-based Inkatha turned from a "cultural movement" founded in 1975 to the Inkatha Freedom party in 1990. The IFP, anti-Communist,

1999: A Proportional Representation System in Action

In 1999, South Africa stayed with its proportional representation system, which had been introduced in its first nonracial elections in 1994. Each South African voter casts two ballots, one for a national party list, the other for a provincial party list. Of the four hundred seats of the lower house—the National Assembly—two hundred are proportional to votes from the national list, and two hundred are proportional to votes from the provincial lists, which are also used to elect provincial legislators (who in turn choose senators).

As expected, the ANC again won nationwide to totally dominate parliament, but it fell one seat short of the two-thirds necessary to amend the constitution. Some breathed a sigh of relief. The big losers were the Nats, now renamed the New National party, who slumped from second place with eighty-two seats to twenty-eight. The new official opposition is the Democratic party, which tries to be multiracial but is heavily white. With only thirty-eight seats, it can do little to block the ANC.

South Africa's PR system, like all PR systems, fragmented the parliament into several parties, and that is just what South Africa needs. A single-member system exaggerates the rewards to the largest party, and in South Africa's case would have given parliament to the ANC with the ability to amend the constitution. From there it is but a few easy steps to rebellion by minority groups who feel they've been disenfranchised and then to dictatorship by the leading party. PR, especially with South Africa's extremely low minimum of 0.25 percent, makes sure all important groups win seats, and this can have a calming effect. The white separatists of the Freedom Front, who shrank from nine seats in 1994 to three in 1999, and the Zulu chauvinists of Inkatha, who dropped from forty-three seats to thirty-four, dislike the ANC majority, but they must ask themselves if they get a better deal by being in parliament or by leaving. (Correct answer: Stay in.) In this way, the fragmenting tendencies of PR paradoxically help South Africa hang together.

	Percent of Vote	*Lower House Seats*
ANC	65.7	266
Democrats	10.2	38
Inkatha	8.0	34
New Nationalists	7.5	28
United Democratic Movement	3.4	14
Freedom Front	0.8	3
others	17.0	

Home for Four Million People?

KwaZulu (meaning the "place of the Zulus") was supposed to be home to nearly half of the 8 million Zulus. Broken into twenty-nine fragments and overpopulated, there is no way it could have survived unless many of its people worked outside the homeland, and white industry set up facilities to take advantage of the plentiful, cheap labor. It is now part of KwaZulu/Natal province.

KwaZulu. (Michael Roskin)

pro-self-determination, and procapitalist, is well-organized and has a territorial base in KwaZulu, where IFP and ANC adherents murdered an estimated 12,000 of each other in virtual civil war. In voting, IFP controls the countryside of KwaZulu/Natal while the ANC controls its urban areas. Inkatha leader Mangosuthu Buthelezi, a Zulu chief, jealously guards his provincial power base. Inkatha attracts few non-Zulu Africans, and radical blacks despise Buthelezi as a sellout and Zulu fascist. Some Natal whites support and even belong to the IFP as protection against the danger of the ANC turning South Africa into a one-party state.

The National party dominated South Africa from 1948 to 1994. Originally a purely Afrikaner party, it crafted most of the institutions of apartheid. In the 1990s, F. W. de Klerk totally transformed the Nats by turning to a program of serious reform and welcoming all voters into National ranks. In short order, many English-speakers, Coloureds, and Indians concluded the Nats were their best ticket to survival. The Nats in 1994 became the leading nonblack party. Renaming itself the New National party, it shrunk greatly from 1994 to 1999.

Much of the white vote in 1999 went to the Democratic party, which was formed in 1989 from the old Progressive Federal party. A classic liberal party—free society, free economy—its votes are in English-speaking cities such as Johannesburg, Cape Town, and Durban. Much earlier than the Nats, the Democrats worked to dismantle apartheid and share power with blacks, Coloureds, and Indians. The Democrats now keep the ANC government on its toes by calling attention to corruption.

In protest at rolling back the apartheid system, in 1982 the right wing of the National party walked out to form a new Conservative party that ran well in the farming districts where the Nats used to hold sway. In the elections of 1994 and 1999 much of this electorate joined the Freedom Front, which sometimes talked about withdrawing to form a separate whites-only state. Further right, the small Afrikaner Resistance Movement (AWB), which used to wave Nazilike flags and vowed violence to preserve white power, did not run in 1994 or 1999 and has all but disappeared.

Is there no party that seriously brings together black and white? In 1997 the United Democratic Movement was formed to do that, but it enjoyed little success in the 1999 election. The symbolism was good: Its leaders were former ANC and Nat officials, Bantu Holomisa and Roelf Meyer, respectively. And its issues were good: Fight crime and unemployment, all within a framework of "national moral regeneration." But the UDM lacked a significant tribal base, the foundation of most of Africa's parties. The ANC, however, smelling competition, lashed out angrily at the UDM, several of whose officials were gunned down.

Farewell to the Homelands

One aim of apartheid, or separate development, was to make Africans citizens only of their homelands and not of South Africa. This policy permitted South Africa to treat blacks as temporary workers in the Republic without voting or residency rights. Some of the homelands were native reserves left after the Kaffir Wars of the last century. (Americans would call them Indian reservations.) Policy was gradually to turn the territorially fragmented black areas into homelands and then into "independent republics," one for each tribe.

These ten homelands, supposedly home to all of South Africa's black population, accounted for only 13 percent of RSA territory. Half of Africans did not live in the homelands but in the cities and on white farms. Many had never seen their homeland and didn't want to. The law let authorities forcibly send Africans to their homelands if they were not needed in an urban area or formed a "black spot" in a farming area designated for whites. Some 3.5 million were thus "resettled" on hopeless, overcrowded, marginal lands. Even with large RSA subsidies, the homelands stayed terribly poor.

Four homelands, under pliant, handpicked leadership, opted for nominal independence: Transkei in 1976, Bophuthatswana in 1977, Venda in 1979, and Ciskei in 1981. Aside from South Africa, no country granted them diplomatic recognition. Other homeland leaders, following the lead of KwaZulu chief minister Buthelezi, rejected independence as a sham designed to deprive Africans of their national birthrights. In 1994, in time for elections, all the homelands were legally merged back into the RSA; in reality, they had never left.

South African Political Culture

The Africans

There is some truth to the view that the Africans are still tribal in outlook. Voting is heavily on tribal lines: Xhosas go ANC, Zulus IFP. Chiefs are still strong; they settle disputes and can deliver much of the rural vote. When asked their nationality in a 1994 survey, 63 percent of South African blacks named their tribe; only 16 percent said South African. But for the many millions—about one-third of all Africans—who reside in urban areas to work in mines, factories, homes, or offices, this is changing. Here, under modern economic conditions, Africans from many tribes integrated with Africans from other tribes and see themselves as Africans suffering a common fate in addition to their continuing identity as Xhosas, Tswanas, or others. The Zulus—the largest group of Africans—see themselves as a superior, warrior race and tend to go their own way. Murderous fighting, helped along by the white police of the old regime, has broken out between Zulus and members of other tribes.

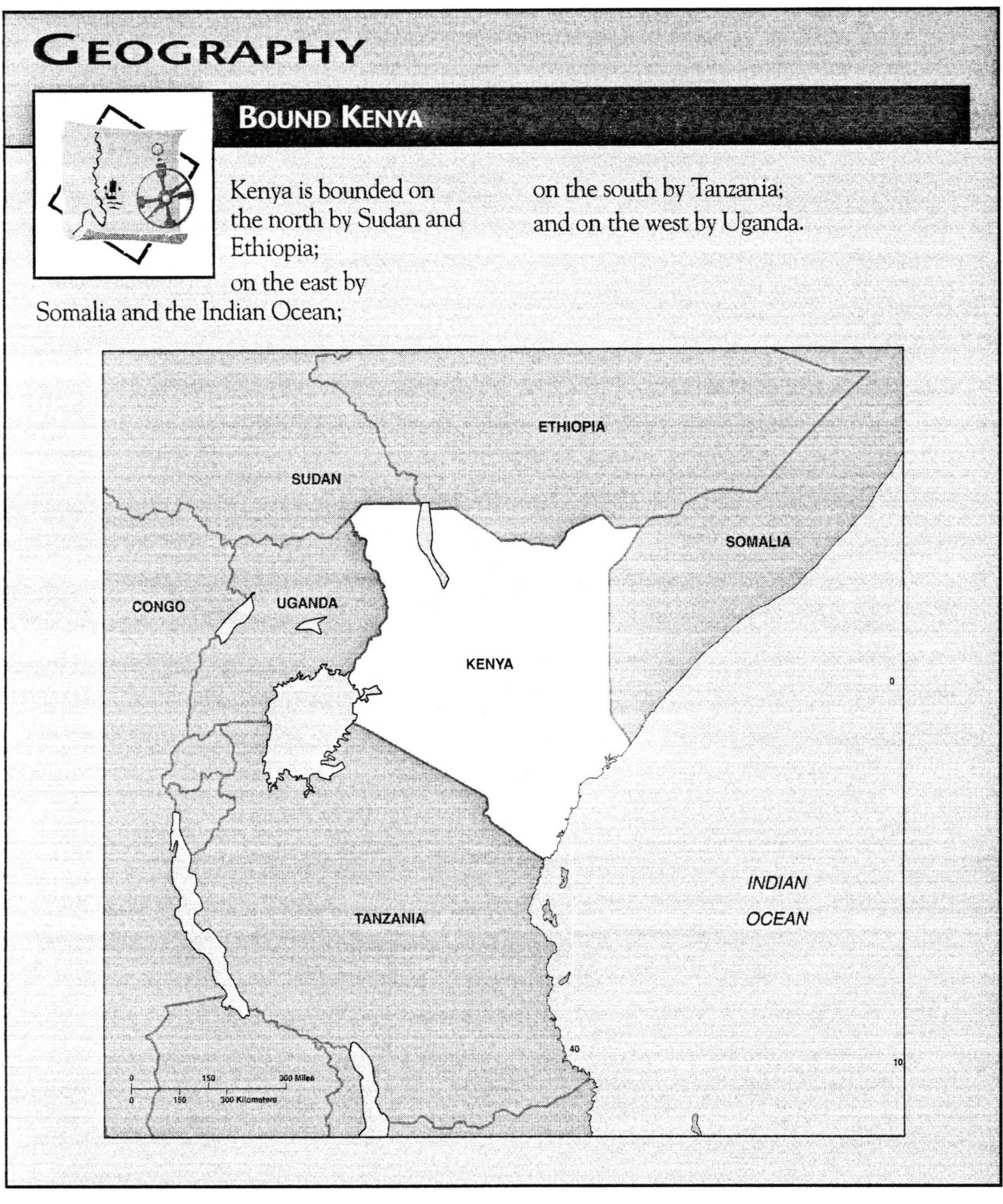

GEOGRAPHY

BOUND KENYA

Kenya is bounded on the north by Sudan and Ethiopia;
on the east by Somalia and the Indian Ocean;
on the south by Tanzania;
and on the west by Uganda.

It is white industry that helped break down tribalism and integrate Africans into a whole. During World War II, South African industry mushroomed, and the ensuing labor shortage led to a major black influx into the cities and factories. (Their squatter towns alarmed whites into voting for the Nats in 1948). Rapid black urbanization produced greater African education, sophistication, and integration. In the mines, for example, work teams composed of only one tribe were prone to fight teams of other tribes. When the work crews were integrated, the fighting stopped. The mining companies even invented a synthetic work language so men from different tribes could communicate. Many urban blacks (including Thabo Mbeki) are fluent in several African languages and generally get along with people from other tribes. Most also speak English, although they were long reluctant to learn Afrikaans, "the language of the oppressor."

Are all Africans revolutionaries? Far from it. African political opinion spans the range from mild, even conservative, to violent and radical. Older Africans especially tend to think in terms of specific problems: the long commute from the black township, decent housing, making ends meet, and so on. Some black South African religions teach submission to authority. A number of young black South Africans, especially in urban areas, are, however, radicalized. They want and expect speedy change. It was, in fact, high school students who led the massive 1976 Soweto riots—triggered by a government order to teach Afrikaans in school—that left some seven hundred dead. Thousands of young blacks then sneaked out of the country to join the ANC. Decades of school boycotts subsequently left a generation of black youths uneducated.

The Afrikaners

Over the nineteenth century, the Boers began to think of themselves as Afrikaners rather than Dutch, German, or French. Their language, Afrikaans, had evolved from the original Dutch. No longer citizens of the Netherlands, they felt Holland had turned its back on them. They had become Africa's white tribe, *die volk* (the people), as they called themselves.

And Afrikaner attitudes are indeed tribal. Until recently, they frowned on marriage to English-speakers. Like tribes throughout Africa, they did not like to share power with other tribes. A dour people, Afrikaners take pride in their steadfastness, religiosity, strength, and determination. Until recently, most were convinced they were right and were rarely willing to compromise or admit they might be wrong. They are not, however, arrogant or elitist; among themselves they are quite democratic. Toward foreigners they are friendly if somewhat reserved.

Political Culture

From Euphoria to Dysphoria

Great was the outpouring of joy and emotion at the election of South Africa's first African (or, more precisely, nonracial) government in 1994. Africans stood in line hours and even days to cast their first ballot, mostly for the ANC. All things seemed possible. Soon, many believed, Africans would enjoy improved living standards, education, and employment. They were euphoric.

But little improved; much of the change was superficial. Crime and corruption grew. Wealth seemed to stay mostly in white hands. Elected leaders tried to explain there were no funds to fix everything immediately. It would take time and patient building up of the economy. Many Africans felt let down and lapsed into dysphoria, the opposite of euphoria.

In actuality, South Africans were passing through the standard psychological stages that accompany most revolutions. The ouster of a bad or repressive regime almost always brings euphoria. Soon, however, reality settles in. Life, amid scarcities and economic disruption, often gets worse. Now comes dysphoria, the letdown after the euphoric high. We will see parallel attitudes in Iran.

Political Culture

A Lost Generation of African Youth

From the Soweto riots of 1976 until the ANC electoral victory of 1994, a large portion of urban African youth dropped out of school and sought no employment. Instead, they busied themselves with revolutionary protests. Many wore ANC or PAC insignia and T-shirts, gave clenched-fist salutes, and called each other "comrade." They enforced rent-boycott programs and gave suspected police spies (and there were many) a grisly death: a "necklace" of a burning car tire around their head. And many just hung out and did little.

What to do with them now? Observers see them as a lost generation that is increasingly bitter that life has passed them by. Many have neither education nor skills. Upon release from prison, Nelson Mandela urged African youths to return to school. Unless integrated into the new South Africa, these urban Africans, many of them no longer "youths," are a potential disruptive and destabilizing force that could wreck the new democracy.

Afrikaners treat blacks firmly but (they think) fairly; on a personal level they may esteem individual blacks but are convinced blacks need white supervision. Although they no longer say so publicly, they see blacks as behind whites in civilization, work habits, and level of organization. Because blacks are still largely tribal, Afrikaners supposed until recently that they must not be accorded political equality with whites. Blacks are still, the Afrikaner believed, happiest with their own people; that's why the homelands struck Afrikaners as a plausible solution.

Afrikaner views of English-speaking whites have softened since the end of apartheid. They used to consider English liberals hypocrites and cowards who saw blacks exactly the way Afrikaners did but lacked the guts to say so. One important factor eluded outside critics of South Africa: The Afrikaners never saw themselves as oppressors but rather as the aggrieved party, the hurt victims of historical injustice at the hands of the British. Afrikaners expected ethnic solidarity from their fellow Afrikaners. An Afrikaner who criticized apartheid broke the laager, the voortrekkers' ring of ox wagons, and thus betrayed die volk. Actually, Afrikaners were never monolithic in their views. Some, such as novelist André Brink, Reverend Beyers Naude, and Afrikaner members of the Democrats were among the regime's severest critics. With de Klerk's takeover of the National party and the country's presidency in 1989, the Nats and many Afrikaners shifted to a reformist position that in five years led to the Mandela presidency. Hardline Afrikaners joined more conservative parties.

The English-Speakers

English-speaking people constitute about 40 percent of South Africa's whites. In terms of ethnic origin, English-speakers can be Greek, Irish, Italian, Jewish, Portuguese, German, or even Dutch. As in Canada, most new immigrants elect to learn English. Sometimes referred to as "the English" for short, they are a diverse group who clustered around the original British colonials.

The English, after winning the Boer War, walked away from politics, preferring business instead. As a result, they lost most political power but they continue to dominate commerce and

Political Culture

Do Afrikaners Change?

Not long ago the conventional wisdom was that Afrikaner attitudes were set in concrete, that they had always been white supremacists and always would be. The common supposition that racial superiority was part of the Dutch Reformed faith of Afrikaners erred by looking at too narrow a time period. Afrikaner historian Hermann Giliomee examined the historical record and found that, over the centuries, Afrikaner thought on race changed quite a lot to accommodate new situations. Whatever seemed the way for Boers and later Afrikaners to survive soon turned into their religious and social teachings.

Accordingly, Giliomee suggested in the 1970s, Afrikaners were capable of adapting to the new situation of black political participation and were already beginning to change. Giliomee was right. Even at the time, one of the foundations of the Afrikaner community, the Dutch Reformed Church ("the National party at prayer," as it was called), was rethinking the church's position on race and finding racial inequality inherently unchristian. This shift in attitude enabled many Afrikaners to accept and even support the new political system. For example, in 1994 Wilhelm Verwoerd, grandson of Hendrik Verwoerd, chief architect of apartheid, campaigned for the ANC, and his wife, Melanie, was elected as an ANC member of parliament! These people do know how to survive.

industry. The rural Afrikaners discovered capitalism relatively recently; the urban English were capitalists from the start. This gave them a more liberal outlook: Let economics and market forces take care of social problems, rather than imposing numerous controls and regulations as the Nationalists have done. The English never formed an exclusively "English party" but were happy to join with Afrikaners in fusion parties, such as the old South Africa and United parties, which were usually Afrikaner-led.

The Afrikaners' scorn for English liberals was at least partly justified. Few protested as the Nationalists built the apartheid system, and many English-speaking business persons benefited from the cheap, controlled labor supply it produced. English liberals questioned the form but not the substance of apartheid. With the Nats' move to reform, many English switched to them. The English are more likely than the Afrikaners to voice their fears openly. Some wonder if South Africa is a safe place for their children; some ask visitors about jobs in other countries. Every year, several thousand quietly emigrate. (Favorite destination: Australia.) Some secretly retain British passports for a possible speedy escape.

Indians and Coloureds

Perhaps the saddest, most worried South Africans are neither the whites nor the blacks but the Indians and Coloureds. They are neither in the economically privileged position of whites nor in the numerical superiority with blacks. They are the middlemen, squeezed between forces they can't control. Held to an inferior status by whites, they are not particularly liked by blacks.

There is little feeling of solidarity between the Coloureds, most of whom live in the Cape, and the Indians, most of whom live in Natal. The Coloureds, who once had the vote in the Cape, became more politically restless and resentful. Sometimes counted as a subgroup among the Coloureds are the Cape's "Malays," descended largely from Indonesians the Dutch brought over who still practice Islam (some fiercely). The Indians—some Hindu, some Muslim—inched their way up from indentured sugar-cane workers to prosperous merchants. They are more inclined to leave national politics alone and settle for self-governance within the Indian community. The Indians brought with them a strong sense of identity and culture from their native country. The Coloureds have identity and culture problems: Most speak Afrikaans and wanted to be the little brown *baas* (Afrikaans for boss) but were rejected by the apartheid system.

What then happened is both amazing and logical. Many Coloureds and Indians went to the Nats, the party that had made them victims along with the black majority. As the 1994 election neared, Indians and Coloureds grew worried that black radicals would seize their property; some received threats. Quickly, they perceived their interests were with the party that might give them some protection, the Nats, who welcomed their votes. In 1999, many of them stayed with the New Nats. The two top leaders of the Western Cape, which includes Cape Town, are Coloured and New Nats.

Patterns of Interaction

Politics within the ANC

The African National Congress is a broad "catchall" party, including everything from black-power extremists, militant trade-unionists, moderate Africans, black entrepreneurs, conciliatory persons, and Communists of every hue. So far, the ANC has hung together amazingly well. With Nelson Mandela as its head, it had one of the most attractive and charismatic figures of all Africa.

The ANC, to a considerable extent, is required to be two-faced. To its black voters it must promise jobs, housing, and education rapidly, no matter what the cost to whites. Moderate as it tries to be, the demands of Africans are so urgent that if the ANC delays, it risks losing its black supporters either to more radical movements—such as Winnie Mandela (divorced second wife of Nelson) and her militant wing of the ANC or the PAC—or to apathy and nonvoting.

The other face of the ANC, required under the circumstances, is to calm and reassure whites, especially white capitalists, who are their only hope for making the economy grow rapidly. Many ANC leaders understand the weaknesses of socialism and strengths of capitalism. They meet with white capitalists and favor a vigorous private sector in South Africa. But if they go for the economic rationality of free markets and private enterprise, they make white capitalists a little richer and move the ANC away from the urgent needs of black masses. What's good economics is sometimes bad politics.

One classic way to retain the loyalty of party activists is to hire them: **patronage**. The Nats over the decades of *apartheid* created bureaucratic monstrosities and gave Afrikaners a lock on civil-service jobs. Now the ANC is keeping the bureaucracies but bumping out the Afrikaners in favor of ANC loyalists. The South African government estimates that it has 54,000 unneeded civil servants on the public payroll. This sort of cronyism hurts in three ways: It leads to corruption; it builds an undemocratic party-state; and it builds a large class of civil servants with a strong incentive to block change.

Key Term

patronage Using political office to hire supporters.

Key Concepts

Cross-Cutting Cleavages

One of the puzzles of highly pluralistic or multiethnic societies is why they hold together. Why don't they all break down into civil strife? One explanation, offered by the German sociologist Georg Simmel early in the twentieth century, is that successful pluralistic societies develop **cross-cutting cleavages**. They are divided, of course, but they are divided along several axes, not just one. When these divisions, or cleavages, cut across one another, they actually stabilize political life.

In Switzerland, for example, the cleavages of French-speaking or German-speaking, Catholic or Protestant, and working class or middle class give rise to eight possible combinations (for example, German-speaking, Protestant, middle class). But any one of these eight combinations will have at least one attribute in common with the other seven (for example, French-speaking, Protestant, working class). Therefore, the theory goes, Swiss always have some kindred feelings with other groups.

Where cleavages do not cross-cut but instead are **cumulative**, dangerous divisions grow. A horrible case is ex-Yugoslavia, where all Croats are Catholic and all Serbs are Eastern Orthodox. The one cross-cutting cleavage that might have helped hold the country together—working class versus middle class—had been outlawed by the Communists. The several nationalities of Yugoslavia had little in common.

Many of Africa's troubles stem from an absence of cross-cutting cleavages. Tribe counts for everything, and religious or social class differences do not cut across tribal lines. It will take both skill and luck for South Africa to build cleavages that cut across the color line. A few appear in voting, such as the Coloureds who went for the previously white parties and the white intellectuals who voted ANC.

The ANC and the Whites

The ANC leadership now has plenty of contact with the great economic engines of South Africa, such as the Anglo-American Corporation (which recently moved its headquarters to London). The dialogue goes both ways. The capitalists explain investment and growth to the former ANC radicals, and the ANC explains to the capitalists that if they wish to retain wealth and position in the new South Africa they will have to quickly deliver new jobs and mass economic improvement and promote blacks to the executive level. Otherwise, black discontent will give rise to radical politicians who preach nationalization of private industry and redistribution of wealth. This, of course, would lead to massive white flight and the impoverishment of South Africa. The ANC tries to persuade white capitalists to invest for rapid economic growth, putting jobs for blacks ahead of immediate profit. This will not be easy, as capitalists are by nature careful investors who aim precisely for profit.

Paradoxically, it is the richer, English-speaking white liberals of the Democratic party that are more likely to understand and accept this argument. As professionals and executives, they have little worry about their economic and social status. Much of the white working class, however, has to pay the price of rapid improvement for Africans. Working-class whites are being leveled downward. The "color bar" that kept blacks out of their jobs is over, their taxes

Key Terms

cross-cutting cleavages Multiple splits in society that make group loyalties overlap.

cumulative Reinforcing one another.

rise, and government jobs (including schoolteachers) now go to Africans. The white resentment these shifts engender comes automatically with a regime dedicated to making blacks equal.

Initially, the Nats tried to cooperate with the ANC in the 1994–96 coalition, but it was strained from the outset. Mandela and de Klerk angrily blamed each other for South Africa's difficulties. In mid-1996 de Klerk (who was also second deputy president) and his Nats pulled out of the government. White confidence in the government declined.

Key Term

consociation General agreement and power sharing among the leaders of all major groups.

The ANC versus Inkatha

The bloodiest interaction in South Africa was not black against white but black against black, namely the turf war between the ANC and the Inkatha Freedom party in its stronghold of KwaZulu/Natal. Inkatha staked out a claim to represent gradual, moderate change but engaged in a great deal of violence, mostly against ANC members. Outside of KwaZulu/Natal, the struggle was between Zulus and non-Zulu Africans. In the Rand townships, where Zulus live mostly in single-men's hostels, white authorities had long encouraged them to crush protest movements and break strikes. The authorities played to the Zulus' sense of warrior superiority over other tribes and pointed out that disturbances meant lost wages. Accordingly, in the

Key Concepts

Consociational Democracy

Another explanation of why pluralistic democracies hold together focuses less on the social level (see box on "Cross-Cutting Cleavages" on page 98) and more on the political level. University of California at San Diego political scientist Arend Lijphart finds certain deeply divided countries can work if the elites of the several groups share executive power. This is quite different from conventional "majoritarian" democracy, where the majority rules. If there is too big a gap between the majority and minorities, civil strife may result. The majority thinks it can get its way, and minorities feel no need to obey.

Clever political leaders may calm such situations by making sure all important groups have a share not only of seats in parliament but of executive power as well. In a consociational democracy, the elites of each major group have struck a bargain to share power and restrain their followers from violence. Every group gets something; no one group gets everything.

Lijphart's chief example of **consociation** is his native Netherlands; he thinks it suitable for South Africa, where a straight majoritarian system would invite minority rebellion. Notice the consociational element in the 1994–96 interim constitution: Parties got one ministry in the cabinet for every 5 percent of the vote they won. Thus the Nats (representing whites, Coloureds, and Indians) got four portfolios, and Inkatha (representing Zulus, the largest tribe) got two. The 1996 constitution abandoned this consociational concept for a majoritarian one. But de facto consociation continued with Inkatha leader Buthelezi serving as home affairs minister in Mandela's and Mbeki's cabinets along with two deputy ministers from Inkatha. The appointments helped hold down ANC-Inkatha violence, exactly what consociation is supposed to do.

Key Term

Inkatha Zulu nationalist political movement, mainly in KwaZulu/Natal.

townships the Zulus became extralegal enforcers of the status quo. Furthermore, the police, practicing the ancient tactic of divide and rule, quietly armed, funded, and sided with **Inkatha**.

In Natal, the Zulu home area, things are even worse. As noted, Buthelezi built up a power base in the Inkatha movement, which was never outlawed. Membership was to some degree coerced, and rival movements were not tolerated. Not all Africans in Natal are Zulus, however, and not all Zulus wish to join a Zulu nationalist movement. In the 1980s, many joined the ANC. Sensing ANC encroachment on its turf, Inkatha reacted violently, slaughtering any blacks suspected of ANC sympathy. ANC supporters defended themselves, leading to virtual civil war in Natal. Thousands were slain for political reasons, mostly in Natal, many by clubs and spears. At a somewhat lower level, the killing continues.

The real horror here is that violence got worse as the white regime eased its controls. The big increase in violence came after Nelson Mandela was released from prison and the ANC was unbanned in 1990. When all black politics were suppressed, there was relative calm, at least on the surface. With the legalization of black political parties in 1990, an immoderate struggle for turf and predominance broke out. Major reforms by themselves do not prevent bloodshed. Chief Buthelezi had no intention of giving up his power to Mandela (who is also of chiefly lineage, as a Xhosa, a tribe which has long fought the Zulus). Is this a political struggle or a tribal struggle? It is both, for in Africa, all politics is tribal.

A parallel with the ANC-Inkatha violence is that visited upon the small, new interracial party, the United Democratic Movement. The ANC views the UDM officials as scoundrels who were thrown out of the ANC and now serve reactionary white interests by dividing the black community. Although no one has taken responsibility, clearly the gunmen who assassinate UDM figures work for the ANC. The ANC, like most African parties, lashes out when it sees encroachments on its turf.

DEMOCRACY

SOUTH AFRICA'S BLOODSHED

Black-on-black violence causes some South African whites to smirk: "You see, we told you liberal foreigners that apartheid was the only workable system. Thought it was so easy, did you? Just abolish the old system and everything will be fine, eh? This bloodshed is your fault." This charge should make some critics of old South Africa think things over. To what extent did well-intentioned liberals naively underestimate the difficulty of achieving freedom and democracy?

The ultimate finding of fault has to carefully consider the steps—or nonsteps—the white government took in preparing black South Africans for political participation. Democracy needs an educated population. Why was black education so inferior? Democracy needs a substantial middle class. Why did apartheid all but prohibit black entrepreneurship? Democracy requires "cross-cutting cleavages," whereby members of different groups have some things in common. Why did apartheid prohibit contacts across the color line? Yes, there is black-on-black violence, but much of it could have been avoided if the white regime had, starting decades ago, begun preparing its black majority for full citizenship.

Geography

Bound Niger

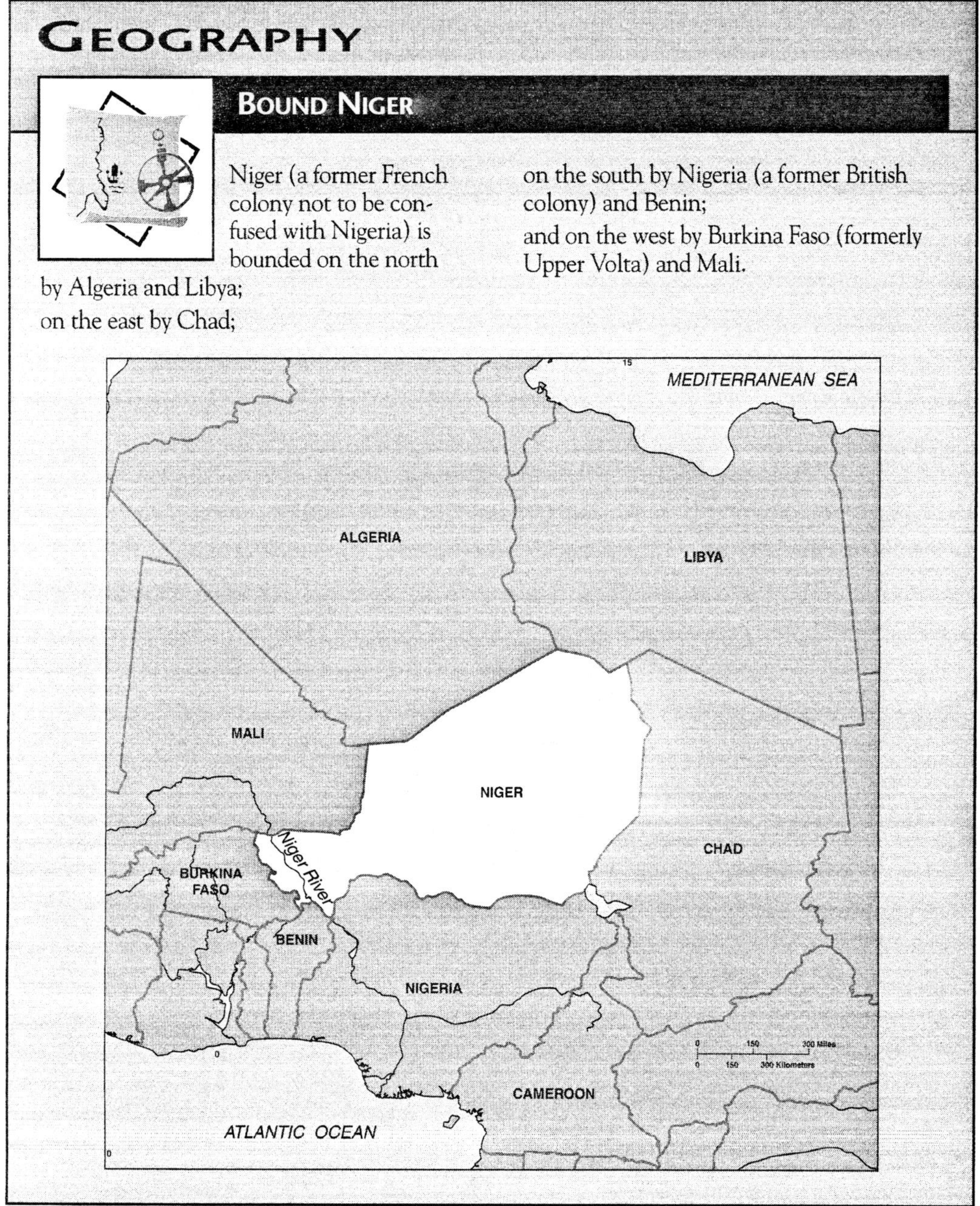

Niger (a former French colony not to be confused with Nigeria) is bounded on the north by Algeria and Libya;
on the east by Chad;
on the south by Nigeria (a former British colony) and Benin;
and on the west by Burkina Faso (formerly Upper Volta) and Mali.

A Dominant-Party System?

South Africa's party system looks like bad news for several reasons. First, the ANC with its big majority does not alternate in power. It seems likely to win elections well into the future, maybe forever. Even if all the other parties merged (an impossibility) they would still form a minority.

Second, in South Africa, we need not only a left-to-right axis but a black and nonblack one as well. In a rough schematic, the South African party system looks like this figure:

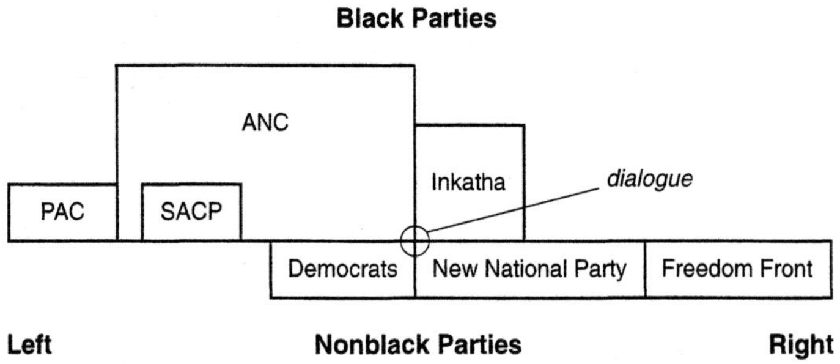

Black Parties

	ANC	Inkatha	
PAC	SACP		
	Democrats	New National Party	Freedom Front

dialogue

Left — **Nonblack Parties** — **Right**

The areas where black and nonblack parties touch—where the ANC and Inkatha and the Democrats and New Nats intersect—enables them to dialogue although not necessarily agree. This area is crucial to South Africa's political stability. If the two predominantly black parties and the two predominantly white parties can continue their dialogue, we may yet see a free and democratic South Africa. If not, we may see bloodshed, white flight, and a black dictatorship.

Third, no party links Africans and nonblacks in a serious way. Fourth, the black political spectrum is further left than the nonblack spectrum, making policy consensus difficult. Fifth, the ruling ANC faces **bilateral opposition**, with forces tugging it left and right. The ANC has Inkatha on its right and PAC on its left. The small Communist party, not the most-left element working within the ANC, is actually rather moderate in its views. Faced with either being pulled apart or into immobilism, African party leaders tend to opt for strengthening and centralizing their power, eventually becoming dictatorial. Thabo Mbeki could go this route, and South Africa could become a dominant-party system, where the ANC holds perpetual sway.

Key Term

bilateral opposition Centrist parties or governments being undermined from both sides.

New Player: COSATU

In 1985, black South African unionists merged thirty-four black labor unions into an umbrella organization called the Congress of South African Trade Unions, COSATU. With some 1.8 million members, COSATU works for higher wages, better conditions, and an end to all vestiges of South Africa's segregated system. Long a front for the ANC, COSATU runs on a joint ANC-SACP-COSATU alignment. COSATU leaders serve in ANC and cabinet positions.

COSATU's biggest component is the National Union of Mineworkers, which claims a membership of a quarter of a million and has greatly boosted miners' pay. The trouble is, with the world price of gold now low, many mines are losing money and laying off workers.

COSATU General Secretary Sam Shilowa likes to quote Lenin and dislikes privatization of state-owned enterprises. COSATU is in a Latin American situation of a pampered government-related union speaking for a comparatively well-off black working class, blocking change rather than demanding it. With COSATU keeping wages too high, there are no new jobs for the millions of black unemployed, and foreign investment looks elsewhere.

President Nelson Mandela attempted to preserve good relations with former President de Klerk, then a deputy president. (South African Consulate General)

Harvest of Hatred

For over four decades, there was no constructive dialogue between South Africa's blacks and whites. The regime simply governed by coercion and repression. Avenues of legal protest were systematically closed off; black protests were automatically illegal and brutally stopped by the police. It was a virtual prescription for violence: plenty of injustice but no way to protest it legally. Riot police used dogs, whips, tear gas, clubs, shotguns, and automatic rifles to disperse crowds of Africans. Secret police and army "hit squads" assassinated dozens of regime opponents.

South Africa made its own contribution to the art of coercion with the **ban**, an order from the justice minister prohibiting a suspected troublemaker from normal contacts. A typical banning order might specify that for five years the subject would not be allowed to work in a large group (such as in a factory); might not have more than one visitor at a time; could not be quoted by others or by the press; and must be home by 6 P.M. Banning also could include exile to remote villages or round-the-clock surveillance by the security police. Since no court was involved, no banning order could be appealed.

Key Term

ban Apartheid punishment of isolating alleged troublemakers.

South Africa jailed prodigious numbers each year; those jailed for simple passbook violations could be released after a short time. Political detainees, on the other hand, could be held indefinitely without charges, beaten to death in jail, or shipped off to Robben Island for life. Under apartheid, life imprisonment meant life.

When some of the worst police-state restrictions eased in 1990 and black movements became legal, there were still few constructive interactions between blacks and whites. Instead of building bridges between the two groups, the Nationalists had deliberately, over the decades, destroyed them. Few whites had contact with Africans outside of a master-servant or boss-employee relationship. For decades there had been no church, club, university, sports association, or political party to serve as a meeting ground. Today, most whites wish a constructive dialogue with blacks. This is difficult. After decades of abuse, many blacks are angry. Their leaders have difficulty keeping them in check. In its dreadful way, the apartheid program worked: Now black and white South Africans really are apart.

What South Africans Quarrel About

How to Manage a Revolution

As political philosopher Hannah Arendt observed, rage is the indispensable ingredient for revolution, but it is absolutely worthless in building anything after the revolution. Such is President Mbeki's difficult task: to carry out a virtual revolution without spilling blood, and retain his government's legitimacy among all population groups. Blacks and whites are still deeply split. Africans call for "transformation," meaning shifting power in essentially all institutions from whites to blacks; change so far has been minor. Whites think they've already ceded a lot.

The government is pulled in different directions: Many black militants want "socialism," although they have a poor understanding of what that means, whereas whites generally want capitalism. Without paying much attention to theory, the impoverished black masses demand a rapid improvement in their living standard, and they recall the ANC promising precisely that.

Income inequality in South Africa is high, about at the level of Brazil. Black wages are about a fifth of white wages. Over a third of black South Africans are unemployed and below the poverty line, and there is only the beginnings of welfare or a social safety net. The white minority owns almost all the land and wealth. Nearly all young whites (along with most Indians and Coloureds) graduate high school; only one-third of blacks do. Black infant mortality is high, white low.

Campaigning in 1994 was easy for Mandela and the ANC. They simply promised African crowds free medical care and education, jobs for all, inexpensive houses, pensions for the old, loans for African entrepreneurs, and land for African farmers. This was subsequently called the Reconstruction and Development Program (RDP). "Each and every person will be entitled to decent housing, like the whites have now," Mandela told crowds. He admitted it couldn't happen overnight; "It is going to take a year, two years, even as much as five years" to lift up Africans to decent levels. It is taking much longer, even though more than half a million new homes were built under Mandela and millions more got water, electricity, and phones.

During the 1999 election Mbeki tried to deflect attention away from 1994 promises by stressing redistribution of executive-level jobs in favor of Africans. This is already happening; indeed, there is a shortage of educated Africans for managerial positions. Business sought African executives, especially the relatives of ANC leaders. This helps only a handful of Africans and leads to corruption. For most Africans, the grinding inequality still makes them wonder why abundance has not been redistributed. If all the wealth and land of South Africa now in white hands could suddenly be redistributed, it would make blacks only a little better off, and that would be temporary, for the white-run economic machine would shut down and poverty would increase.

Capitalism for South Africa?

For many decades the ANC and its SACP junior partner denounced capitalism and vowed a socialist future for South Africa. For a black South African, the capitalism practiced by whites looked an awful lot like brutal exploitation. Actually, South Africa never had a free-market economy; much of it was controlled and state-owned. When they took power in 1948, the Nats thought the law of supply and demand was strange and dubious. They fixed farm prices, severely restricted black labor mobility and entrepreneurship, and developed huge state industries. By the time Mandela took over, an incredible 50 percent of South Africa's fixed assets were state-owned. South Africa's white capitalists were the big liberals and progressives. When, in the late

1980s, white business leaders visited the ANC in Zambia to seek assurances against nationalization, they could get none. It looked like the ANC was committed to socialism.

But the release of Mandela and legalization of the ANC in 1990 came at an interesting time. Communist governments had just collapsed in Eastern Europe, and the Soviet economy was revealed as a failure. Socialism (meaning here state ownership of industry) simply had no success

GEOGRAPHY

BOUND GUINEA

Guinea, a former French colony in West Africa (not to be confused with Guyana in South America), is bounded on the north by Guinea-Bissau, Senegal, and Mali; on the east by the Ivory Coast; on the south by Liberia and Sierra Leone; and on the west by the Atlantic Ocean.

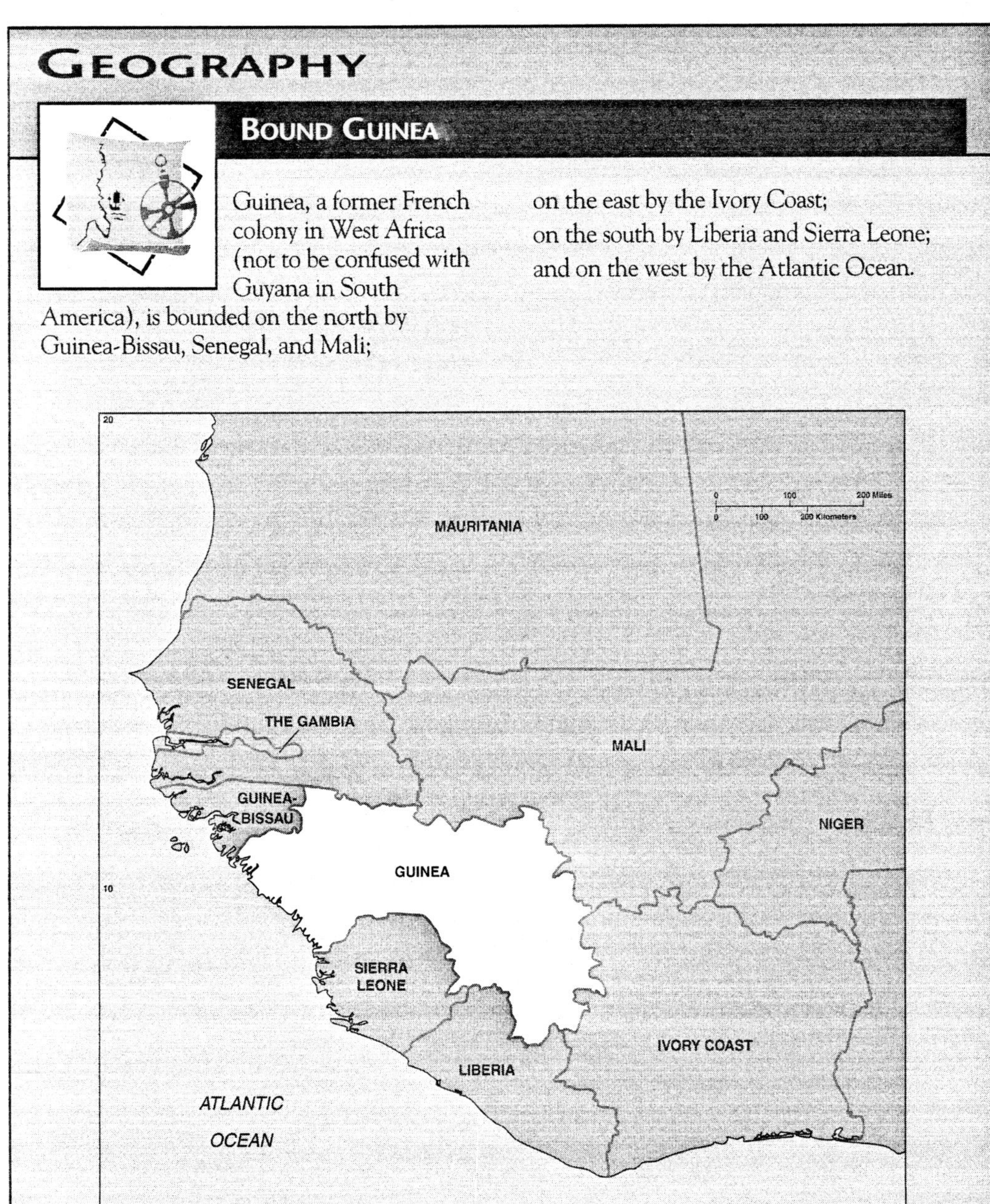

Democracy

How Much Truth Can South Africa Take?

For years South African police and army units secretly bombed, tortured, beat to death, assassinated, and provoked black-on-black violence. How did postapartheid South Africa handle these horrors? In 1996 a Truth and Reconciliation Commission began work aimed at healing the wounds. It sought to get all the facts and publish them. Those who came forward with facts—including naming who their bosses were—could apply for amnesty.

The truths that came out were shocking. Witnesses from the police and army said orders came from the very top—including the defense minister and Presidents Botha and de Klerk—to coldly "eliminate" antiapartheid "targets." Torture and beating to death was routine. The commission also found that the ANC had practiced "extrajudicial killing" in its struggle with the apartheid regime.

The commission concluded its work in 1998 with little reconciliation. South Africans on both sides faulted it. The doers, uncertain if they would get amnesty, were reluctant to testify. The Nats said it was just opening old wounds. And many black victims and their families wanted criminal prosecutions and civil lawsuits brought against former officials; amnesty was too good for these people. Argentina and Chile had earlier tried such commissions after brutal dictatorships with similar unsatisfying results.

stories. Gradually, the lesson began to penetrate the ANC. Maybe free markets and private initiative should be given a chance, especially if blacks could get in on the capitalist deal. By 1996, Mandela had come out in favor of privatizing South Africa's extensive state-owned sector. Some ANC members, however, still think state-owned industries are the way to go.

A government committed to socialism or statism could inflict economic catastrophe on South Africa. White people, with their skills and capital, are already quietly moving abroad. In 1998, for example, the giant Anglo-American Corporation moved its headquarters from Johannesburg to London. Black unemployment is around 40 percent (white: 4 percent). Highly productive white farms are folding before trained black farmers can run them. White farmers are murdered to drive them off the land. Starvation could break out. Responsible black leaders are increasingly aware of these dangers. As black politics came home from exile and out of the underground, it engaged in less ideological debate and in more pragmatic debate.

Tyrants-in-Waiting?

Actually, the Brazilianization of South Africa—crime and inflation—is not the worst thing that could happen. A greater possibility—and one feared by many South Africans—is to become like Zimbabwe, the formerly white-ruled Rhodesia to the north of South Africa. After a long and bitter guerrilla war plus an international embargo (which leaked through Mozambique and South Africa), in 1980 the white regime turned over power to Robert Mugabe, who revived the ancient name of Zimbabwe. Mugabe, intelligent and well-educated, keeps winning six-year terms as president, because his party is based on the country's largest tribe, the Shona.

After strife and looming violence between the Shona party and the parties of smaller tribes,

COMPARISON

THE BRAZILIANIZATION OF SOUTH AFRICA?

One point of resemblance between Brazil and South Africa is the shantytowns that spring up at an increasing rate around South Africa's cities. Much like Brazilians from the impoverished Northeast, poor Africans stream in from the countryside looking for work in the cities. With South Africa's terrible passbook, influx, and residential controls now scrapped, shantytowns grow.

Many critics of apartheid never understood that the original purpose of "influx control" was to prevent the black shantytowns that started with the rapid industrialization of World War II. The Nats bulldozed these shantytowns and offered "townships" instead: neat, planned rows of spartan cottages (without plumbing or electricity, so the "temporary workers" wouldn't get too comfortable) set up several miles from the main cities to be easily controlled by police and army. With the townships, the largest of which is Soweto (South West Townships) near Johannesburg, South Africa's white cities could have black labor by day but have them out of town by night.

"Why, without influx control," the Nats used to say with horror, "we'll become like Brazil." Now they have. Their influx controls just stored up people in the impoverished hinterlands; now they rush to the cities in a flood. They delayed the shantytowns so characteristic of the Third World; they did not prevent them. South Africa vies with Brazil for the dubious honor of having the world's biggest gap between rich and poor. With the rapid printing of excess currency to pay its bills and fulfill some of its promises, the South African rand, once worth more than a U.S. dollar, is now seven to the dollar. With massive patronage hiring, corruption multiplies.

South Africa's crime rate, always high, is skyrocketing. Some twenty thousand people are murdered annually. On average, a South African is eight times more likely to be murdered than an American. Especially common and horrifying: car-jacking. (A recent South African invention: mini-flame throwers built into the sides of cars.) The old, white-dominated police have been thoroughly discredited for brutal illegality and covertly aiding Inkatha against the ANC. Now hundreds of police officers a year are accused of everything from corruption and robbery to murder, just like in Brazil. With uncontrolled influx and plentiful firearms, unemployed young men form criminal gangs. Whites hunker behind razor wire and security systems; crime pushes many to emigrate. Township dwellers form vigilante groups, and the security business booms. Every year, South Africa becomes more like Brazil.

Mugabe strongarmed them into joining his Zimbabwe African National Union (ZANU). Zimbabwe, which started as a multiparty democracy, has thus been a one-party state since 1987 under what seems to be a president-for-life. White farms are seized (with government approval) by poor blacks, opposition is silenced, and the media is muzzled. The problem is not simply individuals with dictatorial leanings. The underlying problem is a country with many poor people, a no-grow economy, and tribe-based politics. Under such circumstances, democracy is likely to fail and power go to the strongest, the story of much of Africa.

Could South Africa go this way? The ANC doesn't like checks and balances or the sharing of power. Its wars with Inkatha and the UDM demonstrate that. If an ANC government ever controls two-thirds of parliament, it could change the constitution and build a dictatorship.

Geography

A Separate KwaZulu?

Inkatha chief Buthelezi was always at odds with the ANC and half-hearted about joining the national unity government of Mandela. What matters for Buthelezi is control of KwaZulu/Natal. His cooperation with the Mandela and Mbeki governments—in which he served as home affairs minister—was purchased at the price of ceding him control of this province. He hates ANC inroads into this area and goes to any lengths to stop them. Most of the bloodshed has been over this.

But if Buthelezi feels control slipping from him, he is likely to bolt from the Pretoria cabinet. In a bizarre move, Buthelezi once pulled his IFP deputies out of parliament but stayed in the cabinet. Conceivably, he could demand an independent KwaZulu/Natal. If it comes to that, what should South Africa do? Let the entire province go? Or fight a war to keep it? Neither is a very pretty choice. Either way there would be a great deal of bloodshed, as Zulus in other provinces come under pressure to flee homeward and as non-Inkatha people in KwaZulu/Natal are eradicated. South Africa has the potential of becoming a sort of Yugoslavia.

Thabo Mbeki is bright and well-educated, but the situation inclines South Africa toward dictatorship, if not under Mbeki then under someone else. As Archbishop Desmond Tutu, who fought apartheid for decades, put it, "Within the ANC are numerous tyrants-in-waiting."

Whatever the regime, South Africa's great challenge is how to shift from a revolutionary mode to a constructive postrevolutionary mode. One of the biggest challenges is education. Many of South Africa's black young people are enraged, uneducated, and unskilled. Education is also needed to stem the tide of AIDS that is engulfing Africa.

Black unemployment was earlier disguised by forcing many of them to live in the homelands. South Africa desperately needs rapid economic growth to create two million new jobs a year. In the mid-1990s, the economy did grow, but not the number of jobs. Hemmed in by labor restrictions, tough unions, high wages, and low productivity, businesses hired few new workers. Foreign investment is the key.

For this, South Africa must make up its mind on privatizing its gigantic state sector. State industries tend to generate little job growth, but in order not to arouse ANC and unionists still inclined to socialism, the government avoids the "p-word" but speaks of "restructuring of state assets." Although the ANC government needs foreign investment, it has gone slowly in selling off industries such as its airlines, railroads, buses, arms industries, energy industries (electricity, oil, gas), television stations, and the telephone company. Some economists say the sooner these are privatized the better; they will bring in new money, new technology, and new jobs.

As part of this, the regime must encourage white capitalists, who already know their futures are on the line, to invest and reinvest, especially in ways that employ more labor. For this, they must be firmly assured that they will keep their property. The unions and their friends in the ANC must understand that the high costs of South African labor and its low productivity relative to other economies doom it to slow growth and fewer jobs. The previously protected, high-cost South African economy now faces bruising international competition. Investment flows to where wages are low and productivity is high; South Africa has the opposite.

South Africa has intriguing economic possibilities. It has the only substantial industrial plant south of the Sahara. It has a treasure of minerals, some rare and important. It now has trade access to a potentially large market in all of Africa. It has a good infrastructure of highways, railroads, electric power, and communications. Will South Africa more resemble the economic tigers that rim Asia or the stagnant economies typical of much of the Third World?

Key Terms

African National Congress (p. 83)
Afrikaners (p. 81)
apartheid (p. 82)
ban (p. 103)
bilateral opposition (p. 102)
colonialism (p. 78)
consociation (p. 99)
cross-cutting cleavages (p. 98)
cumulative (p. 98)
Inkatha (p. 100)
lingua franca (p. 87)
patronage (p. 97)
Zulu (p. 80)

Further Reference

Abel, Richard L. *Politics by Other Means: Law in the Struggle Against Apartheid, 1980–1994*. New York: Routledge, 1995.

Adam, Heribert, Frederik van Zyl Slabbert, and Kogila Moodley. *Comrades in Business: Post-Liberation Politics in South Africa*. Concord, MA: International Books, 1998.

Alden, Christopher. *Apartheid's Last Stand: The Rise and Fall of the South African Security State*. New York: St. Martin's, 1996.

Holland, Heidi. *The Struggle: A History of the African National Congress*. New York: George Braziller, 1990.

Johnson, R. W., and Lawrence Schlemmer, eds. *Launching Democracy in South Africa: The First Open Election, April 1994*. New Haven, CT: Yale University Press, 1996.

Karis, Thomas G., and Gail M. Gerhart. *From Protest to Challenge: A Documentary History of African Politics in South Africa, 1882–1990. Vol. 5: Nadir and Resurgence, 1964–1979*. Bloomington, IN: Indiana University Press, 1997.

Lowenberg, Anton D., and William H. Kaempfer. *The Origins and Demise of South African Apartheid: A Public Choice Analysis*. Ann Arbor, MI: University of Michigan Press, 1998.

Marx, Anthony W. *Making Race and Nation: A Comparison of South Africa, the United States, and Brazil*. New York: Cambridge University Press, 1998.

May, Julian, ed. *Poverty and Inequality in South Africa: Meeting the Challenge*. New York: Zed Books, 1999.

O'Meara, Dan. *Forty Lost Years: The Apartheid State and the Politics of the National Party*. Athens, OH: Ohio University Press, 1996.

Sampson, Anthony. *Mandela: The Authorized Biography*. New York: Knopf, 1999.

Sparks, Allister. *Tomorrow Is Another Country*. New York: Hill & Wang, 1995.

Taylor, Stephen. *Shaka's Children: A History of the Zulu People*. New York: HarperCollins World, 1996.

Thompson, Leonard. *A History of South Africa*. New Haven, CT: Yale University Press, 1990.

Waldmeir, Patti. *Anatomy of a Miracle: The End of Apartheid and the Birth of the New South Africa*. New York: Norton, 1997.

CHAPTER 5

Iran

DEMOCRACY

Questions to Consider

1. What has geography contributed to Iran's development?
2. How does Iran differ from Arab countries?
3. What is a "modernizing tyrant"? Why do they fail?
4. What factors brought Iran's Islamic Revolution?
5. Explain Iran's dual executive. Who is more powerful?
6. Does secularization always come with modernization?
7. What kind of Iranians wish to liberalize their system?
8. Explain the power struggle in Iran.
9. How is attire a political debate in Iran?
10. How have America and Iran misunderstood each other?
11. Why is the Persian Gulf region strategic?

The Impact of the Past

Much of Iran is an arid plateau approximately 4,000 feet above sea level. Some areas are rainless desert; some get sufficient rain only for sparse sheep pastures. In this part of the world, irrigation made civilization possible, and whatever disrupted the waterworks had devastating consequences. Persia's location, though, made it an important trade route between East and West, one of the links between the Middle East and Asia. Persia thus became a crossroads of civilizations and one of the earliest of the great civilizations.

A crossroads country becomes a natural target for conquest. Indo-European-speaking invaders took over Persia about the fifteenth century B.C. and laid the basis for subsequent Persian culture. Their most famous kings: Cyrus and Darius in the sixth century B.C. The invasions never ceased, though: the Greeks under Alexander in the third and fourth centuries B.C., the Arab-Islamic conquest in the seventh century A.D., Turkish tribes in the eleventh century, Mongols in the thirteenth century, and many others. The repeated pattern was one of conquest, the founding of a new dynasty, and its falling apart as quarrelsome heirs broke it into petty kingdoms. This fragmentation set up the country for easy conquest again.

Iran, known for most of history as Persia (it was renamed only in 1925), resembles China in that it is heir to an ancient and magnificent civilization that, partly at the hands of outsiders, fell into "the sleep of nations." When it awoke, it was far behind the

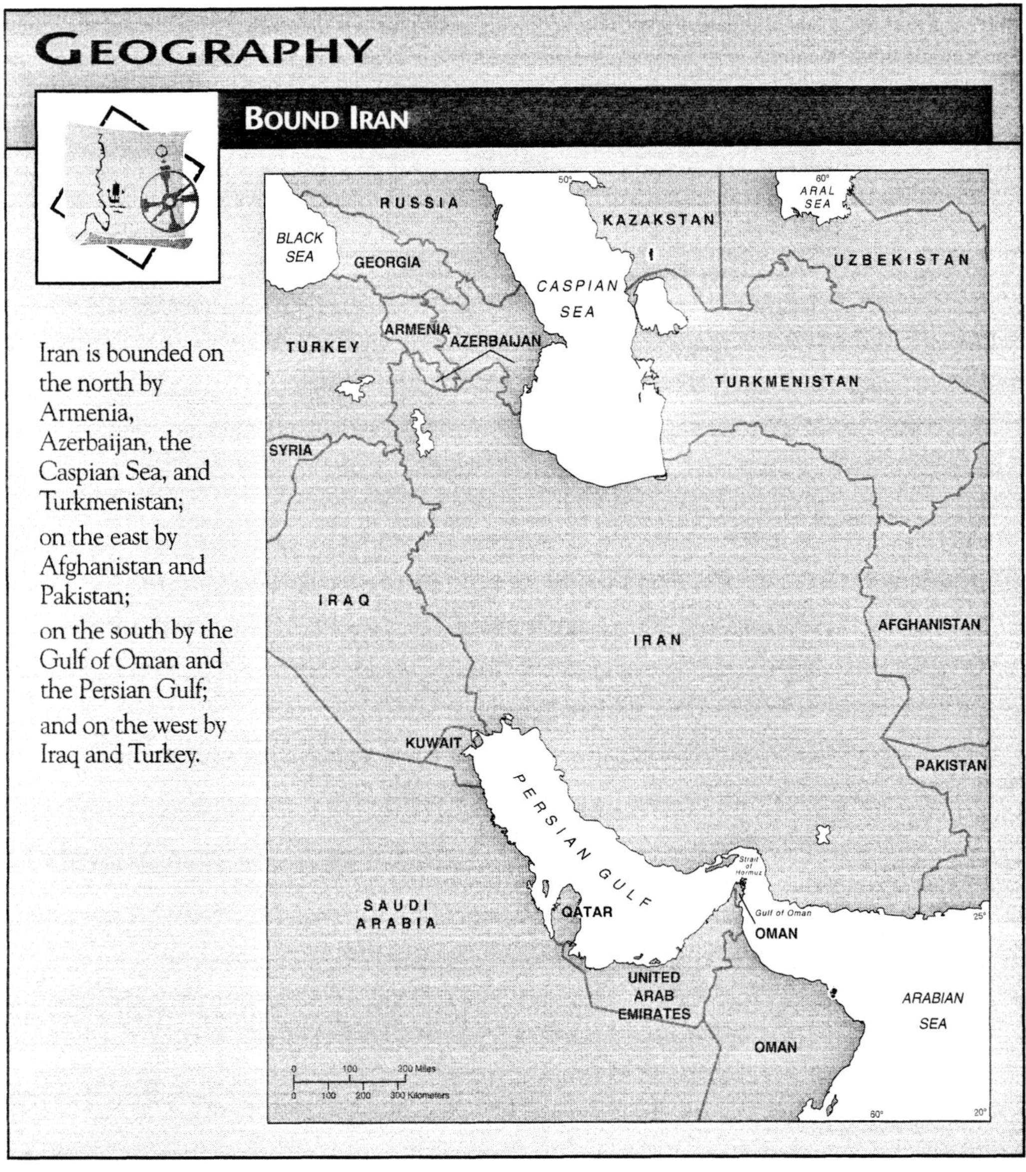

West, which, like China, Iran views as an adversary. If and how Iran will move into modernity is a major question.

Although it doesn't look or sound like it, Persian (*Farsi*) is a member of the broad Indo-European family of languages; the neighboring Arabic and Turkic tongues are not. Today, Farsi is the mother tongue of about half of Iranians. Another fifth speak Persian-related languages (such as Kurdish). A quarter speak a Turkic language, and some areas speak Arabic and other tongues. The non-Farsi speakers occupy the periphery of the Farsi-speaking heartland

and have at times been discontent with rule by Persians. In Iranian politics today, to be descended from one of the non-Persian minorities is held against politicians.

The Arab Conquest

Allah's prophet Mohammed died in Arabia in 632, but his religion spread like wildfire. **Islam** means "submission" (to God's will), and this was to be hastened by **jihad**. Islam arrived soon in Iran by the sword. The remnant of the Sassanid empire, already exhausted by centuries of warfare with Byzantium, was easily beaten by the Arabs at Qadisiya in 637 and within two centuries Persia was mostly **Muslim**. Adherents of the old religion, Zoroastrianism, fled to India where today they are a small, prosperous minority known as Parsis.

The Arab conquest was a major break with the past. In contrast to the sharp social stratification of Persian tradition, Islam taught that all Muslims were, at least in a spiritual sense, equal. The Arabic script was adopted, and many Arab words enriched the Persian language. Persian culture flowed the other way, too, as the Arabs copied Persian architecture and civil administration. For six centuries, Persia was swallowed up by the Arab empires, but in 1055 the Seljuk Turks invaded from Central Asia and conquered most of the Middle East. As usual, their rule soon fell apart into many small states, easy prey for Genghis Khan, the Mongol "World Conqueror" whose horde thundered in from the east in 1219. One of his descendants who ruled Persia embraced Islam at the end of that century. This is part of a pattern Iranians are proud of: "We may be conquered," they say, "but the conqueror ends up adopting our superior culture and becomes one of us."

A major step toward establishing a distinctly Iranian identity was the coming of the Safavid dynasty in 1501. The Safavids practiced a minority version of Islam called **Shia** (see box on page 126) and decreed it Persia's state religion. Most of their subjects switched from **Sunni** Islam and are *Shi'ites* to this day. Neighboring Sunni powers immediately attacked Safavid Persia, but this enabled the new regime to consolidate its control and develop an Islam with Persian characteristics.

Western Penetration

It's too simple to say Western cultural, economic, and colonial penetration brought down the great Persian empire. Safavid Persia was attacked from several directions, mostly by neighboring Muslim powers: the Ottoman Turks from the west, Uzbeks from the north, and Afghans from the northeast. It was in the hope of saving themselves from the Ottomans that Safavid rulers sought to make common cause with the early Portuguese, Dutch, and English sea traders in the late sixteenth and early seventeenth centuries. As previously in the region's history, the outsiders were able to penetrate because the local kingdoms had seriously weakened themselves in ruinous warfare, a pattern that continues in our day.

In 1722, Afghan invaders put an end to the Safavid dynasty, but no one was able to found a new dynasty or effectively govern the whole country. After much chaos, in 1795 the Kajar dynasty emerged victorious. Owing to Persian weakness, Britain and Russia became dominant in Persia, the Russians pushing in from the north, the British from India. Although never a colony, Persia, like China, slid into semicolonial status, with much of its political and

Key Terms

Islam The religion founded by Mohammed.

jihad Muslim holy war.

Muslim A follower of Islam; also adjective of *Islam*.

Shia Minority branch of Islam.

Sunni Mainstream branch of Islam.

economic life dependent on what foreigners wanted, something Persians strongly resented. A particularly vexatious example was an 1890 treaty turning over to British traders a monopoly on tobacco sales in Persia. Mass hatred of the British tobacco concession was led by Muslim clerics, and the treaty was repealed.

At this same time, liberal, Western ideals of government seeped into Persia, some brought, as in China, by Christian missionaries (who made very few Persian converts). The Constitutional Revolution of 1906–07 (in which an American supporter of the popular struggle was killed) brought Persia's first constitution and first elected parliament, the **Majlis**. The struggles over the tobacco concession and constitution were led by a combination of two forces: liberals who hated the monarchy and wanted Western-type institutions and Muslim clerics who also disliked the monarchy but wanted a stronger role for Islam. This was the same combination that brought down the **Shah** in 1979; now these two strands have turned against each other over the future of Iran.

Key Terms

Majlis Arabic for assembly; Iran's parliament.
shah Persian for king.
modernizing tyrant Dictator who pushes country ahead.

Notice how at almost exactly the same time—1905 in Russia, 1906 in Persia—corrupt and weak monarchies promised somewhat democratic constitutions in the face of popular uprisings. Both monarchies, dedicated to autocratic power and hating democracy, only pretended to deliver, a virtual prescription for increasing mass discontent. A new shah inherited the throne in 1907 and had his Russian-trained Cossack bodyguard unit shut down the Majlis. Mass protest forced the last Kajar shah to flee to Russia in 1909; he tried to return in 1911 but was forced back as Russian troops occupied Tehran. The 1907 Anglo-Russian treaty had already cut Persia in two, with a Russian sphere of influence in the north and a British one in the south. During World War I, Persia was nominally neutral, but with neighboring Turkey allied with Germany, Russia and Britain allied with each other, and German agents trying to tilt Persia their way, Persia turned into a zone of contention and chaos.

The First Pahlavi

As is often the case in such situations, military officers come to see themselves as the saviors of their nation. (See the box on page 67 on "praetorianism.") In 1921 an illiterate cavalry officer, Reza Khan, the commander of the Russian-trained Cossack brigade, seized power and in 1925 had himself crowned shah, the founder of the short-lived (1925–79) Pahlavi dynasty. The nationalistic Reza took the pre-Islamic surname Pahlavi and told the world to start calling the country by its true name, Iran, from the word *aryan*, indicating the country's Indo-European roots. (Nazi ideologists also loved the word aryan, which they claimed indicated genetic superiority. Indeed, the ancient Persian Zoroastrians preached racial purity.)

Like Ataturk, Reza Shah was determined to modernize his country (see box on page 114). His achievements were impressive. He molded an effective Iranian army and used it to suppress tribal revolts and unify Iran. He invented a modern, European-type civil service and a national bank. He replaced traditional and Islamic courts with civil courts operating under Western codes of justice. In 1935 he founded Iran's first Western-style university. Under state supervision and fueled by oil revenues, Iran's economy grew. Also like Ataturk, Reza Shah ordered his countrymen to adopt Western dress and women to stop wearing the veil. But Reza also kept the press and Majlis closely obedient. Troublemakers and dissidents often died in jail. Reza Shah was a classic **modernizing tyrant**.

World War II put Iran in the same situation as World War I had. It was just too strategic

Key Terms

secular Non-religious.
mosque Muslim house of worship.
Ottoman Turkish imperial dynasty, fourteenth to twentieth centuries.

to leave alone. As an oil source and important conduit for U.S. supplies to the desperate Soviet Union, it could not possibly stay neutral. As before, the Russians took over in the north and the British (later the Americans) in the south. Both agreed to clear out six months after the war ended. Reza Shah, who tilted toward Germany, in September 1941 was exiled by the British to South Africa, where he died in 1944. Before he left, he abdicated in favor of his son, Mohammed Reza Pahlavi.

The Americans and British cleared out of Iran in 1945; the Soviets did not, and some argue this incident marked the start of the Cold War. Stalin claimed that Azerbaijan, a Soviet "republic" in the Caucasus, was entitled by ethnic right to merge with the Azeris of northern Iran and refused to withdraw Soviet forces. Stalin set up puppet Communist Azeri and Kurdish governments there. In 1946 U.S. President Truman delivered some harsh words, Iran's prime minister promised Stalin an oil deal, and Stalin pulled out. (Then the Majlis canceled the oil deal.)

The Last Pahlavi

Oil has determined much of Iran's twentieth-century history. Oil has been the great prize for the British, Hitler, Stalin, and the United States. Who should own and profit from Iran's oil—foreigners, the Iranian government, or Iranians as a whole? Major oil deposits were first discovered in Iran in 1908 and developed under a British concession, the Anglo-Persian (later Anglo-Iranian) Oil Company. Persia got little from the oil deal, and Persians began to hate this rich foreign company in their midst, one that wrote its own rules. Reza Shah ended the lopsided concession in 1932 and forced the AIOC to pay higher royalties.

COMPARISON

ATATURK AND REZA SHAH

During the 1920s, two strong personalities in adjacent Middle Eastern lands attempted to modernize their countries from above: Kemal Ataturk in Turkey and Reza Shah in Iran. Both were nationalistic military officers and Muslims but **secular** in outlook and both wished to separate **mosque** and state.

In economics, both were *étatiste* (French for "statist"; see page 52) and made the government the number-one investor and owner of major industries. Both pushed education, the improved status of women, and Western clothing. As such, both aroused traditionalist opposition led by Muslim clerics. Both were authoritarian. Both thundered "You will be modern!" But religious forces opposed their reforms, and do to this day.

Their big difference: Ataturk ended the **Ottoman** monarchy and firmly supported a republican form of government in Turkey. He pushed his reforms piecemeal through parliament, which often opposed him. Reza Shah rejected republicanism and parliaments as too messy; he insisted on an authoritarian monarchy as the best way to modernize an unruly country, as did his son. Although Turkey has had plenty of troubles since Ataturk, it has not been ripped apart by revolution. Ataturk built some political institutions; the Pahlavi shahs built none.

The United States and Iran: The Big U.S. Mistake

We were much too close to the Shah. We supported him unstintingly and unquestioningly. The Shah was anti-Communist and was rapidly modernizing Iran; he was our kind of guy. Iranian unrest and opposition went unnoticed by the U.S. Embassy. Elaborate Iranian public relations portrayed Iran in a rosy light in the U.S. media. Under Nixon, U.S. arms makers sold Iran "anything that goes bang." We failed to see that Iran and the Shah were two different things, and that our unqualified backing of the Shah was alienating many Iranians. We didn't notice the Shah governed by means of a dreaded secret police, the SAVAK. We failed to call a tyrant a tyrant. Only when the Islamic Revolution broke out did we learn what Iranians really thought about the Shah. We were so obsessed by communism penetrating from the north that we could not imagine anything like a bitter, hostile Islamic revolution coming from within Iran.

The AIOC still rankled Iranians, who rallied to the radical nationalist Prime Minister Mohammed Mossadegh in the early 1950s. With support from Iranian nationalists, liberals, and leftists, Mossadegh nationalized AIOC holdings. Amidst growing turmoil and what some feared was a tilt to the Soviet Union, Shah Mohammed Reza Pahlavi fled the country in 1953. The British urged Washington to do something, and President Eisenhower, as part of U.S. **containment**, had the CIA destabilize the Tehran government. It was easy: The CIA's Kermit Roosevelt arrived with $1 million in a suitcase and rented a suitable mob. Mossadegh was out, the Shah was restored, and the United States won a battle in the Cold War. We thought we were very clever.

Like his father, the Shah was a modernizing tyrant, promoting what he called his "White Revolution" from above (as opposed to a red revolution from below). Under the Shah, Iran had excellent relations with the United States. President Nixon touted the Shah as our pillar of stability in the Persian Gulf. We were his source of money, technology, and military hardware. Some one hundred thousand Iranian students came to U.S. universities, and forty-five thousand American businessmen and consultants surged into Tehran for lucrative contracts. This point shows that person-to-person contacts do not always lead to good relations between countries.

What finally did in the Shah? Too much money went to his head. With the 1973 Arab-Israeli war, oil producers worldwide got the chance to do what they had long wished: boost the price of oil and take over oil extraction from foreign companies. The Shah, one of the prime movers of the Organization of Petroleum Exporting Countries (**OPEC**), gleefully did both. What Mossadegh tried, the Shah accomplished. Oil prices on the world market quadrupled. With more cash than ever, the Shah went mad with vast, expensive schemes. The oil revenues were administered by the state for the greater glory of Iran and its army, not for the Iranian people. This resentment was one of the prominent factors in the Islamic Revolution. Oil led to turmoil.

The sudden influx of new wealth caused great disruption. The Shah promoted education, but the more education people got, the more they could see the Shah was a tyrant. Some people got rich fast while most stayed poor. Corruption grew worse than ever. Millions flocked from the countryside to the cities where, rootless and confused, they turned to the only institution they understood, the mosque, for guidance. In their rush to modernize, the Pahlavis alienated the

Key Terms

containment U.S. policy throughout Cold War of blocking expansion of communism.

OPEC Cartel of oil-rich countries designed to boost petroleum prices.

GEOGRAPHY

CRUISING THE PERSIAN GULF

The countries bordering the Persian Gulf contain some two-thirds of the world's proven petroleum reserves. Some of you may do military service in the Gulf, so start learning the geography now. Imagine you are on an aircraft carrier making a clockwise circle around the Gulf. Upon entering the Strait of Hormuz, which countries do you pass to port? Oman, United Arab Emirates, Qatar, Saudi Arabia, Bahrain (an island), Kuwait, Iraq, and Iran.

Muslim clergy. Not only did the Shah undermine the traditional cultural values of Islam, he seized land owned by religious foundations and distributed it to peasants as part of his White Revolution. The **mullahs** also hated the influx of American culture, with its easy toleration of alcohol and sex. Many Iranians saw the Shah's huge military expenditures—at the end, an incredible 17 percent of Iran's GDP—as a waste of money. As de Tocqueville observed, economic growth paves the way to revolution.

Key Terms

mullah Muslim cleric.
ayatollah "Sign of God"; top Shia religious leader.

One of Iran's religious authorities, **Ayatollah** Khomeini, criticized the Shah and incurred his wrath. He had Khomeini exiled to Iraq in 1964 and then forced him to leave Iraq in 1978. Khomeini took up residence in a Paris suburb, from which his recorded messages were telephoned to cassette recorders in Iran to be duplicated and distributed through mosques nationwide. Cheap cassettes bypassed the Shah's control of Iran's media and helped bring him down.

In the late 1970s, matters came to a head. The Shah's overambitious plans had made Iran a debtor nation. Secular intellectuals and Islamic clerics alike were discontent. And U.S. President Jimmy Carter made human rights a foreign-policy goal. As part of this, the Shah's dictatorship was subject to U.S. criticism. Shaken, the Shah began to relax his grip, and that is when all hell broke loose. As de Tocqueville observed, the worst time in the life of a bad government is when it begins to mend its ways. Compounding his error, Carter showed his support for the Shah by exchanging visits, proof to Iranians that we were supporting a hated tyrant. In 1977, Carter and the Shah had to retreat into the White House from the lawn to escape the tear gas that drifted over from the anti-Shah protest (mostly by Iranian students) in Lafayette Park.

By late 1978, the Shah, facing huge demonstrations and (unknown to Washington) dying of cancer, was finished. Shooting into the crowds of protesters just made them angrier. The ancient Persian game of chess ends with a checkmate, a corruption of the Farsi *shah mat* ("the king is trapped"). On January 16, 1979, the last Pahlavi left Iran. *Shah mat.*

The Key Institutions

A Theocracy

Two and a half millennia of monarchy ended in Iran with a 1979 referendum, carefully supervised by the Khomeini forces, that introduced the Islamic Republic of Iran and a new constitution. As in most countries, the offices of head of state and head of government are split. But instead of a figurehead monarch (as in Britain) or weak president (as in Germany), Iran now has two heads of state, one its leading religious figure, the other a more standard president. Ultimately, the religious chief is the real power. That makes Iran a **theocracy**.

Theocracy is rare and tends not to last. Even in ancient times, priests, shamans, and holy men filled supporting rather than executive roles. Russia's tsar, head of both church and state, emphasized the state side; he wore military, not priestly, garb. Iran (plus Afghanistan and Sudan) tried a theocratic system. The principle of political power in the system devised by Khomeini is the **velayat-e faqih**. This leading Islamic jurist, the *faqih*, serves for life. *Jurist* means a legal scholar steeped in Islamic, specifically Shia, religious law. (The closest Western equivalent is **canon law**. In medieval Europe, canon lawyers were leading intellectuals and politicians.) Allegedly the *faqih*, also known as the "Spiritual Guide," can use the Koran and related Islamic commentaries to decide all issues, even those not connected to religion. (An **Islamist**, of course, would say everything is connected to religion.)

Key Terms

theocracy Rule by priests.

velayat-e faqih "Guardianship of the religious jurist"; theocratic system devised by Khomeini.

canon law The internal laws of the Roman Catholic Church.

Islamist Someone who uses Islam in a political way.

Iran's 1997 Presidential Election

In a surprising landslide, a relative moderate came from obscurity to win Iran's presidential election in May 1997. Mohammed Khatami, age fifty-four, took nearly 70 percent of the vote to less than 25 percent for conservative Ali Akbar Nateq-Noori, the Speaker of the Majlis, who had been favored. Khatami's election, which had an amazing 90 percent turnout, showed that a big majority of Iranians were fed up with economic decline and clerical supervision of private life. Educated, urban Iranians, women, and young people ignored the urgings of the top mullahs to vote for Nateq-Noori and went strongly for Khatami. The Council of Guardians (see box on page 119) let only four candidates run out of more than two hundred hopefuls.

Khatami ran on a platform of greater personal freedoms, legalization of political parties, more jobs, and less male dominance, issues aimed at women and young people. Nateq-Noori ran on improving the economy and following strict Islamic law. All Iranians (male and female) age sixteen or older were eligible to vote. Both candidates, it should be noted, were Islamic clerics and in no sense opposed the Islamic Revolution. They just held different versions of that revolution, Nateq-Noori a harsh version and Khatami a tolerant one aiming at "civil society."

Indeed, Khatami is the son of a famous Islamic teacher and wears a black turban, permitted only to clerics who can prove they are direct descendants of the Prophet Mohammed. Khatami criticized the Shah's regime in the 1970s and in 1978 headed the Islamic Center in Hamburg, Germany. He speaks some German and English. With the triumph of the revolution in 1979, Khatami returned to Iran and served as Minister of Islamic Guidance from 1982 to 1992 but was forced out for allowing too much media and artistic freedom. Largely out of sight as head of Iran's national library, he advocated rights for workers, women, and young people. His views became known only during the last few weeks before the election but spread rapidly.

Within the limits set by the Council of Guardians, it was a fair and democratic election. Although party labels were not allowed, people knew where the candidates stood and voted accordingly. Not a liberal in our sense of the word, Khatami probably qualifies as a moderate, a cautious reformer.

Khomeini, the first and founding *faqih*, died in 1989. He was nearly all-powerful. His successor—now referred to in the constitution as the "Leader"—is chosen by an elected Assembly of Experts. These eighty-six Muslim clerics, elected every eight years, choose from among the purest and most learned Islamic jurists. The man they elect (Islam permits no female religious leaders) will likely already be an ayatollah, one of a handful of the wisest Shi'ite jurists, or he will be named an ayatollah.

Iran's current *faqih* is Ayatollah Ali Hoseini-Khamenei. He names the heads of virtually all major state and religious organizations and may declare war. He therefore controls, at least indirectly, the judiciary, armed forces, security police, intelligence agencies, radio, and television. He is more powerful than Iran's president. Khamenei has neither the spiritual depth nor forceful personality of Khomeini, but he and his followers can still block any liberalizing moves.

Iran's Executive

Iran's working chief is a U.S.-type executive president, elected by popular vote for up to two four-year terms. The constitution specifies that this president is "the holder of the highest official power next to the office of the *faqih*," indicating he is inferior in power to the Leader. Khatami continually had to defer to the conservative policies of Khamenei. There was no open disagreement between the two, but it meant that Iran got stuck between Khomeini's original revolutionary design and attempts to reform and stabilize the country.

Both Khatami and his predecessor are Muslim clerics. Ali Akbar Hashemi-Rafsanjani, who earlier was the powerful Speaker of the parliament, served two terms as president (from 1989 to 1997), and was himself a *hojatolislam*, an Islamic jurist ranked just below *ayatollah*. An extremely shrewd and pragmatic individual, however, Rafsanjani served to quietly calm and secularize the Islamic revolution, never, of course, going directly against the top clerics. The cabinet conducts the real day-to-day work of governance. Practically all new laws and the budget are devised by the cabinet and submitted to parliament for approval, modification, or rejection.

Iran's Legislature

Iran has a unicameral (one-house) legislature, the Islamic Consultative Assembly (Majlis), consisting of 290 deputies elected for four-year terms. Iran uses single-member districts, like Britain and the U.S. Congress. Iran is divided into 265 constituencies, and each Iranian seventeen (raised from sixteen in 2000) and older has one vote for a representative. An additional five seats are reserved for non-Muslim deputies (one each for Assyrian Christians, Jews, and Zoroastrians; two for Armenian Christians; none for Baha'is).

Majlis elections are semifree. The actual balloting is free and fair, but all candidates must be approved by the Council of Guardians, which disqualifies candidates they suspect might not support the Islamic Revolution. Out-and-out liberals are thus discouraged from even putting forward candidates. The 2000 elections, however, produced a clear reformist majority.

The Speaker of parliament has emerged as a major position, first filled by Rafsanjani and now by the leader of the conservative Islamist forces that predominate in the Majlis, Ali Akbar Nateq-Noori, who lost the 1997 presidential election to the moderate Khatami. Nateq-Noori blocked President Rafsanjani's and Khatami's proposals for moderate liberalization.

Iran's Strange "Council of Guardians"

Iran's Council of Guardians is strange among political institutions, combining features of an upper house, a supreme court, an electoral commission, and a religious inquisition. It has twelve members; they serve six years each with half of them changed every three years. The *faqih* chooses six Islamic clerics; Iran's supreme court (the High Council of Justice) names another six, all Islamic lawyers, who must be approved by the Majlis.

The Council examines each Majlis bill to make sure it does not violate Islamic principles. If a majority decides it does, the bill is returned to the Majlis to be corrected. Without Council approval, a bill is in effect vetoed. Several important pieces of legislation have been blocked in this way. To settle conflicts between the Majlis and the Council, an "Expediency Council" appointed by the Leader has become like another legislature.

Perhaps more important, the Council of Guardians examines all candidates for the Majlis and has the power to disqualify them without explanation. Their criteria are unclear for rejecting candidates; anyone deemed not "politically correct" in their support of Islamic rule may be rejected. In the 1996 and 2000 Majlis elections, the Council scratched a large fraction of the candidates. While not as strict as Communist control over Soviet elections, the Council makes sure there is no serious opposition in the Majlis.

Emerging Parties?

Parties are legal under Iran's constitution, but the government does not allow them; only individual candidates run. This also makes Iranian elections less than totally free, for without party image the electorate cannot clearly discern who stands for what. It was not even possible, in the 1996 and 2000 parliamentary elections, to count which "tendencies" exactly won how many seats. In practice, however, candidates are linked through alignments, "lists," and "fronts." Over time, these may turn into legal parties. Observers see four main political groupings, all of which contain many factions and individual viewpoints.

Radicals, the most extreme supporters of the Islamic Revolution, want to adhere to what they perceive as Khomeini's design for an Islamic republic. Socialist in economics, they also favor state control over the economy. They wish to keep out all Western influences and continue Islamic supervision of society, such as squads who dictate women's attire.

Conservatives, more moderate than the radicals, want a nonfanatic Islamic Republic with special consideration for the economic needs of small merchants. They still oppose any U.S. contacts.

Moderates are reformers in Iranian terms, but are cautious and work within the system. They tend to be the educated middle class and favor privatization of state enterprises, fewer Islamic controls on society, elections open to most candidates (not just those approved by the Council of Guardians), and an end to confrontations with the West.

Liberals would go farther. Popular among Iranian students, they emphasize democracy and civil rights and want totally free elections. They would like to eliminate the social controls imposed by the Islamists. In economics, however, they are a mixed bag, ranging from free-marketeers to socialists. In the 2000 legislative elections, moderate and liberal reformists won a majority of Majlis seats.

A Partly Free System

Iran could be described as a partially free political system or one trying to become free. The 2000 elections were heartening. The spirited debates of the Majlis (mostly about the direction of the economy, statist or free-market), televised nationwide, show a parliament and society that wants to guide its future in a democratic way. Elections are lively and, within the limits imposed by the Council of Guardians, contested. The press is constitutionally free but a law also requires it "to enjoin the good and forbid the evil," as defined by the mullahs. Newspapers and magazines criticize some government policies and charge some high officials, mullahs, and their relatives with corruption. Critical papers are frequently closed, their editors tried, and dissidents mysteriously killed. As in much of the Third World, Iran's political institutions are vague and chaotic. It's hard to tell who has the power to do what. Much depends on personalities. Furthermore, researchers are not permitted to investigate Iran's government first-hand. We probably know more about the government workings in Russia and China—and we don't know much about them—than we do about how power flows in Iran.

Iranian Political Culture

As is often the case in the Third World, many Iranians do not wish to see their traditional culture erased by Western culture. "We want to be modern," say many citizens of the Third World, "but not like you. We'll do it our way, based on our values and our religion." Whether you can be a modern, high-tech society while preserving your old culture is a key question for much of the globe today. Will efforts to combine old and new cultures work or lead to chaos? In some cases, like Japan, it has worked. For Islamic nations, so far it has not. The key factor may be the flexibility and adaptability of the Third World culture, which is very high in the case of Japan. Japan learned to be modern but still distinctly Japanese. Can Muslim countries do the same?

Beneath all the comings and goings of conquerors and kingdoms, Persian society changed little over the centuries. As in China, the dynastic changes little disturbed the broad majority of the population, poor farmers and shepherds, many of them still tribal in organization. As in much of the Third World, traditional society was actually quite stable and conservative. Islam, the mosque, the mullah, and the **Koran** gave solace and meaning to the lives of most Persians. People were poor but passive.

Then came modernization, mostly under foreign pressure, starting late in the nineteenth century, expanding with the development of petroleum, and accelerating under both the Pahlavi shahs. Iran neatly raises the question of whether you can modernize and still keep your old culture. According to what political scientists call "modernization theory," a number of things happen more or less simultaneously. First, the economy changes, from simple farming to natural-resource extraction to manufacturing and services. Along with this comes urbanization, the movement of people from country to city. At the same time, education levels increase greatly; most people become at least literate and some go to college. People consume more mass media—at first newspapers, then radio, and finally television—until many people are aware of what is going on in their country and in the world. A large middle class emerges along with a variety of interest groups. People now want to participate in politics; they do not like being treated like children.

It was long supposed that secularization comes with modernization, and both Ataturk and the Pahlavis had tough showdowns with the mullahs.

Key Terms

Koran Muslim holy book.
sharia Muslim religious law.

Political Culture

Is Islam Anti-Modern?

Most Middle-East experts deny there is anything inherent in Islamic doctrine that keeps Muslim societies from modernizing. Yet one finds no Islamic countries that have fully modernized. Under Ataturk, Turkey made great strides between the two wars, but Islamic militants constantly try to undo his reforms. In Huntington's terms, Turkey is a "torn" country, pulled between Western and Islamic cultures. Recently Malaysia, half of whose people are Muslim, has scored rapid economic progress. Generally, though, Islam coincides with backwardness, as we define it. Some Muslim countries are rich but only because oil has brought them outside revenues.

Does Islam cause backwardness? By itself, no. The Koran does prohibit loaning money at interest, but there are ways to get around that. Historically, Islamic civilization was for centuries more advanced than Christian Europe in most areas (e.g., science, philosophy, medicine, sanitation, architecture, steelmaking). Europe got reacquainted with classic Greco-Roman thought, especially Aristotle, through translations from the Arabic, which helped trigger the Renaissance and Europe's modernization. Go back a millennium and you would find Muslims wondering if it wasn't Christianity that kept Europe backward.

But something happened; Islamic civilization faltered and European civilization modernized. By the sixteenth century, when European merchant ships arrived in the Persian Gulf, the West was ahead of Islam. Why? There are some historical causes. The Mongol invaders of the thirteenth century massacred the inhabitants of Baghdad and destroyed the region's irrigation systems, something the Arab empire never recovered from. (The Mongols' impact on Russia was also devastating.) Possibly because of the Mongol devastation, Islam turned to mysticism. Instead of being flexible, tolerant, and fascinated by learning and science, Islam turned sullen and rigid. When the Portuguese first rounded the southern tip of Africa in 1488, they opened up direct trade routes between Europe and Asia, bypassing the Islamic middlemen. Trade through the Middle East declined sharply and with it the region's economy.

Islam also has a structural problem in its combining of religion and government. The two are not supposed to be separate in Islam, and it is very difficult to split mosque and state in a Muslim country; those who try (such as Ataturk) are strongly resisted. Even today, many Muslims want **sharia** to be the law of the land. This sets up the kind of hostility Iran saw between secular modernizers and religious traditionalists, who compete for political power, with the latter constantly trying to reverse the efforts of the former. Until Muslim countries learn to separate mosque and state, this destructive tug-of-war will block progress.

Perhaps most important, the domination of European (chiefly British) imperialists starting in the nineteenth century created the resentment of a proud civilization brought low by upstart foreigners: "You push in here with your guns, your railroads, and your commerce and act superior to us. Well, culturally and morally we are superior to you, and eventually we'll kick you out." This attitude—which has some historical validity—spurs hatred of anything Western and therefore opposition to modernity, because embracing modernity would be admitting the West is superior. Islam teaches it is superior to other civilizations and will eventually triumph worldwide. Devout Muslims do not like evidence to the contrary.

If Muslim countries do not discard their antipathy toward the West and modernity in general, their progress will be slow and often reversed. Look for reforms in Islam that will make this possible; such movements are already afoot. Eventually, we could see societies that are both modern and Muslim. One of the best ways to promote this: Educate women.

Key Term

Islamism Islam turned into a political ideology.

But Iran's Islamic Revolution and other religious revivals now make us question the inevitability of secularization. Under certain conditions—when things change too fast, when the economy declines and unemployment grows, and modernization repudiates traditional values—people may return to religion with renewed vigor. If their world seems to be falling apart, church or mosque give stability and meaning to life. This is as true of the present-day United States as it is of Algeria. In the Muslim world, many intellectuals first passionately embraced modernizing creeds of socialism and nationalism only to despair and return to Islam. (Few intellectuals, however, embraced free-market capitalism, which was too much associated with the West.)

The time of modernization is a risky one in the life of a nation. If the old elite understands the changes that are bubbling through their society, they will gradually give way toward democracy in a fashion that does not destabilize the system. A corrupt and foolish elite, on the other hand, that is convinced the masses are not ready for democracy (and never will be), hold back political reforms until there is a tremendous head of steam. Then, no longer able to withstand the pressure, they suddenly give way, chaos breaks out and ends in tyranny. If the old elite had reformed sooner and gradually, they might have lowered the pressure and eased the transition to democracy. South Korea and Taiwan are examples of a favorable transition from dictatorship to democracy. Iran under the Shah is a negative example.

The Shah was arrogant: He alone would uplift Iran. He foresaw no democratic future for Iran and cultivated no important sectors of the population to support him. When the end came, few Iranians did support him. Indeed, the Shah scorned democracy in general, viewing it as a chaotic system that got in its own way, a view as old as the ancient Persian attack on Greece. The mighty Persian empire, under one ruler, could surely beat a quarrelsome collection of Greek city-states. (Wrong!) The Shah, repeating the millennia-old mistake, supposed that Iran, under his enlightened despotism, would soon surpass the decadent West. When a Western journalist asked the Shah why he did not relinquish some of his personal power and become a symbolic monarch, like the king of Sweden, the Shah replied: "I will become like the king of Sweden when Iranians become like Swedes." By this he indicated that unruly, tumultuous Iranians need a strong hand at the top.

The answer to this overly simple view is that, yes, when your people are poor and ignorant, absolute rule is one of your few alternatives. Such a country is far from ready for democracy. But after considerable modernization—which the Shah himself had implemented—you've got a different country, one characterized by the changes discussed earlier. The educated middle class especially resents one-man rule; the bigger this class, the more the resentment builds. By modernizing, the Shah was sawing off the tree limb on which he was sitting. He modernized Iran until it no longer wanted him.

Islam as a Political Ideology

Ayatollah Khomeini developed an interesting ideology that resonated with many Iranians. Called by some **Islamism**, it was not only religious but also social, economic, and nationalistic. The Shah and his regime, held Khomeini, not only abandoned Islam but also turned away from economic and social justice. They allowed the rich and corrupt to live in Westernized luxury while the broad masses struggled in poverty. They sold out Iran to the Americans, exchanging the people's oil for U.S. weapons. They permitted large numbers of Americans to live in Iran with their "unclean" morals, corrupting Iran's youth with their alcohol, sex, and rock music. By returning to the Koran, as interpreted by the mullahs, Iranians would not only

Key Concepts

Is "Islamic Fundamentalism" the Right Name?

Some object to the term "Islamic fundamentalism." First used to describe U.S. Bible-belt Protestants in the nineteenth century, "fundamentalism" stands for inerrancy of Scripture: The Bible means what it says and is not open to interpretation. But that's the way virtually all Muslims view the Koran, so Muslims are automatically "fundamentalists." Some thinkers propose we call it "Islamic integralism" instead, indicating a move to integrate the Koran and sharia with government. "Integralism," too, is borrowed, from a Catholic movement early in the twentieth century whose adherents sought to live a Christ-like existence.

Political scientists, of course, like to stress the political angle. Some use the term "political Islam," indicating it is the political and nationalistic use of religion to gain power. Along this line, it has been called "sacral nationalism," indicating that its underlying impulse is a nationalistic resentment of the West. And the term "Islamism," a religion turned into a political ideology, has been gaining favor for the simple reason that it's shorter.

cleanse themselves spiritually but also build a just society of equals. The mighty would be brought low and the poor raised up by extensive welfare benefits administered by mosques and Islamic associations. Like communism, Islamism preaches leveling of class differences, but through the mosque and mullahs rather than through the Party and *apparatchiks*.

Islamism is thus a catchall ideology, offering an answer to most things that made Iranians discontent. It's a potent brew, but can it work? Probably not. Over time, its many strands fall apart and start quarreling among themselves. Islamism's chief problem is economics (as we shall consider in greater detail later). As Islamism recedes as a viable ideology, look for the reemergence of other ideologies in Iran.

Democracy and Authority

If rule by the mullahs is someday overturned, can Iranians establish a stable democracy, or was the Shah right—do Iranians need a strong hand to govern them? There were two impulses behind the 1979 revolution: the demands of secularist intellectuals to become a democracy and the demands of Islamists to become a theocracy. The secular democrats, always a small minority, threw in with the more-numerous Islamists, figuring they would be an effective tool to oust the Shah and that the two would form a sort of equal partnership. But the Islamists, better organized and knowing exactly what they wanted, used the secular democrats and then dumped them (in some cases, shot them). Many fled to other countries. Learning too late what was happening to them, some democratic supporters of the Revolution put out the slogan: "In the dawn of freedom, there is no freedom."

But these secular democrats did not disappear; they simply laid low and went along outwardly with the Islamic Revolution. To have opposed it openly could have earned them the firing squad. Among them are the smartest and best-educated people in Iran, the very people needed to make the economy function. With Iran's drastic economic decline, many either lost their

Political Culture

Are Iranians Religious Fanatics?

Only some Iranians are religious fanatics. Not even the supposed Islamic fundamentalists are necessarily religious fanatics. Many Iranians are perfectly aware that religion is a political tool (more on this in the next section) and are fed up with it. Neither are Iranians anti-American on a personal basis. Despite massive regime propaganda depicting the United States as the "great satan," most Iranians are very friendly to the few Americans who visit. Some have been in the United States or have relatives there; many remember that when Iran was allied with America, Iraq didn't dare invade. Do not confuse regime propaganda with the attitudes of ordinary citizens.

Ironically, Iranians labeled the Taliban government of neighboring Afghanistan as Muslim extremists. Far stricter than Iranian Islamists, the Taliban confine women to the home and require all men to have beards. Why the conflict with Iran? Like most of Afghanistan, the Taliban are Sunni and attacked the Shia minority, some 1.5 million of whom fled to Iran. When Iranian diplomats tried to aid Afghan Shi'ites, the Taliban killed them. Dangerous stuff, religious extremism.

jobs or decided it was more prudent to develop private practices as consultants and specialists, working out of their apartments. Many of them—once they are sure you are not a provocateur for the regime—speak scathingly in private of the oppression and economic foolishness of the rule of the mullahs. "I believe in Islam, but not in the regime of the mullahs," said one Iranian.

People like these—who voted for Khatami in 1997—believe Iranians are capable of democracy. They argue that the anti-Shah revolution was hijacked by the Islamists but that its original impulse was for democracy, not theocracy, and this impulse still remains. Especially now that people have tasted the economic decline, corruption, and general ineptitude of the mullahs, they are ready for democracy. Look for the secular democrats to increasingly make their arguments public and to demand open elections with no parties declared ineligible.

Persian Nationalism

Islam is not the only political force at work in Iran. Remember, Islam was imposed on Persia by the sword, and Iranians to this day harbor folk memories of seventh-century massacres by crude, barbaric invaders. Iranians do not like Arabs and look down on them as culturally inferior and lacking staying power. By adopting Shia, Iranians were and are able to distinguish themselves from their mostly Sunni neighbors. "Yes, of course we are Muslims," is the Iranian message, "but we are not like these other Muslim countries." Accordingly, not far under the surface of Iranian thought is a kind of Persian nationalism, affirming the greatness of their ancient civilization, which antedates Islam by a millennium.

The Shah especially stressed Persian nationalism in his drive to modernize Iran. The Shah was a nominal Muslim and had himself photographed in religious devotion, as on his **hajj**, required of all Muslims who can possibly afford it

Key Term

hajj Muslim pilgrimage to Mecca.

once in their lifetime. But the Shah's true spirit was secular and nationalistic: to rebuild the glory of ancient Persia in a modern Iran. If Islam got in the way, it was to be pushed aside. The Shah was relatively tolerant of non-Muslim faiths; Baha'is (a universalistic and liberal offshoot of Islam), Jews, and Christians were generally unharmed. Since the Islamic Revolution, non-Muslims have been treated harshly, especially the 300,000 Baha'is, Iran's largest minority religion, who are regarded as dangerous **heretics**. For centuries, Iran's sense of its unique Persianness coexisted uneasily with its Islam. The Shah's modernization program brought the two strands into open conflict.

Key Term

heretic Someone who breaks away from a religion.

But if you look closely, even the Islamic Revolution of 1979 did not totally repudiate the Persian nationalist strand of Iranian thought. Rather, it put the stress on the religious side of Persianness. The long and horrible war with Iraq, 1980–88, especially brought out the Persian nationalist side of the Islamist regime. They were fighting not only for their faith but for their country and against a savage, upstart Arab country, Iraq, that didn't even exist until the British invented it in the 1920s. Iran celebrates two types of holidays, Persian and Muslim. The Persian holidays are all happy, such as New Year (*Now Ruz*). The Islamic holidays are mostly mournful, such as the day of remembrance of the martyrdom of Hussein at Kerbala, during which young Shi'ite men beat themselves until they bleed. In analyzing Iranian political attitudes, remember that Persianness is about as strong as Islam, and Iranian regimes typically base themselves on both, although often giving more weight to one. As the Islamic Revolution tires, be on the lookout for an Iranian switch back to greater emphasis on Persianness.

DEMOCRACY

IRAN'S ANGRY STUDENTS

In the late 1970s, Iranian students, most of them leftists, battled to overturn the old regime. Twenty years later, Iran's students—who number over one million—are again willing to turn to street demonstrations for civil rights. Many students are outspoken liberals and want to push President Khatami to pluralism, a free press, and free elections. As before, they also protest the serious lack of jobs.

In 1999, when a hard-line court closed a relatively liberal daily, *Salaam* (Peace), and convicted its editor, Tehran students erupted in a week of street protests that spread to several cities. Some were killed. The editor was himself a Muslim cleric, helper of Khomeini, and ally of Khatami. To say one is Muslim in Iran doesn't say much; there are Muslim liberals and Muslim conservatives. Newspapers are closed all the time for showing too much "tolerance and leniency," that is, support for pluralism.

Both Ayatollah Khamenei and President Khatami, who must maintain good relations with the Leader and the conservative Majlis, denounced the student riots. To repeat: Khatami operates within the the system, not against it. Could students one day pave the way to democracy? By themselves, probably not. They are too few and not organized. But in combination with other groups, they could push moderates like Khatami to take stronger reformist stances.

Key Concepts

Sunni and Shia

Over 80 percent of all Muslims practice the mainstream branch of Islam, called Sunni. Scattered unevenly throughout the Muslim world, however, is a minority branch (of 100 million) called Shia. The two split early over who was the true successor (*caliph*) of Mohammed. Shi'ites claim the Prophet's cousin and son-in-law Ali has the title, but he was assassinated in 661. Shia means "followers" or "partisans," hence Shi'ites are the followers of Ali. When Ali's son, Hussein, attempted to claim the title, his forces were beaten at Karbala in present-day Iraq (now a Shia shrine) in 680, and Hussein was betrayed and tortured to death. This gave Shia a fixation on martyrdom; some of their holidays feature self-flagellation.

Shia also developed a messianic concept lacking in Sunni. Shi'ites in Iran hold that the line of succession passed through a series of twelve *imams* (religious leaders) of whom Ali was the first. The twelfth imam disappeared but is to return one day to complete the Prophet's mission on earth. He is referred to as the Hidden Imam and the Expected One. Such believers are thus sometimes called "Twelver" Muslims. Shi'ites are no more "fundamentalist" than other Muslims, who also interpret the Koran strictly.

Although the origin and basic tenets of the two branches are identical, Sunnis regard Shi'ites as extremist, mystical, and crazy. Only in Iran is Shia the majority faith and state religion. With their underdog status elsewhere, Shi'ites sometimes become rebellious (with Iranian money and guidance), as in southern Lebanon, southern Iraq, and scattered through Arabia. Shia imparts a peculiar twist to Iranians, giving them the feeling of being isolated but right, beset by enemies on all sides, and willing to martyr themselves for their cause.

Patterns of Interaction

Religion as a Political Tool

Manipulate, use, dump. This is how Khomeini's forces treated those who helped them win the Revolution. Like turbaned Bolsheviks, the Islamists in the late 1970s hijacked the Iranian revolution as it unfolded. First, they captured the growing discontent with the Shah and his regime. By offering themselves as a plausible and effective front organization, they enlisted all manner of anti-Shah groups under their banner—the democratically inclined parties of the National Front, the Iran Freedom Movement, the Marxist (and Soviet-connected) Tudeh party, and Islamic guerrilla movements. They had some of these groups do their dirty work for them, and then got rid of them, sometimes by firing squad. The flowering of democratic, Islamic, secular, and socialist parties that accompanied the Shah's overthrow was crushed within three years. As an example of revolutionary technique, Lenin would have admired their skill and ruthlessness.

In doing all this, the Islamists used their religion much as the Bolsheviks used Marxism, as a tool, a recruiting and mobilizing device, a means of gaining authority and obedience, and a way to seize and consolidate power. This is not to say they were not serious about their religion, but rather that in a revolutionary situation the instrumental uses of their faith predominated over the devotional. If you want to seize state power, you can't be otherworldly; you've got to be very shrewd and practical. There's nothing "crazy" about the Islamists who run Iran; they are perfectly capable of calm and rational decisions calculated to benefit themselves. They only look crazy.

After some time immersed in the world of politics, the power side takes over and the original religious (or ideological) side takes a back seat. As with the Bolsheviks, this soon leads to opportunism and cynicism among the politically involved and ultimately to regime decay. The ruling group turns into a self-serving new class. This is why regimes that base themselves on ideology or religion (Islamism combines both) have finite lifespans. After a while, the power and greed of the ruling class is noticed by all, and mass disillusion sets in; the regime loses its legitimacy. This is happening in Iran. Eventually Iran's Islamic revolution will burn out.

Radicals and Moderates in Iran

After the 1986 Iran-contra fiasco, in which White House aides attempted to secretly sell U.S. missiles to alleged Iranian "moderates," the term "Iranian moderate" disappeared from Washington's vocabulary. The Americans, led by Marine Lt. Col. Oliver North, fell for a sucker play by Iranian revolutionary leaders, who set up the deal and then leaked word that the United States was trading with Iran, illegal under U.S. law. These people never miss a chance to embarrass the United States. There are Iranian moderates; it's just that they've learned to keep their mouths shut and do nothing stupid, like having contact with Americans. Instead, the Iranians who fit under the labels "moderates" and "liberals" discussed earlier play a cautious game, not directly opposing the Islamic revolution while trying to tone it down. They are in a permanent power struggle with conservative forces.

Those who fit under the labels "radicals" and "conservatives" want an Islamic republic, one based on religious law and presided over by the *faqih*. Anything else means giving in to

POLITICAL CULTURE

DOES ISLAM DISCRIMINATE AGAINST WOMEN?

Iran is actually one of the better Muslim countries when it comes to the treatment of women. Unlike the Arab kingdoms on the southern shore of the Gulf, Iranian women drive cars, go to school, work outside the home, and participate in politics. But even in Iran there are tough restrictions on dress, contact with males, and travel.

Devout Muslims swear women are deeply honored in their societies; it's just that their place is in the home and nowhere else. Women are indeed kept at a subservient status in most Islamic countries; often they get little education, cannot drive a car, and their testimony is worth half of men's in courts of law. But such discrimination does not always come from the Koran. In some Muslim countries (not Iran), such customs as the seclusion of women, the veil, and female genital mutilation are pre-Islamic and were absorbed by Islam (much as Europeans adopted for Christmas the pagan worship of trees). These non-Koranic imports can therefore be discarded with no harm to the faith, maintain Muslim feminists. Yes, there are such people, and increasingly they are speaking out and organizing. If they succeed, they will greatly modernize their societies. The widespread education of Iranian women suggests social and legal change will arrive there before long.

Iran's enemies—the West in general, the United States in particular—with eventual loss of Iran's independence, culture, and religion. They do anything they can to block liberalizing reforms, from closing newspapers to voting out ministers to putting allies of Khatami on trial.

In a parallel with what we did earlier for Russia and China, we can construct a list of Iranian moderate and Islamist views (see table on page 130). On at least a couple of points there is no clear divergence between moderates and Islamists. First, both groups are Muslim and want to preserve a generally Islamic emphasis in public life, including the judicial system. Second, both groups want economic growth, both for the sake of Iran's national power and to improve the lot of its people. It's how to do this that is the bone of contention: free market or state controlled? In elections no one runs on an opposition platform; all seem to be supporting at least a version of the Islamic revolution. In Iran, direct opposition could be hazardous to your health. It is in the nuances among groupings that differences begin to appear.

There are some Iranians, both inside and outside the country, who would like to get rid of the whole Islamic revolution. A few monarchists, mostly people who got rich under the Shah, would like to restore the son of the last Pahlavi, a young man now living in the West, to the throne.

The United States and Iran: The U.S. Embassy Takeover

The seizure of the U.S. embassy in Tehran by student militants in November 1979 brought American cries of outrage and a complete break in relations. The embassy takeover and holding of fifty-two American officials for 444 days indeed broke every rule in the diplomatic book and seemed to prove Iran was governed by mad fanatics.

Looked at more closely, the incident was a domestic Iranian power play, cynically manipulated by the Khomeini forces. The ayatollah had no further use for the prime minister he had appointed early in 1979, Mehdi Bazargan, a relative moderate. How to get rid of him and other moderates? The occasion was the admission of the ailing Shah to the United States for cancer treatment. Khomeini's cadres whipped up mass rage in Iran, claiming that this U.S. humanitarian gesture proved the United State still supported the Shah's ousted regime. Then they had a group of student militants invade and take over the U.S. embassy, which had already been reduced to a skeleton staff. No shots were fired; the U.S. Marine guards were ordered not to shoot. They took sixty-six Americans prisoner—but killed none and released fourteen—and published classified embassy documents (pieced together from the shredder) purporting to show how dastardly the Americans were.

The Islamic activists, using anti-American hysteria ("Death to USA!"), consolidated their hold on the country. Humiliated and powerless, Bazargan resigned. Anyone opposed to the embassy takeover was fired or worse. One foreign-ministry official (who had dropped out of Georgetown University to promote revolution) helped some Americans escape via the Canadian embassy. He was tried and shot. Khomeini's followers seemed to enjoy watching President Carter squirm, especially after the aborted U.S. rescue mission in April 1980. Carter's apparent weakness on Iran hurt him in the 1980 election, which he lost to Reagan.

At that point, the holding of U.S. diplomats had exhausted its utility for Khomeini. Knowing Reagan was not averse to military measures, Tehran released the diplomats just as he was inaugurated. The militants who had seized and held the Americans had also served their purpose. Considered unreliable, some were arrested and executed. Others were sent to the front in the war with Iraq, where they died in the fighting. The revolution devours its children.

COMPARISON

IS SAUDI ARABIA NEXT?

The bombings of U.S. servicemen in Saudi Arabia remind us that not all is well in the Kingdom, as Saudis call their country. Not far under the surface are the same kind of antiregime forces that overthrew the Shah in Iran. The Saudi regime, which established itself in the 1920s based on the Wahhabi brand of strict Islam, is vulnerable for the same reasons we reviewed earlier in Iran. The legitimacy of the royal family has come into question, because many of them play around, Western-style, in a non-Islamic fashion. The House of Saud has some four thousand princes, with more than five hundred of them eligible to become king, an invitation for a succession struggle.

Oil created some very rich people, including the princes, but left many poor Saudis behind. Earlier, oil revenues allowed the regime to buy off discontent with subsidies for everyone from wheat farmers (who use expensive desalinated seawater) to students (who got scholarships to study overseas). But oil prices dropped, and the Kingdom paid much of the cost of the 1991 Gulf War. Saudi Arabia now has a debt and budget deficit; it is no longer nearly so rich. Cushy jobs no longer await young Saudis, who must now work for a living.

Making matters worse, in the oil-producing Eastern Province are Shi'ites, who (with Iranian backing) carry out acts of terrorism. In 1979 Sunni fanatics (also with Iranian help) seized the holiest Islamic shrine in Mecca until dislodged by French special forces. News from the Kingdom is rigorously censored—nothing negative is allowed—and Washington never utters a word critical of or worried about our good friends, the House of Saud. It was the same way we treated the Shah.

What can be done? It may be too late to do anything, as attempting reforms can easily trigger revolution. Still, drawing lessons from the Iranian revolution, we might suggest that the Saudi government do the following:

Allow some opposition parties: Make sure they are moderate, and let them criticize the regime in a constructive way. Make sure there are many parties (some conservative, some liberal, none radical) to divide public discontent.

Permit a semifree press: Make it along the same lines as parties—limited criticism only.

Crush and suppress revolutionaries: Don't ease up on them. They are out to destroy you, and if they take over they will not be moderate or democratic. Be especially ruthless with any group getting Iranian or Iraqi support.

Hold legislative elections: But make them elections with a list of parties limited to the authorized ones (i.e., ranging from conservative to moderate). Gradually, over many years, you can expand the list.

Have the new legislature redistribute wealth in the form of heavy taxes on the rich: Impose taxes especially on members of the royal family, who must be seen taking a financial hit. This is to defuse mass anger over the great and unfair wealth of the royals. The princes don't like paying taxes? Point out to them they could lose everything—including their heads—if they aren't careful.

Limit the American presence; it is a cultural irritant: Women soldiers, American media, and foreigners on holy Islamic soil offer natural fodder for Islamic extremists. The handful of Americans left should be nearly invisible.

Crack down on corruption, especially among the highest officials and princes: Show that you mean business here, and that the crackdown will be permanent.

Have we learned anything from Iran? Would any of this work to head off a revolution? Maybe, but it would require the willingness of the House of Saud to cut its own wealth and power, and that is something ruling classes rarely do. But if Saudi Arabia cannot make the transition to some kind of democracy, revolution and then U.S. military involvement is likely. The Persian Gulf and its oil is one place we do not walk away from.

The spirit of Iran's Islamic Revolution lives on in this Tehran cemetery memorial to the fallen of the Iran-Iraq war of 1980–88. Losses were horrifying—some three-quarters of a million killed, many of them boys. Note the women in chadors in the foreground. (Mehrdad Madresehee)

Only in conditions of extreme domestic chaos is this even dimly feasible. Even Iranians who think the Shah's rule was not so bad do not consider this option. The times are against monarchy; every decade there are fewer and fewer ruling (as opposed to figurehead) monarchs.

On the other side, some Marxist-type revolutionaries, the *Mujahedin-e Khalq* (Fighters for the People), who earlier worked with the Islamists to overthrow the Shah now try to overthrow the Islamists. Among them were some of the young militants who seized the U.S. embassy. Subsequently, it is estimated that over 10,000 Mujahedin were executed by the Khomeini forces. Their survivors have a headquarters in Paris and are sheltered in and sponsored by Iraq, which invaded and massacred Iranians (sometimes with poison gas), during the 1980s, so these Mujahedin have little resonance among Iranians.

Change is coming from the struggle between Iranian militants and moderates, not the influence of monarchists, leftists, or outside forces. For example, one of the key alliances of the 1979 Iranian revolution was between the mullahs, the Muslim clerics, and the *bazaaris*, the small merchants whose shops are often in a bazaar (a Persian word). Suffering under the Shah's top-heavy modernization—bakers were put out of business by bread factories, clothiers by department stores, cobblers by shoe factories, and so on—the *bazaaris*' shift to the Islamic revolution

Moderates	***Islamists***
shift power to Majlis	preserve power of *faqih*
permit all parties	outlaw non-Islamic parties
free press	controlled press
permit Western women's attire	Islamic attire only (veil)
improve relations with West	keep distant from West
stop hating America	keep hating America
don't spread Islamic revolution	keep spreading it
liberalize economy	keep economy statist

guaranteed its success. But now many *bazaaris* are also fed up with the mullahs, whose corruption and amassing of wealth has betrayed the revolution. Accordingly, some *bazaaris* back moderates in the Majlis, especially those who understand the needs of small businesspeople. Even in revolutionary Iran, interest groups are alive and well.

The Revolution Burns Out

Crane Brinton's classic theory of revolution fits the Iranian revolution well. To recapitulate: The old regime loses its legitimacy. Antiregime groups form, rioting breaks out, and the old regime folds. Initially moderates seize power, but they are soon dumped by more ruthless radicals, who drive the revolution to a frenzied high point. But people can't take that forever; eventually a "Thermidor," or calming down, arrives. Iran passed through each of these stages almost as if Iranians had read Brinton. Every stage, that is, except the last, and even that seems to have happened without a clear-cut Thermidor. Instead, there may be a low-key, rolling Thermidor that led to Khatami's election in 1997.

No revolution lasts forever. In Iran we see an effort to become stable and normal, disputed, to be sure, by Islamic revolutionary militancy. Time is probably on the side of the normalizers. In the first place, many mullahs have corrupted themselves. Mullahs were placed in control of *bunyads*, foundations originally set up to redistribute the wealth of the Shah and his supporters. These *bunyads* now control billions of dollars and much of Iran's industry. They are supposed to be run for the good of all, a sort of Islamic socialism, but in practice they have made their mullahs rich, powerful, and corrupt while their industries are run poorly. As Lord Acton observed, power corrupts.

Aware of this, many Iranians want the mullahs to return to the mosque and get out of government and the economy. Even some mullahs wish to return to the mosque. Here we have a parallel with the Brazilian generals, who bowed out when they came to realize that running a country was ruining their reputation and their mission in life. Chanted Iranian students in 1999: "The mullahs have become God, and the people have become poor." Another factor is that now half of Iranians were born after the Shah and have no personal commitment to the Islamic revolution. They want jobs and more freedom and they can vote at age seventeen. (In raising the voting age from sixteen to seventeen in 2000, the mullahs kept out some 1.5 million young voters, most of them favoring reforms.)

Will there be a point at which we can say the Iranian revolution has burnt itself out? The reestablishment of diplomatic ties between the United States and Iran would indicate that point had passed. Khatami has mentioned "dialogue" with Americans (but not with Washington) but pulled back when conservative forces objected. Other indications would be the mullahs giving up control of the *bunyads* and the *faqih* becoming a figurehead or "dignified" office.

What Iranians Quarrel About

Which Way for Iran's Economy?

Iran has changed rapidly, partly under the Shah and partly under the Islamic Revolution. The countryside has received schools, electricity, health care, and tractors. Infant mortality, a key measure of health care, fell from 169 per 1,000 births in 1960 to 33 in 1996. Average life expectancy

How Many Iranians?

Islam frowns upon family planning: The more babies the better. After the revolution, Iran's mullahs urged women to produce a generation of Muslim militants; subsidized food helped feed them. Iran's rate of population growth for several years averaged 3.7 percent a year, one of the world's highest. Despite the murderous war with Iraq, in less than two decades after the Revolution Iran's population doubled from 34 million to 68 million.

By the early 1990s, though, the government, realizing it could not subsidize or employ the vast numbers of young Iranians, reversed the high-births policy. Amid economic decline, families now can afford fewer children. Clinics now offer all manner of contraception free of charge (but not abortions). Women agents go door-to-door to promote family planning. Food and other family aid is decreased after a family has three children. One Muslim cleric even issued a *fatwa* in favor of smaller families. From an average 7 births per woman during her life in 1986, the fertility rate dropped to half, to 3.6 births per woman over her life in 1993, actually much lower than before the revolution. By 1995, the rate of population growth was down to a more reasonable 2.3 percent (which, if held, would still double the population in thirty years.) The turnaround on births is an indication the revolution is over.

jumped thirteen years, from 56 to 69. Literacy has climbed from less than half to two-thirds. More Iranian women than ever are in schools (segregated from males, of course) and universities.

The Iranian economy—ruined by revolution, war, isolation, and mismanagement—declined steeply in the 1980s until now per capita income is about a third of what it was under the Shah. There is some growth, but inflation, although somewhat tamed, is still hefty. Many Iranian workers are unemployed. Pay is low so people hold two and three jobs to make ends meet. Many jobs and business dealings, as in Russia, are off the books. Even the oil industry, once the pride and basis of the Iranian economy, has suffered from lack of replacement parts and up-to-date technology. U.S. pressure has kept most oil companies from cooperating with Iran. The mullahs who run the *bunyads* run them badly and corruptly, and increasingly Iranians notice this.

By giving all Iranians a welfare floor—including subsidized food and gasoline—while simultaneously damaging Iran's great source of revenue, its petroleum connection with the West—Tehran has run out of money. Iran runs large annual budget deficits, which translate into persistent inflation. The Shah left a foreign debt of $8.4 billion, which the Khomeini regime, amid great hardship, repaid, swearing Iran would never fall into imperialist clutches again. But by 1996, Iran's foreign debt was a dangerous $33 billion. Under worsening material conditions, many of the early adherents of Islamism have dropped out or even come to oppose it. The true believers, the **hezbollahis**, still try to supervise much of Iranian society, but they are an increasingly resented minority, the functional equivalent of the old Soviet Communist party. And you recall what happened to them.

Key Term

hezbollahi "Partisan of God"; fanatic supporter of Islamism.

The Islamic Revolution did not dismantle the Shah's statist economy. State-owned businesses (the biggest: oil) still produce 86 percent of Iran's GDP. And much of the rest is in the hands of the *bunyads*. Theoretically, foreigners can invest in Iran, but the limits and regulations are so many and so tangled that most investors are scared off. To get anything done requires numerous bribes. Iran's is not a free-market economy. The big question: Should it become one?

Opposing arguments show up in Majlis debates over economic policy, which have become thinly disguised battles over the future of strict Islamic rule. As we have considered, Islamism is a surrogate socialism; that is, it blends Islamic correctness with collectivist economics. In the minds of many Islamists, socialism is the logical extension of Islam, for Islam preaches equality and leveling of class differences. Thus, they claim, Islam is the true and best path to a just society of equal citizens, where no one is either rich or poor. What the Marxists, Socialists, and Communists talked about, they say, we can deliver.

Most moderates respond that socialism and/or statism is not the way to go, that they just keep Iran poor and backward. The collapse of the Soviet system demonstrates socialism doesn't work, and the decline of Iran's economy demonstrates statism doesn't work. Besides, they note, there is no Koranic basis for government control of the economy. It is perfectly feasible to combine free-market capitalism with the alms-giving required of faithful Muslims to achieve social justice. If we keep declining economically, moderates also worry, we'll never be able to build a first-class army and so will be vulnerable to hostile

The United States and Iran: America, Don't Mess with Iran

We don't understand the Iranian revolution and have not been clever in dealing with it. Part religious, part nationalistic, part cultural, and part antityrannical, the Iranian revolution defied our predictions and efforts to tame it. When we tried to deal with alleged "Iranian moderates" in 1986, we were humiliated. When we tilted toward Iraq in its war against Iran, we supported a fiendish dictator (Saddam Hussein) whom we soon had to fight ourselves. In 1988 a U.S. destroyer mistook an Iranian jetliner for an attacking fighter, shot it down with a missile, and killed all 290 aboard. (Some specialists believe the downing of Pan Am 103 over Scotland later that year was a retaliation.) Iran, and indeed the whole Persian Gulf, is a tar baby: Once you punch it, you get stuck worse and worse.

But if we leave Iran alone, things may break our way. As pointed out in these pages, Iran's Islamic revolution is waning and relative moderates have a chance to take over. In the long term, Iran needs us. We can provide the petroleum technology and other means to modernize the country. If an aggressive Russia starts rebuilding its Caucasian empire, Iran would find U.S. support awfully handy. Historically, Russia always had territorial designs on Persia; the United States never did. We need not be enemies forever.

Anthropologists have pointed out that when two Iranian *bazaaris* quarrel, by long tradition they simply shun and ignore each other for some years. Gradually, the quarrel fades and they cautiously reestablish relations with each other. After a while, the quarrel is forgotten. Actually, it's a rather civilized way to handle a quarrel. We might take a leaf from a Persian folkway in dealing with Iran and avoid another Cold War.

The United States and Iran: Iran, Don't Mess with America

You Iranians don't understand American culture very well. Americans are in many ways the opposite of Iranians; we are direct, unsubtle, and prone to violence: cowboys. When we see something stamped "enemy," we destroy it. We like black and white, not shades of grey. Our presidents are especially afraid of appearing weak; it hurts their chances for re-election. Americans like tough, decisive action, especially if accompanied by good TV film clips.

Accordingly, Iranians, do not let yourselves be seen as hostile or dangerous to America. Do not chant *Marg bar Amrika!* ("Death to America!"), as we take it literally. The U.S. commitment to making sure the oil of the Persian Gulf flows in a friendly fashion is one point Americans agree on in foreign policy. No amount of bombings can persuade us to abandon this policy. And we can "make your economy scream." Those were Kissinger's words describing what we did to Chile when it came under Marxist rule. (We're probably doing it to you now.)

So end all sponsorship and encouragement of terrorist activity, especially that aimed at Americans. Do not develop a nuclear device; remember, we have thousands of them. Turn to your tradition and simply shun America, doing nothing against us. And when you're ready to resume contact and economic growth, let us know in a public way. We understand that you are going through a terrible power struggle between conservatives and reformers and that you can't move prematurely. Eventually, there will be a thaw. We were friends once and can be again. One area of possible cooperation: an oil pipeline from Central Asia to the Persian Gulf. Another area: our mutual enmity toward Iraq. The Middle East, after all, is the origin of the famous diplomatic dictum: "The enemy of my enemy is my friend."

outside forces. And if our towering unemployment problem is not solved soon, the whole Islamic revolution could be doomed. The best and quickest way to solve these problems is the free market. State ownership of major industries, especially petroleum, is what the Shah tried, and we certainly don't want to follow in his footsteps. Such are the arguments of Iranian moderates. Notice that outright rejection of the Islamic revolution is not one of their points.

The Veiled Debate on Islam

Iran will always be a Muslim country, but what kind of Islam will it have? A relatively moderate kind that largely keeps out of direct political involvement or a militant kind that seeks to guide society by political means? Judging by the victories of reformists in elections, most would opt for the first kind.

Because outright liberal candidates are barred by the Council of Guardians, public debate on the religion question is muted. No one wants to risk being branded "anti-Islamic." Still, one can infer that such a debate is taking place. One of the stand-ins for a discussion of Islam in public life is the debate on what kind of clothing is admissible, especially for women. Even for men, though, blue jeans were frowned upon, partly because they represent American culture. Liberals say, no, they don't; jeans are simply a comfortable and international garment with no political connotations.

Before the Islamic revolution, urban and educated Iranian women dressed as fashionably as European women. Then suddenly they could wear no makeup and had to wear the veil and *chador*, the single-piece head-to-toe garment designed to cover feminine attractiveness. Devout Muslims, including many women, say this attire is better than Western clothing as it eliminates lust, vanity, and distinctions of wealth. (Notice how some U.S. schools are coming to similar conclusions about school uniforms.) Western clothes and makeup are the first steps toward debauchery and prostitution, they argue, and anyone who thinks otherwise is deemed anti-Islamic. But in subtle ways urban Iranian women dress in a manner that pushes to the limit of the permissible in public (and in private dress as they wish). The veil and *chador* are no longer mandatory on the street, so long as a woman is dressed modestly without makeup and with hair and forehead covered by a kerchief. Push beyond this and women run the risk of Islamic *komitehs* (morals police) stopping them on the street and sending them home or to jail. These volunteer squads have become one of the most obnoxious features of the Islamic revolution and have pushed urban and educated Iranians away from the revolution. The lifting of Islamically correct clothing requirements will mark an overall retreat in the political power of the mullahs.

Geography

Strategic Waterways

These are mostly narrow choke points connecting two bodies of water. Hostile control of them causes one or more countries discomfort or fear. Here are the main ones:

- Turkish Straits (Dardanelles and Bosporus), connecting the Black and Mediterranean Seas.
- Strait of Gibraltar, connecting the Atlantic and the Mediterranean.
- Suez Canal, connecting the Mediterranean and Red Seas.
- Bab al Mandab, connecting the Red Sea and Indian Ocean.
- Strait of Hormuz, connecting the Persian Gulf and Indian Ocean.
- English Channel, connecting the Atlantic Ocean and North Sea.
- Skagerrak, connecting the Baltic and North Seas.
- North Cape, dividing the Atlantic from the Barents Sea.
- Cape of Good Hope, where the Atlantic and Indian Oceans meet off the southern tip of Africa.
- Strait of Malacca, connecting the Indian Ocean and South China Sea, the oil lifeline of East Asia.
- Korea (Tsushima) Strait, connecting the East China Sea and Sea of Japan.
- Panama Canal, connecting the Atlantic and Pacific Oceans.

You are the captain of a small tanker that has just loaded oil in Kuwait for delivery in Umea, Sweden. Which bodies of water—including seas, oceans, straits, and canals—do you pass through? (Note: Supertankers are too big for Suez; they have to go around Africa. But small tankers still pass through Suez.)

What Kind of Foreign Policy?

The guiding lights of the Islamic revolution had aspirations beyond Iran. Some still have. They saw themselves as the revitalizers of the entire Islamic world and tried to spread their revolution, especially among Shi'ites but also among Muslims in general. One of

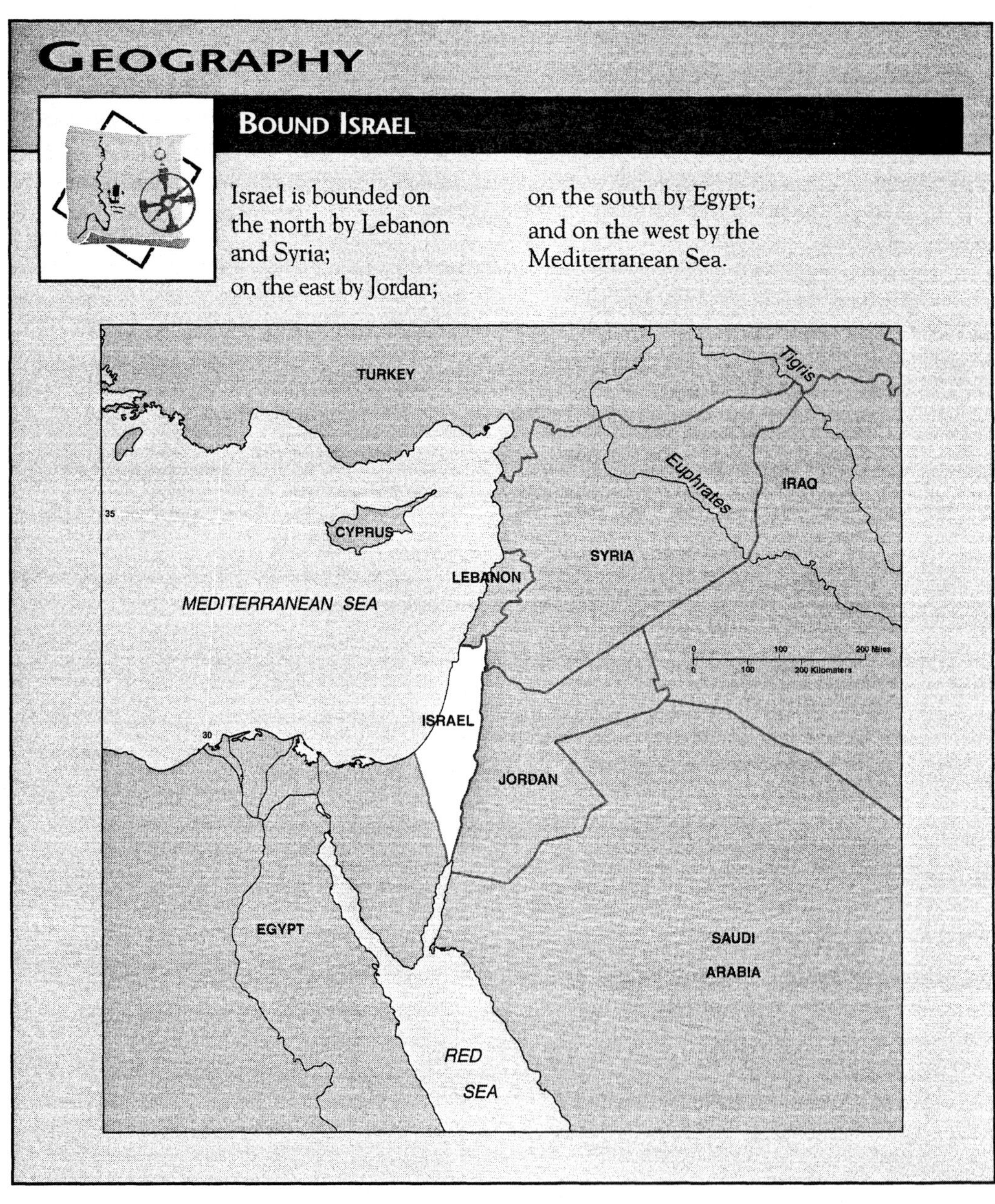

Political Culture

A Fatwa on Rushdie

One of the more horrifying examples of the Iranian revolution was the turning of a **fatwa** into an international death warrant. In 1989 Khomeini issued a *fatwa* ordering the execution of British author Salman Rushdie, a lapsed Muslim of Indian origin. Rushdie had just published his *Satanic Verses*, a fantasy on the life of Mohammed that was extremely offensive to devout Muslims. A semi-official Tehran foundation offered a reward of $1 million (later raised to $2.8 million) for killing Rushdie, who went into hiding for years. Even now, he appears rarely and cautiously; he knows they mean it.

The Western world was aghast at this order to kill someone in a faraway country for writing a book. The entire concept of the *fatwa* underscores the vast cultural differences between Islamic and Western civilizations. (In 1993, the top Saudi cleric issued a *fatwa* that the earth is flat and anyone claiming it round should be punished as an atheist.) Iran's relations with most of Europe deteriorated. Even many Iranians are embarrassed and apologetic over the *fatwa* and wish it rescinded. Khomeini's successors claim that he's the only one who can rescind it, and he died a few months after issuing it. Even though the Tehran government says it has dissociated itself from the *fatwa* on Rushdie, it continues as a block to improved Iranian relations with other countries.

their earliest areas of concern were the Shi'ites of southern Iraq, long a large, suppressed minority. Actually, by the time you subtract the Shi'ites of the south and Kurds of the north of Iraq, the Sunni Arabs of the middle of Iraq are a minority, but political power has always been in their hands, and they don't share it. Many of the main shrines of Shia are in southern Iraq, the area Khomeini was exiled to in 1964. Upon taking power in Tehran, the Khomeini people propagandized Iraqi Shi'ites and urged them to join the Islamic revolution. This was one of the irritants—but hardly a sufficient excuse—for Iraqi dictator Saddam Hussein to invade Iran in 1980.

Wherever there are Shi'ites, Iranian influence turns up: southern Lebanon, Kuwait, Bahrain, and Saudi Arabia. Funds, instructions, and explosive devices flow through this connection. Iran, along with Iraq, Syria, and Libya, were placed on the U.S. State Department's list of countries sponsoring terrorism. Iran feels it must take a leading role in destroying Israel, which it depicts as a polluter of Islamic holy ground (Jerusalem is also sacred to Muslims) and outpost of Western imperialism. Under the Shah, Tehran had good (but informal) relations with Israel and quietly sold it most of its oil. Suddenly that totally changed, and Iran supports Lebanon's *Hezbollah* ("Party of God"), which harasses Israel's northern border. (One of the best information sources for critical Iranians is Israeli radio, which broadcasts to Iran in Farsi.)

How many enemies can a country handle at once? On all sides but one—the northeast, namely the ex-Soviet Muslim republics of Central Asia—Iran now faces enemies. To a considerable extent, by trying to spread its revolution, it has made these enemies.

Key Term

fatwa A ruling issued by an Islamic jurist.

And it has no allies that can do it any good. This has put Iran into a tight squeeze, limiting its economic growth and requiring it to maintain armed forces it cannot afford. Many thinking Iranians want to call off any attempt to spread the Islamic revolution. It brings nothing but trouble and no rewards. A few militant mullahs want to keep going, no matter what it costs the country. The ending of Iranian support for militant Shi'ites elsewhere will be another sign that Iran's moderates have prevailed.

Another nasty pattern revolutionary Iran has fallen into is terrorism, both as victim and practitioner. Antiregime forces, particularly the Mujahedin-e Khalk, assassinated several Iranian leaders, including one prime minister. In return, Iranian hit squads in Europe took out several regime opponents, including a former prime minister and the leaders of a breakaway Kurdish movement. This kind of "war in the shadows" simply deepens Iran's isolation from the world community.

Do Revolutions End Badly?

Burke was right: Revolution brings in its wake tyranny far worse than that of the regime it toppled. Iran is a good example: The Shah was a dictator, but rule of the mullahs is worse. Only in America did revolution lead to the establishment of a just, stable, democracy—and the American revolution was a very special, limited one, aimed more at independence than at revolution. The twentieth century is littered with failed revolutions: fascist, communist, and now Islamist. The few remaining Communist countries that still celebrate and base their legitimacy on an alleged revolution, Cuba and North Korea, are hungry and isolated. Communist China and Vietnam, by partly integrating their economies with world trade, have so far been spared this fate.

Why do revolutions end badly? Several writers have attempted to answer this question. Burke argued that the destruction of all institutional and political structures leaves people confused and ripe for dictatorial rule. François Furet wrote along similar lines that the French Revolution unleashed such chaotic forces that it had to "skid out of control." Crane Brinton wrote that revolutions fall into the hands of their most ruthless element, who then proceed to wreck everything until they are replaced in a "Thermidor." Hannah Arendt wrote that revolution goes astray when revolutionists try to solve the "Social Question" (how to bring down the rich and help the poor); to do this they must institute a tyranny. It is interesting to note all these writers were, to some extent, conservatives. Radicals and leftists often refuse to admit revolutions end badly; if something goes wrong they tend to blame individuals for "betraying" the revolution.

The unhappy revolution is something Iranians ponder. Although few want a return of the Pahlavis, many Iranians—in private conversation with people they can trust—indicate the Islamic revolution has turned out wrong. At least under the Shah there was economic growth, however unfairly distributed, and modernization. Now there is economic decline and unemployment. Most Iranians live more poorly now than before. Certain mullahs and their friends, those in charge of the *bunyads*, are doing well. Given a chance, many Iranians would be delighted to throw these rascals out. The mullahs, their security forces, and their *komitehs* try to make sure this won't happen. They have some bases of support—more than the Shah had—among the religious and certain groups of the poor who have benefited from Islamic handouts. President Khatami must fight a two-front war, against the conservatives and militants on his right and against the liberals and students on his left.

And what should we do? Only wait. Direct interference just gives the Islamists more nationalistic propaganda points: "You see, the U.S. imperialists are trying to destroy poor little Iran." Time and economic difficulties are breaking the Iranian revolution, just as it broke the Communist revolution in the Soviet Union.

Key Terms

ayatollah (p. 116)
canon law (p. 117)
containment (p. 115)
fatwa (p. 137)
hajj (p. 124)
heretic (p. 125)
hezbollahi (p. 132)
Islam (p. 112)
Islamism (p. 122)
Islamist (p. 117)
jihad (p. 112)
Koran (p. 120)
Majlis (p. 113)
modernizing tyrant (p. 113)
mosque (p. 114)
mullah (p. 116)
Muslim (p. 112)
OPEC (p. 115)
Ottoman (p. 114)
secular (p. 114)
shah (p. 113)
sharia (p. 120)
Shia (p. 112)
Sunni (p. 112)
theocracy (p. 117)
velayat-e faqih (p. 117)

Further Reference

Arjomand, Said Amir. *The Turban for the Crown: The Islamic Revolution in Iran.* New York: Oxford University Press, 1988.

Bahrampour, Tara. *To See and See Again: A Life in Iran and America.* New York: Farrar, Straus & Giroux, 1999.

Baktiari, Bahman. *Parliamentary Politics in Revolutionary Iran: The Institutionalization of Factional Politics.* Gainesville, FL: University of Florida Press, 1996.

Esposito, John L., ed. *Political Islam: Revolution, Radicalism, or Reform?* Boulder, CO: Lynne Rienner, 1997.

Halliday, Fred. *Islam and the Myth of Confrontation: Religion and Politics in the Middle East.* London: I. B. Tauris, 1996.

Keddie, Nikki R. *Iran and the Muslim World: Resistance and Revolution.* New York: New York University Press, 1995.

Mackey, Sandra. *The Iranians: Persia, Islam, and the Soul of a Nation.* New York: Dutton, 1996.

Miller, Judith. *God has Ninety-Nine Names: Reporting from a Militant Middle East.* New York: Simon & Schuster, 1996.

Moin, Baqer. *Khomeini: Life of the Ayatollah.* London: I. B. Tauris, 1999.

Rahnema, Saeed, and Sohrab Behdad, eds. *Iran After the Revolution: Crisis of an Islamic State*. New York: St. Martin's, 1994.

Ramazani, R. K. *Revolutionary Iran: Challenge and Response in the Middle East*. Baltimore, MD: Johns Hopkins University Press, 1994.

Schirazi, Asghar. *The Constitution of Iran: Politics and the State in the Islamic Republic*. London: I. B. Tauris, 1998.

Watt, William Montgomery. *Islamic Political Thought*. New York: Columbia University Press, 1998.

Index